95¢

THE ANATOMY OF
SATIRE

BY GILBERT HIGHET

PRINCETON, NEW JERSEY

PRINCETON UNIVERSITY PRESS

PREFACE

IN THE SPRING of 1960, at the invitation of President Goheen, I delivered four lectures on satire at Princeton University under the sponsorship of the Spencer Trask Lecture Fund. This book has grown out of them.

I am grateful to Princeton for its hospitality, to the Trask Lecture Fund for giving me the opportunity to analyze some ideas which had long been in my mind, and to many friends with whom, in conversation and through correspondence, I have discussed the problems of satiric literature.

My special thanks go to Professor James Clifford of Columbia, Mr. Clifton Fadiman, Sir Alan Herbert, my son Keith Highet, Professor William Jackson of Columbia, Miss Ada Pesin of *Horizon*, Professor Walter Silz of Columbia, and Miss Constance Winchell of the Columbia University Library Reference Department, with her efficient and courteous staff.

Columbia University, New York   G. H.
August 1961

CONTENTS

I. INTRODUCTION   3-23

Satire is not the greatest form of literature but
    one of the most energetic and memorable
    forms   3

Examples of satire: 3-13
    Monologue: Juvenal on traffic   3
    Parody: Pope on the Dark Age   5
    Narrative: Voltaire on optimism   8

These are the three main patterns of satire   13-14

How to determine whether a work is satire or
    not: 14-23
    The author names his genus   15
    The author quotes a satiric pedigree   16
    The author chooses a traditionally satiric
        subject   16
    The author quotes an earlier satirist   16
    The theme is concrete, personal, topical   16
    The vocabulary is forcible and the texture
        varied   18
    Typical satiric devices are used   18
    The satiric emotion is present   21

II. DIATRIBE   24-66

1. THE SATIRIST'S MONOLOGUE   24-52

The beginnings of satire in Rome: 24
    Lucilius and Horace   24

The satiric spirit in Greece: 25
    Old Comedy   25
    Bion of Borysthenes   30
    Philosophical criticism   35
    Personal abuse   37
    Social satire   38

CONTENTS

Satire as the monologue of the satirist: 39
  Rome: Lucilius, Horace, Persius,
    Juvenal, Claudian   41
  Greece: Lucian, Julian the Apostate   42
  Dark Age and Middle Age   44
  Renaissance and Baroque   47
  Modern times: Byron, Hugo, Campbell,
    and contemporaries   48

2. VARIATIONS OF THE SATIRICAL
    MONOLOGUE   52-66

Satire as the monologue of the victim: 52
  Erasmus, Browning   53

Satire as an ironic monologue: 55
  Swift's *Modest Proposal*   57

Satire as a letter   61

Satire as a prearranged dialogue   62

Introvert and extravert monologues   65

III. PARODY   67-147

1. PARODY AND MIMICRY   67-80

Parody differs from distortion and imitation by its
    intention and its effect   67

Sometimes it is possible to distinguish formal
    parody from material parody: 69
  Housman's *Fragment of a Greek Tragedy*   69
  Burns's *Holy Willie's Prayer*   71
  Pegler's *My Day*   73
  Standard Speech to the United Nations   75
  Abraham a Sancta Clara   76
  Labouchere's *God Save the Queen*   77
  Wordsworth and self-parody   78

2. PARODY OF FORM AND PARODY OF
    CONTENT   80-92

Form and matter interpenetrate in most good
    parodies: 80

CONTENTS

The *Battle of Frogs and Mice*   80
Byron's *Vision of Judgment*   83
Titian's *Laocoon*   89
Musical parodies   90

3. THE HOAX AS SATIRE   92-103

Montgomery's double   92
The Captain of Köpenick   93
The "Dreadnought" hoax   94
Rabelais' prophecies   97
Swift and Partridge   98
Hyacinthe Maglanovitch   99
Spectra   100
Romains' *The Pals*   102

4. TYPES OF LITERARY PARODY   103-147

Mock-heroic and burlesque   103

Parodies of different literary forms:

EPIC: 107

Lucilius and Juvenal   107
Battles of animals   107
Boileau's *Lectern*   107
Dryden's *Absalom and Achitophel* and
    Mac Flecknoe   108
Pope's *Rape of the Lock* and *Dunciad*   109
Swift, De Callières, Fielding   109
Joyce's *Ulysses*   109
Tassoni's *Rape of the Bucket*   110
Scarron's *Vergil Travestied*   112
Voltaire's *Maid of Orleans*   112

ROMANCE: 113

Petronius's *Satyrica*   114
Rabelais and Ariosto   115
Cervantes' *Don Quixote*   116
Butler's *Hudibras*   119

DRAMA: 120

Aristophanes   120
The *phlyakes*   120
Fielding's *Tom Thumb the Great*   121

CONTENTS

Shelley's *Oedipus Tyrannus*   122
Beerbohm's "*Savonarola*" *Brown*   122
Shakespeare's *Troilus and Cressida*   123
Gay's *Beggar's Opera*   124
Gilbert and Sullivan   124
"Myra Buttle" 's *Sweeniad*   125

DIDACTIC POETRY: 128
Parini's *Day*   129

LYRIC: 131
Aristophanes and the young Vergil   132
Chaucer's *Sir Thopas*   132
Swift   133
The Anti-Jacobin   133
Rejected Addresses   134
Calverley and Swinburne   135
Wilson's *Omelet of A. MacLeish*   136

PROSE: NON-FICTION: 136
Plato's *Menexenus*   137
Letters of Obscure Men   138
The Menippean Satire   140
Knox's *Essays in Satire*   142
Jensen's *Gettysburg Address in Eisenhowese*   143

PROSE: FICTION: 143
Fielding's *Joseph Andrews*   143
Harte's *Condensed Novels*   144
Beerbohm's *Christmas Garland*   145
Fadiman on Wolfe   146
De Vries on Faulkner   147

IV. THE DISTORTING MIRROR   148-230

1. SATIRE AND TRUTH   148-159
Narrative is the third main form of satire   148
The neighbors of satire: 151
   Invective and lampoon   151
   "Flyting"   152
   Comedy and farce   154
The shapes of satirical narrative   156

CONTENTS

2. OUT OF THIS WORLD   159-177

   STRANGE LANDS: 159
   Swift's *Gulliver's Travels*   159
   Jean de Hauteville's *Man of Many Sorrows*   160
   Butler's *Erewhon*   161
   Maurois' *Articoles*   161
   More and Rabelais   162

   OTHER WORLDS: 162
   Menippus   163
   Ariosto and Milton   163
   Rabelais' Epistemon   164
   Seneca's *Pumpkinification of Claudius*   165
   Julian's *Drinking-Party*   167
   Quevedo's *Visions*   168

   EXTRA-TERRESTRIAL VISITS: 169
   Voltaire's *Micromegas*   170

   VISIONS OF THE FUTURE: 171
   Bellamy and Wells   171
   Orwell's *Nineteen Eighty-Four*   171
   Huxley's *Ape and Essence*   173
   Huxley's *Brave New World*   174
   Mayakovsky's *Bedbug*   174

   FANTASTIC VOYAGES: 175
   Raspe's *Munchausen*   175
   Carroll's *Alice*   175
   Lucian's *True History*   176

3. ANIMAL TALES   177-190
   Reynard the Fox   178
   Nigel's *Fools' Mirror*   179
   The Prisoner's Exit   180
   Apuleius' *Metamorphoses*   181
   Swift's Houyhnhnms   183
   France's *Penguin Island*   184
   Orwell's *Animal Farm*   185
   Aristophanes' *Birds* and *Wasps*   186
   The Čapeks' *Insect Comedy*   187
   Ionesco's *Rhinoceros*   187
   Peacock's Sir Oran Haut-Ton   189
   Collier's *His Monkey Wife*   189

CONTENTS

4 · DISTORTED VISIONS OF
THIS WORLD   190-206

    Flaubert's *Bouvard and Pécuchet*   191
    Waugh's *Decline and Fall*   193
    Lewis, Peacock, Huxley   195
    McCarthy and Jarrell   196
    Dramatic satire   196

    TALES OF TRAVEL AND
    ADVENTURE: 198
    Dickens's *Pickwick Papers*   198
    Waugh's *Scott-King's Modern Europe*   199
    Cervantes' *Don Quixote*   199
    Grimmelshausen's *Simplicissimus*   200
    Byron's *Don Juan*   201
    Horace's journey to Brindisi   201
    Linklater's *Juan in America*   204
    Waugh's *Black Mischief* and *The Loved
    One*   204
    Montesquieu's *Persian Letters*   205

5 · THE STRUCTURE OF SATIRIC
STORIES AND PLAYS   206-213

    Episodic: *Till Owlglass*   207
    Improbable: Romains' *Dr. Knock*   208
    Shocking: Rabelais' Panurge   210
    Comical: Petronius's *Satyrica*   211

6 · HISTORY AND BIOGRAPHY   213-219

    Gibbon's *Decline and Fall of the Roman
    Empire*   213
    Strachey's *Eminent Victorians*   216
    Le Sage's *Gil Blas*   218
    Morier's *Hajji Baba of Ispahan*   218
    Fielding's *Jonathan Wild the Great*   218

7 · DESCRIPTIVE SATIRE   219-230

    THE HORRIBLE PARTY   221

    Petronius's *Banquet of Trimalchio*   221
    Régnier and Boileau   222
    Dickens, Waugh, Proust   222

CONTENTS

CARICATURES   224
  Brant's *Ship of Fools*   224
  Boccaccio's *Courbash*   224
  Lucretius, Boileau, Swift on women   226
  Hogarth's "Gin Lane"   228

V. CONCLUSION   231-244

1. NAME   231-233

Meaning of the word "satire"   231

2. FUNCTION   233-238

Satire tells the truth; but which truth?   234
Two types of satirist   235

3. MOTIVES   238-243

Motives of the satirist: 238
    Personal grudges   238
    Sense of inferiority and injustice   240
    Wish to amend vice and folly   241
    Desire to make an aesthetic pattern   242
    Idealism   243

ABBREVIATIONS   245

NOTES   247-278

BRIEF BIBLIOGRAPHY   279-281

INDEX   283-301

THE ANATOMY OF SATIRE

ATIRE is not the greatest type of literature. It cannot, in spite of the ambitious claims of one of its masters, rival tragic drama and epic poetry.[1] Still, it is one of the most original, challenging, and memorable forms. It has been practiced by some energetic minds— Voltaire, Rabelais, Petronius, Swift; by some exquisitely graceful stylists—Pope, Horace, Aristophanes; and occasionally, as a parergon, by some great geniuses—Lucretius, Goethe, Shakespeare. It pictures real men and women, often in lurid colors, but always with unforgettable clarity. It uses the bold and vivid language of its own time, eschewing stale clichés and dead conventions. Where other patterns of literature tend sometimes to be formal and remote, satire is free, easy, and direct. Where they use carefully posed models and work in a skillfully lighted studio, the satirist cries, "I am a camera! I am a tape-recorder!" If the results which he offers us are not always smooth with the contours of perfect art, and if their tints are not harmoniously blended, they at least have the urgency and immediacy of actual life. In the work of the finest satirists there is the minimum of convention, the maximum of reality.

To discover what satire is and what shapes it takes, the best way is to look at some good satirists, dealing with themes which we regard as important.

First, consider the problem of traffic in the big city, described by the Roman poet Juvenal. To most of us today, the streets jammed with crowds and vehicles are merely one more annoyance in our irksome lives, an inevitable price to pay for metropolitan luxury. We scarcely realize that the infuriating frustrations of traffic, by maltreating our emotions, are injuring our health, and that the

noxious gases belched from a million motors are shortening
our lives. Juvenal lived before the age of the internal com-
bustion engine and the motor-horn; but he knew that
megalopolitan traffic was more than a mere inconvenience;
and so, although speaking in a tone of wry humor, he began
his description of the traffic problem in ancient Rome with
chronic illness, and ended it with violent death. This is an
excerpt from his third satire, in which a man who is leaving
the city of Rome forever describes the abuses which are
driving him away. (A few details have been modernized
in the translation, in order to reproduce the intensely topical tone of the original.)

Most sick men here die from insomnia—though first
their illness starts with undigested food, that clogs
the burning stomach. Who can ever sleep in a rented
apartment? Peaceful rest is costly in the city.
There is the root of our sickness: heavy buses squeezing
through narrow twisted streets, and the curses of stalled
    drivers,
would break a deaf man's sleep, or keep a walrus awake.
To make a morning call, the millionaire is driven
easily through the crowds in his long limousine,
reading his paper en route, or writing—yes, or sleeping,
for warmth and closed windows invite him to take a nap;
yet he'll be early. I keep pressing, but I'm blocked
by a mighty surge in front, my hips are squeezed by the
    crowd
shoving behind, an elbow hits me here and a fender
there, now I am banged by a beam, now biffed by a barrel.
My legs are thick with mud, a barrage of coarse shoes
bunts me, upon my toe a soldier's boot stands fast. . . .
My newly mended coat is ripped with a flick from a log
joggling upon a truck; next comes a heavy girder
suspended on a trailer, poised like a threat of doom:
for if the axle beneath a load of heavy granite
snaps, and pours out a rockslide on the moving horde,
what will be left of their bodies? Bones and flesh alike

will disappear. The poor victims' corpses will vanish as utterly as their souls![2]

A gruesome picture. And yet, in a grim way, funny. When the ambulance arrives, the interne will write on his form D.O.A., which stands not for the customary "Dead On Arrival," but for "Disappeared. Obliterated. Annihilated." And, although exaggerated, there is a truth in this satire. Traffic *is* too much with us, late and soon; it is corroding our nerves and afflicting our health; and, one of these days, unless we escape, it will crush us out of existence. In this specimen we recognize the characteristic features of satire: it is topical; it claims to be realistic (although it is usually exaggerated or distorted); it is shocking; it is informal; and (although often in a grotesque or painful manner) it is funny. And this is one of the typical forms assumed by satire: a monologue, spoken virtually without interruption by one man—the author himself, or a mouthpiece of the author.

Another satirist treats a more important theme in a different and more ambitious manner. The history of the human race is a strange succession of light and darkness. Brief and exciting the bright periods usually are, long and stubborn the years of obscurity. In the life of our world one of the gloomiest epochs was the Dark Age of ignorance and barbarism that closed in after the fall of the western Roman Empire. Libraries were destroyed. Schools and universities diminished or disappeared. The sciences were forgotten. The arts shrank to miniature skills or rude crafts. Cities dwindled to groups of villages, towns to sordid hamlets. The population fell away, becoming less numerous and more gross. Illiteracy and superstition flourished in a world made up of warring tribes, lonely settlements, and hopeless "displaced persons." Monarchs could not write; nearly all laymen were unable to read. After long being prosperous and highly civilized, western Europe sank back into half a millennium of poverty, ignorance, and oppression, only to emerge in the twelfth century of our era, and then with vast difficulty and painful effort. Today, when we recall the hideous devastation caused by the Second World War, and realize with horror that the next will be still more destructive, we can easily, too easily, imagine our grandchildren's grandchildren half-barbarized, struggling for a bare existence among ruins and deserts, reduced to the life of primitive man, "solitary, poor, nasty, brutish, and short."[3]

Alexander Pope, like most intelligent men of the eighteenth century, looked back on that early time of troubles with revulsion. In his most ambitious satire, *The Dunciad*, he went so far as to forecast the imminent coming of a new Dark Age, brought on not by war but by the infectious spread of human pride, selfishness, and stupidity; and he made his chief victim, personifying all these vices, glory in a vision of past ignorance triumphing both in Rome and in Britain.

> Lo! Rome herself, proud mistress now no more
> Of arts, but thundering against heathen lore:
> Her grey-haired synods damning books unread,
> And Bacon trembling for his brazen head.
> Padua, with sighs, beholds her Livy burn,
> And even the antipodes Virgilius mourn.
> See the cirque falls, the unpillared temple nods,
> Streets paved with heroes, Tiber choked with gods:
> Till Peter's keys some christened Jove adorn,
> And Pan to Moses lends his pagan horn;
> See graceless Venus to a virgin turned,
> Or Phidias broken, and Apelles burned.
> Behold, yon isle, by palmers, pilgrims trod,
> Men bearded, bald, cowled, uncowled, shod, unshod,
> Peeled, patched, and piebald, linsey-woolsey brothers,
> Grave mummers! sleeveless some, and shirtless others.
> That once was Britain.[4]

Although Pope was a Roman Catholic, he writes here in terms which anticipate Gibbon's famous epigram, "the triumph of Barbarism and Religion."[5] But these lines are not uttered by the satirist himself. They are part of a long prophetic speech delivered by the spirit of a dead poet, himself a champion of Dulness, to the hero of the poem, in a vision of Elysium. Every reader who knows the classics will at once recognize that this speech is a parody of one of the greatest speeches in Latin poetry: the address of the dead Anchises, in Elysium, to his son Aeneas. The main conception is the same in both: a prophecy of a world-wide empire, to be brought into being by the efforts of the hero under the protection of a guardian deity, and sustained by mighty champions who, still waiting to be born, pass before him in a magnificent procession. Feature after feature recalls the sixth book of the *Aeneid*: the hero is led by a Sibyl; he sees the souls of the unborn, multitudinous as bees, moving by the river of Lethe; the mystical doctrine of transmigration is imparted to him; from a hilltop he is shown the heroes of his race. However, the themes of the two passages are dissimilar, indeed contraposed. The subject of the prophecy in the *Aeneid* is the rise of Roman civilization. The subject of the prophecy in *The Dunciad* is, in part at least, the reverse: the invasion, first of ancient, and then of modern, civilization by the forces of stupidity. The former is spoken by a majestic figure, the spirit of Aeneas's father now endowed with preternatural wisdom; the latter, by a ridiculous personage, the third-rate poet Elkanah Settle,

By his broad shoulders known, and length of ears.[6]

Nevertheless, the tone of the speech in *The Dunciad* is grave and at times enraptured, although its subject is both absurd and repellent. This is a fine example of the second main pattern of satiric writing: parody.

From the problem of the city suffering from vehicular thrombosis, and the problem of irrepressible human stupidity, let us turn to a third, much older and more formidable, which has been handled by one of the greatest satirists of all. This is the problem of providence: the question how this world is constructed and governed. Everywhere we look, every day we live, we see and experience evil. Pain and suffering seem to be built into the very structure of the universe. Look through the microscope at the tiniest of living things: they are as savage and cunning as sharks, or leopards, or men. Gaze backward at the physical history of this planet, and see what appears to be a long series of meaningless catastrophes. Think of human history: consider what horrors men have inflicted on one another, and what crimes they are preparing even now to commit. Observe the natural disasters—floods, famines, earthquakes, epidemics—which visit us at irrational intervals, as though the Four Horsemen of the Apocalypse were forever riding around the planet. Can we confidently say that this world is good? Can we easily believe that it was created so that we should be happy in it? Can we call its almost ubiquitous evil merely negative, or incidental, or illusory? For these questions, religions which depend on faith have their own answers. But philosophers also have endeavored to solve them. One philosopher devised an ingenious answer. Unable to say that the world was flawlessly good, yet eager to assert that it was systematically and intelligibly constructed, Gottfried Leibniz argued that, while other types of world-order are thinkable, this which we inhabit is, with all its apparent imperfections, the best possible world. An omnipotent creator could have brought many other kinds of universe into existence; but they would logically have suffered from more and greater peccancies.

As long as human life jogged on with no more than its customary quotient of suffering, this declaration might not evoke any more than a puzzled smile or a logic-chopping debate. But about forty years after its emission, an unusually violent and apparently inexplicable disaster occurred. The city of Lisbon was almost wholly destroyed by a tremendous earthquake, followed by a tidal wave and by fire. Many thousands of innocent people were killed in an instant, buried alive, or roasted to death. Here was the opportunity for a satirist—not to gloat over the sufferings of the victims, but to point out the ludicrous inadequacy of the philosopher who asserted that they lived, and died, in the best of all possible worlds. In 1759 Voltaire published *Candide*.

Once upon a time, he tells us, there was a decent young fellow who had been taught, by an expert in metaphysicotheologocosmolonigology, that the world-order was intelligible, logical, and, philosophically speaking, the best of all possible world-orders. His name was Candide, which means Ingenuous, so he believed this theory. He was born in a castle in Germany; he was exiled when only about twenty; he never saw his home again, but became a "displaced person" and ended his days on a small subsistence-farm in Turkey. Between those two terminals, he traveled half round the world, became fabulously rich and miserably poor, was imprisoned, tortured, threatened a hundred times with death; he saw his pretty young sweetheart changed into a bitter old hag, and the philosopher who had taught him the doctrine of optimism turn into a miserable relic of humanity, like one of the ghastly figures who appeared when the German concentration-camps were liberated. And yet Candide continued, almost until the very end, to believe the metaphysicotheologocosmolonigological theory that everything fell out for the best in this world, and that this was the best of all possible worlds.

It is unnecessary to summarize this brilliant satirical tale, but a few of its episodes will show its special quality.

On a business trip, Candide is shipwrecked. (Nowadays he would be in an airplane where one of the passengers was carrying a heavy brief-case, which ticked.) He swims ashore clinging to a plank and lands on the coast of Portugal. Exhausted and famished, he walks into Lisbon, arriving just in time for the earthquake. He survives; but, because he is overheard discussing the philosophical inevitability of the disaster, he is arrested by the Holy Inquisition, and, to the sound of hymns, flogged. Another earthquake shock follows. Candide is unexpectedly rescued by an old woman, who proves to be the servant of his sweetheart Cunégonde. Learning that Cunégonde, no longer a maiden, is shared by two lovers, a Jewish banker and the Grand Inquisitor, he kills them both and escapes to South America. A little later he is captured by a tribe of Indians who prepare to cook and eat him. (He made the mistake of shooting two apes who were chasing a pair of Indian girls, and were in fact the girls' sweethearts.) A little later again he reaches Eldorado, which he leaves with an immense fortune in gold and jewels (the dirt and pebbles of that country); a little later still, his wealth is stolen by a Dutch sea-captain; and so it goes. Compared with the adventures of Candide, the exploits of the far-wandering and much-experienced hero Odysseus were mild and humdrum.

The story of *Candide* has no pattern—except the elementary pattern of constant change and violent contrast, which can scarcely be called a pattern at all. Indeed, it would be perfectly easy for us, if a new manuscript of the book were discovered containing half a dozen fresh chapters on the adventures of Candide in Africa or in China, to accept them as genuine. Probability is disregarded. Logic and system never appear. Chance, idiotic chance both kindly and cruel, is supreme. True, there is a single dominating theme—the philosophical theory of optimism—and

From Voltaire's *Candide*. Engraving by Jean Dambrun.
Photograph by Giraudon, Paris

a basic plot—Candide loves Cunégonde and at last marries her. But beyond these the story is designed to be illogical, unsystematic, fantastic, and (in the existentialist sense) absurd. A romantic tale which is not satiric may contain wild and unexpected adventures; but they will follow a pattern which, given the premises, could be called reasonable. Allan Quatermain in *King Solomon's Mines* and Robert Jordan in *For Whom the Bell Tolls* move through worlds of extreme fantasy and unguessable peril, but their adventures link into a chain, and the chain forms a design. In *Candide* there is no design. The implicit purpose of the author is to deny that design in life exists. At every moment the regular course of existence is interrupted or distorted, so that nothing, whether good or bad, happens for any comprehensible reason. In two of the biggest scenes of the book, Candide visits the unreal land of Eldorado and the almost equally unreal city of Venice during the Carnival. In Eldorado he finds that our diamonds are common gravel. In Venice six chance-met tourists prove to be dethroned kings—one Russian czar, one British pretender, one Corsican, one Sultan, and, of course, two rival Poles. When four displaced princes appear after dinner, no one pays any attention to them. In the world of satiric fiction, almost anything may happen at any moment. Satire sometimes looks at reality as a tale told by an idiot, full of sound and fury, signifying nothing, deserving nothing but a bitter laugh.

The improbable and the unexpected constantly intrude. The philosopher Pangloss is publicly hanged by the Inquisition; but he turns up again twenty-two chapters later, explaining that the rope was wet and the noose did not choke him to death and he revived on a dissecting table. The brother of Cunégonde is killed by a force of Slavs looting his father's mansion; but he reappears in Paraguay, explaining that after the catastrophe he was restored to life by a priest who found some signs of movement in his eyes and heart. A little later he is run through the body with a sword (Candide is at the other end); but after another dozen chapters, he is rediscovered as a galley-slave in Turkey, explaining that the wound was not fatal.

Now, nearly every one of these adventures is horrible in itself. On the four chief characters in *Candide*, almost every kind of human suffering is inflicted; almost every variety of injustice and outrage, human and divine, falls upon their long-enduring bodies and souls. And yet, when these hideous disasters and cruelties are put all together into a sort of cacophonous fugue, the final effect is not tragic. It is not even sad. It is—satirical. We cannot quite call it comic; but it does not bring agonizing tears to the eyes or icy horror to the soul. The result of reading this short book which, in thirty chapters of accidents, narrates the humiliating collapse of four lives, is neither tears nor hearty laughter, but a wry grimace which sometimes, involuntarily, breaks into a smile. Only a very brave man or a very desperate one can smile at death. But the satirist, and he alone, can make us smile at someone else's. Touching at Portsmouth, Candide sees a blindfolded man kneeling on the deck of a ship. The man is then shot by a firing squad. When Candide asks who and why, he is told that it is a British admiral, who is being killed "to encourage the others."[7]

This is the complex emotion which appears in Juvenal's half-amused and half-indignant description of the hapless pedestrians abolished in the accident of a single minute, squashed to unrecognizable jelly beneath a load of stone; and in the gleeful evocation, in Pope's *Dunciad*, of the barbarous days when the masterpieces of classical sculpture were converted into pious monuments by an age which had forgotten how to carve original statuary, or else discarded as worthless and immoral, thrown into rivers or ground down for road metal. This emotion is the truest product and the essential mark of the genus we call satire.

One of the best ways to study the problem of form in literature is the method used by Aristotle. This is induction. First, collect as many examples of a given phenomenon as possible. Then, by observing resemblances and differences and contrasts and alliances, extract from these particulars a few general descriptive principles. This is the system which Aristotle employed when preparing to analyze tragedy, in the one surviving book of his treatise called *Poetics*. If we use it on the works which, throughout the history of Western literature from Greece and Rome through the Middle Ages to the Renaissance and then to our own time, have been intended, or have been interpreted, to be satires, we shall find that nearly all of them fall into three classes. A satire usually has one of three main shapes.

Some are monologues. In these the satirist, usually speaking either in his own person or behind a mask which is scarcely intended to hide, addresses us directly. He states his view of a problem, cites examples, pillories opponents, and endeavors to impose his view upon the public. Such is Juvenal, denouncing the traffic which makes big city life almost unlivable.

Some, again, are parodies. Here the satirist takes an existing work of literature which was created with a serious purpose, or a literary form in which some reputable books and poems have been written. He then makes the work, or the form, look ridiculous, by infusing it with incongruous ideas, or exaggerating its aesthetic devices; or he makes the ideas look foolish by putting them into an inappropriate form; or both. Such is Pope, making Settle's ghost glorify the Dark Age.

The third main group of satires contains neither monologues, in which the satirist often appears personally, nor parodies, in which his face wears a mask, but narratives, in which he generally does not appear at all. Some of them are stories, such as *Candide*. Others are dramatic fictions: staged satires, such as *Troilus and Cressida*. Narrative, either as a story or as a drama, seems to be the most difficult type of satire—easiest for the author to get wrong, hardest for the reader to understand and to judge. When it is successful—as it is in *Candide* or Aristophanes' *Frogs*—it is likely to be a masterpiece; but even the best writers are apt to waver in their conception of its methods, its scope, or its purpose, while less experienced authors often misconceive it entirely, and ruin what may originally have been a viable satiric idea.

This classification can, it must be admitted, be criticized on the ground that it is not a true trichotomy. Although monologues are generally different from narratives, so that the two types form two equivalent classes, it is clearly possible for a parody to be in the form of a monologue or of a narrative. For instance, there is a delightful parody of the cetacean style of Samuel Johnson, shaped as a dedicatory address spoken by his ghost;[8] and although *Candide* is not, the *Satyrica* of Petronius may well be, a parody of romantic fiction. To be scrupulously exact, we ought to define the patterns of satire as parody, non-parodic fiction (dramatic or narrative), and non-parodic monologue (with its variants); but for the sake of convenience we shall use the simpler terms.

If the three forms of satire are different, and if their material (as we shall see) is omnigenous, what have they in common? What quality or qualities permit us to look at a poem, or a play, or a story, and call it a satire; to examine another, and declare that it has some satirical episodes, but is not wholly or mainly a satire; and to distinguish, between outwardly similar works written by two not dis-similar authors—or even, sometimes, by the same author—asserting that one is, and the other is not, satire? It is not always easy to say. When a satirist writes a parody which closely and delicately reproduces the manner of his victim, or when he depends strongly on the device of irony, or when his smile is subtle and his humor mild, or when he pretends rather convincingly to be telling the truth, the whole truth, and nothing but the truth, then he may easily be mistaken for a dispassionate commentator, an amiable comedian, a frank forthright fellow, a genuine admirer of the stuff he parodies, or even one of its adepts. There was an Irish bishop who read *Gulliver's Travels* soon after it was published and so far missed the satiric implications of the narrative as to declare that he didn't believe a word of it. (Or at least Swift said so to his fellow-satirist Pope.)[9] Plato—who loathed and despised democracy, and Athens, and Athenian patriotism—wrote a parody of a patriotic speech over the Athenian war dead which was so close to orthodox sentiments and the accepted oratorical manner that some good critics took it seriously in antiquity and some modern scholars still believe it was sincerely written—although Plato himself said it was comparable to a dirty joke.[10]

However, there are a number of reliable tests. If some, or most, of them apply to a book, it is likely to be a satire.

First, a generic definition given by the author. When Juvenal looks at corrupt Rome and cries

It is difficult *not* to write satire,[11]

we know the pattern he will use, although in fact he will boldly change and extend it. Hundreds of poets, he says, are writing epics and dramas and elegies; satire is my field—and he goes on in a powerful tirade to justify his choice, to describe his material, and to sketch his special methods.

Second, a pedigree. When Erasmus says that his *Praise of Folly* is justified by *The Battle of Frogs and Mice*, Seneca's *Pumpkinification of Claudius,* and Apuleius's *Metamorphoses* (among other books), he is proclaiming that one line of its descent comes from the classical satirists.[12]

Third, the choice of a theme and method used by earlier satirists. Often this is a disguised statement of pedigree. The first satire of Boileau (published when he was twenty-four) is a monologue spoken by a beggar poet who is leaving Paris forever, since he cannot live and prosper there without being or becoming corrupt. This main theme, and many of its subordinate developments, are adapted from the third satire of Juvenal. Boileau thereby, although he does not even mention Juvenal's name, announces himself as a satirist of the hard bitter Juvenalian school.

Similarly, by quoting the actual words of a distinguished satirist, an author can make it plain, without a more direct statement, that he is writing satire. Peacock opens no less than four of his novels with quotations from the satirist Samuel Butler. Byron begins *English Bards and Scotch Reviewers* with an adaptation of the first sentences of Juvenal's first poem.

Subject-matter in general is no guide. Men have written satire on the gravest of themes and the most trivial, the most austere and the most licentious, the most sacred and the most profane, the most delicate and the most disgusting. There are very few topics which satirists cannot handle. However, we can say that the type of subject preferred by satire is always concrete, usually topical, often personal. It deals with actual cases, mentions real people by name or describes them unmistakably (and often unflatteringly), talks of this moment and this city, and this special, very recent, very fresh deposit of corruption whose stench is still in the satirist's curling nostrils. This fact involves one of the chief problems the satirist has to face. To write good satire, he must describe, decry, denounce the here and now. In fifty years, when he is dead, will not his subjects also be dead, dried up, forgotten? If so, how can he hope to produce a permanent work of art? Open Dryden at one of his most famous satires, *Mac Flecknoe*. Full of good jokes, it is written with infectious gusto, but what is it about? Who is its victim, Sh—? The notes say he was Shadwell, but who now knows, or cares, who Shadwell was? And what is the point of calling him Mac Flecknoe, and relating one nonentity to another? It is all sunk in oblivion now, and utterly unimportant. Open Pope's ambitious *Dunciad*, and read

> Silence, ye wolves! while Ralph to Cynthia howls,
> And makes night hideous—Answer him, ye owls!
> Sense, speech, and measure, living tongues and dead,
> Let all give way—and Morris may be read.
> Flow, Welsted, flow! like thine inspirer, beer,
> Though stale, not ripe, though thin, yet never clear.[13]

Who on earth are these characters? Pope himself was aware that they were obscure even in his own time and would soon be forgotten; apparently he felt the paradox implicit in his work and the work of many satirists, that he was expending his genius on giving a kind of immortality to the unimportant and the ephemeral; but he could not resist one of the satirist's strongest impulses, hatred. Yet this passage shows, in a small way, not only a principal defect of satire, but a principal merit: the energy and originality of its style. To us, Ralph, Morris, and Welsted are quite unknown. But we can still enjoy the biting paradoxes: the bad rhymester singing to the moon louder than howling wolves, a soloist with a choir of ululating owls; the thin stale trickle of Welsted's pale poetic brew. We can admire the deftly turned phrases—"makes night hideous" adapted from *Hamlet*, and the fine line about beer parodied from Denham's famous description of the Thames in *Cooper's Hill*. We can laugh at the mock gravity of his apostrophe to these triflers and bunglers; and, if we are satirically inclined, we can, for Welsted, and Morris, and Ralph, substitute other names, the names of today's howlers and babblers and dribblers.[14] It is in this way that good satire, although essentially topical, becomes general and permanent.

The subject-matter of satire is multifarious. But its vocabulary and the texture of its style are difficult to mistake, and, although sometimes used in other types of literature, are most concentrated and effective in satire. Most satiric writing contains cruel and dirty words; all satiric writing contains trivial and comic words; nearly all satiric writing contains colloquial anti-literary words. All good satires are eminently various. The original Latin word *satura* means "medley," "hotch-potch," and the best satirists have either known this or divined it. In plot, in discourse, in emotional tone, in vocabulary, in sentence-structure and pattern of phrase, the satirist tries always to produce the unexpected, to keep his hearers and his readers guessing and gasping.

Since most satirists have read satiric books published before their own débuts, they are apt to admire satiric devices which have already been worked out. Any author, therefore, who often and powerfully uses a number of the typical weapons of satire—irony, paradox, antithesis, parody, colloquialism, anticlimax, topicality, obscenity, violence, vividness, exaggeration—is likely to be writing satire. If he uses these devices only in certain sections of his work, then those sections alone may properly be satirical; but if they are omnipresent, his work is almost certainly a satire. In nearly all good satire two special methods, or attitudes, are essential.

The first is to describe a painful or absurd situation,

or a foolish or wicked person or group, as vividly as possible. The satirical writer believes that most people are purblind, insensitive, perhaps anaesthetized by custom and dulness and resignation. He wishes to make them see the truth— at least that part of the truth which they habitually ignore. When I was last rereading Juvenal's satire on the horrors of the big city, I was reminded of a passage written in the same spirit, and at least partially for the same purpose, by an author whose name is seldom associated with satire. John Ruskin, while giving a course of lectures on sculpture at Oxford University in 1870, introduced into them a bitter attack on the design and decoration of the newly built Thames Embankment in the heart of London. At the climax of this attack, he described the flight of stairs leading from Waterloo Bridge down to the Embankment, "the descent" (he reminded his hearers with a Victorian magnificence) "from the very midst of the metropolis of England to the banks of the chief river of England."

The steps . . . descend under a tunnel, which [a] shattered gas-lamp lights by night, and nothing by day. They are covered with filthy dust, shaken off from infinitude of filthy feet; mixed up with shreds of paper, orange-peel, foul straw, rags, and cigar ends, and ashes; the whole agglutinated, more or less, by dry saliva into slippery blotches and patches; or, when not so fastened, blown dismally by the sooty wind hither and thither, or into the faces of those who ascend and descend.[15]

Of those who ascended and descended, millions must have seen this repellent sight, but not with the inward eye, not with the mind. Ruskin therefore pictured it with remorseless clarity, so that they and others might for the first time see, and understand what they saw. Although Ruskin is an exquisitely sensitive writer, who habitually delights to dwell on scenes of loveliness and grace, he here uses words and cites details which are repulsive: rags, cigar ends, ashes, dry saliva. This is the direct method used by satirists, to describe what their readers have not clearly seen or fully understood. Only the tone of scornful amusement is lacking from this passage, for it to resemble Juvenal's description of the squalors of the Roman streets.

Second, when a satirist uses uncompromisingly clear language to describe unpleasant facts and people, he intends to do more than merely make a statement. He intends to shock his readers. By compelling them to look at a sight they had missed or shunned, he first makes them realize the truth, and then moves them to feelings of protest. Most satirists enhance those feelings by careful choice of language. They employ not only accurate descriptive words, but also words which are apt to startle and dismay the average reader. Brutally direct phrases, taboo expressions, nauseating imagery, callous and crude slang—these are parts of the vocabulary of almost every satirist.

Thus, in *Candide*, Voltaire achieves one of his most exquisite satirical effects by naming a part of the body which is well-known, which is necessary, and which is sometimes (in certain Greek sculptures and the paintings of Boucher) even decorative, but which is not usually mentioned in literature or even conversation. As Candide's sweetheart is lamenting the miseries which, although still young, she has been forced to endure in this, the best of all possible worlds, she is overheard by a hideous old woman. This creature reproaches her for complaining, and says that Cunégonde has suffered relatively little. She adds, "If I showed you my behind, you would not speak like that."[16]

The old woman was once a beautiful young princess, who by a series of misfortunes was converted into an abject slave; she was sold to an officer in the Turkish janissaries. During a siege, he and the other Turkish soldiers determined, not to eat all the non-combatants, but to eat parts of the non-combatants. So the princess lost one buttock. Starvation and cannibalism are horrible. Voltaire increases their impact by deliberately introducing a word that is meant to shock. And he alters the impact at the same time. In the word "behind," there is something comical. If the poor old thing has lost an arm, or a breast, it would have been pathetic, an atrocity; but part of her behind!

Similarly, death in the afternoon, upon the streets of one's own home city, is miserable; and yet, as Juvenal describes the sequelae of a traffic accident, there is something titillating in the contrast between the dead man's departure from this earth and the unconcern of the people at home.

> Meanwhile, his household, quite at ease, is washing
> the plates, blowing the fire, and clattering the brushes
> for his evening bath, and setting out his soap and towels.
> His servants are all busy variously, while he
> sits on the river's edge, and shudders at the grim
> ferryman: he can't hope to cross the muddy torrent,
> poor newcomer, without a coin in his mouth for the fare.[17]

In the world of death, the ghost, a naked exile, sits forlorn in Limbo, beside the Styx. (He cannot enter Hades until his corpse is reassembled and given a proper funeral.) In the upper world, there are a cheerful fire, and the clink of dishes, and the smells of cooking, and a hot bath, and dinner, waiting for him. It is funny. It is funny because it is so incongruous.

This leads us to the final test for satire. The final test for satire is the typical emotion which the author feels, and wishes to evoke in his readers. It is a blend of amusement and contempt. In some satirists, the amusement far outweighs the contempt. In others it almost disappears: it changes into a sour sneer, or a grim smile, or a wry awareness that life cannot all be called reasonable or noble. But, whether it is uttered in a hearty laugh, or in that characteristic involuntary expression of scorn, the still-born laugh, a single wordless exhalation coupled with a backward gesture of the head—it is inseparable from satire.

Even if the contempt which the satirist feels may grow into furious hatred, he will still express his hatred in terms suitable, not to murderous hostility, but to scorn. Hate alone may be expressed in other kinds of literature; and so may laughter, or the smile of derision. The satirist aims at combining them. Shakespeare could not dismiss Iago with a sneer. Such wickedness was too loathsome to be merely derided: the man was a "demi-devil," a figure fit for tragedy alone. But Pandarus in *Troilus and Cressida* is covered with purely satirical contempt:

> Hence, broker, lackey: ignomy and shame
> Pursue thy life, and live aye with thy name.

This contempt Pandarus himself then turns into scornful laughter by singing a little song and addressing those in the audience who, like himself, are hard-working ill-rewarded pimps.[18]

It is because satire always contains some trace of laughter, however bitter, that it was and still is so difficult to produce an effective satire on Adolf Hitler. Charlie Chaplin mocked him with temporary success in *The Great Dictator* (1940), and David Low produced some good satirical caricatures stressing the contrast between his rather absurd physical appearance and his diabolical malevolence. But after he had conquered most of Europe and initiated his fearsome policy of mass enslavement, torture, and murder, it was impossible to despise him. Swift put it very well, saying, "Satire is reckoned the easiest of all wit, but I take it to be otherwise in very bad times: for it is as hard to satirize well a man of distinguished vices, as to praise well a man of distinguished virtues. It is easy enough to do either to people of moderate characters."[19]

Horror and fear and hate and indignation will not, without contempt, make a satire. If Leibniz's theory of optimism had not been merely a superficial and silly hypothesis which could lead to nothing more than folly and eventual disillusionment, Voltaire would not have written a satire about it. For subjects which were terrible without stirring contemptuous laughter, he adopted a totally different tone and method. Six or seven years after *Candide*, he issued a *Treatise on Toleration*, which opens with a darkly serious description of the trial and execution of Jean Calas on religious grounds, and ends (save for a postscript) with a solemn prayer to the Creator of the universe. No one could write a successful satire on Attila, or Genghis Khan, or Hulagu with his pyramids of skulls. No one could satirize leprosy or cancer. Hermann Goering, Benito Amilcare Mussolini, and even that sinister paranoiac Josef Vissarionovitch Djugashvili, called Stalin, had their ineffective and contemptible aspects, and therefore could, by a powerful writer or artist, be satirized. But some villainies are too awful for us to despise. We can only shudder at them, and in horror turn away—or try to write a tragedy. Against such crimes, satire is almost impotent. Against all lesser crimes and against all follies, it is a powerful weapon.

II DIATRIBE

ATIRE as a distinct type of literature with a generic name and a continuous tradition of its own, is usually believed to have started in Rome. The earliest satirist whose work has survived intact for us to read is Horace (65–8 B.C.). He has left us two volumes of verse satire, with ten poems in the first and eight in the second, together with some poetic letters which are not far removed from satire as he conceived it.

Horace says, however, that in Latin one important satirist came before him.[1] This predecessor's poems have perished, except for a collection of shattered and isolated fragments; but from these fragments, and from the comments of Horace and others, we can do a little to reconstruct his life and achievement. He was a brilliant and charming gentleman who would have fitted excellently well into the Whig society of Great Britain in the early nineteenth century: we can easily see him cracking jokes in competition with Sydney Smith, and even imagine him out-talking Tom Macaulay—at least for half an hour or so. This is Lucilius (c. 180–c. 102 B.C.). In some thirty volumes of poems written in gaily careless, vivid, and unconventional language, he turned a whole world into poetry: contemporary politics and personalities, his own tastes and adventures, the characters of his friends and servants, social fads and fancies, anything that interested him. He even attempted the almost impossible task of teaching the Romans to spell their own language.[2] Horace calls him the real discoverer, inventor, explorer of satire, because it was he, Lucilius, who gave direction and purpose to the genus. In Lucilius's poems, satire was willful and various, and could comment on all

· 24 ·

the activities of human life; but its comment was mainly critical, derisory, destructive. Although he was not the first Roman poet whom we know to have inveighed against his powerful contemporaries in verse (Naevius, that bold plebeian, did so and suffered for it), he was the first who attacked them at considerable length, with artistic elaboration, and apparently with impunity. Even among the meager fragments that survive, we can find several pieces of mockery which must have made their victims clench their fists, and groan, and writhe in pain. From Lucilius onward, verse satire has always had a bite in it.[3]

Every Roman poet of the Republican era knew Greek, and—ruefully, enviously, or worshipfully—admired the grace and power of Greek literature. However original, independent, and carefree he might be, he was bound to have some favorite Greek author whom (even involuntarily) he would imitate and emulate. Now, satire is not usually thought to have existed in Greece. There is no exact Greek word for "satire"; there is no tradition of satirical writing in Greek—nothing, for instance, comparable to the long tradition of lyric poetry or oratory. Yet satire is a natural activity; and the Greeks have always been good haters and they enjoy scornful laughter. Therefore we shall expect to find the satiric impulse coming out somewhere in Greek literature, and thereafter serving as a stimulus to Roman satirists. About this, what do the Romans themselves say?

Among his *disiecti membra poetae*, we cannot find Lucilius mentioning any Greek author as his model and inspiration; but his successor Horace names two who helped to mould Roman satire.

First, very clearly and unequivocally, he says that satire in Lucilius "entirely depends on" the Old Comedy of Athens.[4] Elsewhere he describes his own special type of satire as "talk seasoned with black salt, in the manner of Bion,"[5] the philosophical preacher. Let us look at these two filiations.

The comedies—or should we call them comic operas?—of Aristophanes and his contemporaries were plays of fantasy in verse, often soaring high into beautiful lyric imagination, often crudely vulgar, sometimes downright silly. They were rich with music and dancing, and used many of the technical resources of the theatre. The satires of Lucilius were non-dramatic poems meant to be read. Although they contained lively dialogue, they could scarcely be put on the stage and acted. What then does Horace mean by saying so emphatically that Lucilius "entirely derives from Aristophanes" and the others? He means chiefly that Lucilius writes not about fictitious or mythical characters, but about real contemporary people; and that he does so in a spirit of mocking criticism. Socrates studying the sun from his space-vehicle in Aristophanes' *Clouds*, the demagogue Cleon competing in vulgar abuse with a sausage-seller in Aristophanes' *Knights*—these are the direct ancestors of the pompous politicians and affected fops whom Lucilius pillories. And furthermore, the motives of both poets were identical. If you attack a man in poetry merely because you hate him, you are not properly writing satire. You are writing "lampoon," or sometimes, in a special sense, epigram. (The Greeks generally named such attacks after the meter in which they were habitually couched, "iambics"; and the Romans followed them.) The lampoon wishes merely to wound and destroy an individual or a group. Satire wounds and destroys individuals and groups in order to benefit society as a whole. Lampoon is the poisoner or the gunman. Satire is the physician or the policeman. Aristophanes covered his victims with overwhelming contempt and irresistible laughter: he made the wise Socrates look silly, the tender-hearted Euripides look sickly and degenerate, the bold progressive Cleon look a cheap rabble-rouser. But he did so because he felt that these men were injuring his beloved country, by corrupting the young, demoralizing the women, and dislocating the structure of society. For all his crudity and absurdity, for all his frequent cheapness and Dionysiac wrong-headedness, Aristophanes is a moral and political reformer. Whether Lucilius explicitly imitated any of his big effects, we cannot now tell;[6] but Horace, who knew Lucilius's work, assures us that he modeled his great innovation, the social function of satire, upon the social function of Attic Old Comedy.

Yet how about form? We are investigating the morphology of satire. Did Lucilius, in defining the future development of verse satire, take any formal hints from Greek comedy?

Obviously he did not adopt the dramatic structure of Aristophanes and the other comedians.[7] We can see no sign that he ever expected his satires to be staged, with a troupe of actors dancing and singing. Still, some of his poems contained scenes of brisk comic dialogue, which remind the reader of the lively disputes between embittered opponents in Aristophanes.[8] And he clearly admired and imitated the free-flowing spontaneity of the Old Comedy. Greek tragic drama is, formally, rather rigid: as is natural for a type of literature which displays the arrival of inevitable doom. But Aristophanic comedy is wildly unpredictable and asymmetrical and apparently improvisatorial. It always reminds us that it originated in a drunken revel; indeed, some of the extant comedies end where comedy began, in a wild party, with wine, women, crazy dancing, and gay semi-coherent singing. In the same way, and on that same model, Roman verse satire is capriciously varied and—unlike almost all other types of literature—often looks as though it were improvised, spontaneous, structureless.

There is one more feature, and an important one, which

Lucilius shares with Old Comedy. A play by Aristophanes has a few chief characters, many subordinate figures, and a large singing and dancing chorus. The chorus itself is a collective character: a group of jurymen dressed as wasps, with stings to wound their enemies, or birds, who have their own commonwealth high up in the middle air, or embattled and mutinous women. Throughout most of the comedy, the members of the chorus watch the action, comment on it, and share in it. But at one important point near the middle (when the playwright has established his domination over the audience) the chorus changes its nature. It ceases to pretend that it is a swarm of wasps or a float of clouds. It leaves the action to stand still for a while. It turns its back on the now empty stage. It faces the audience. And it transforms itself from a set of puppets into the playwright himself. In this particular episode of the play, with a special name (*parabasis*, "forward march"), the chorus turns away from the comedy and speaks directly to the spectators. It uses the rollicking anapaests and the bold jolly trochaic rhythms which everyone can feel and enjoy. It performs one of the most difficult feats in all drama, by crossing the barrier between the actors and the audience. Most ancient comedies do this once at least, at the end of the play—appealing to the audience for friendly applause, as Shakespeare often does. But Aristophanes and his competitors addressed the audience in the middle of the play also, not to gain their applause, but to focus their attention on the central message of the play. At this moment the leader of the chorus faced the audience. He spoke, and the chorus spoke, the thoughts of the dramatist. William Shakespeare sometimes played good parts in his own dramas. I wonder whether, in the same way, Aristophanes himself may not have appeared in person, behind a mask and within a disguise, to lead the chorus in some of his own comic inventions, and to say to the audience the message which he himself had written. At any rate, just as he and his rivals, at the end of their plays, often invited the audience to join them in a party, so, at a turning-point in each comedy, while all were enjoying themselves and were elated but still receptive, they addressed their fellow-citizens with a positive and thoughtful message which was meant to remain in their minds long after the wine and the gaiety had blown away. Therefore, when the Roman satirist steps forward boldly to address the public, crying "Listen!" and speaking in his own voice and provoking his hearers to criticism and reflection on important problems of the day, he is copying the address of the chorus and the dramatist to the public, in Athenian Old Comedy.

There are further resemblances between Aristophanic comedy and early Roman verse satire: for instance, the richly unconventional vocabulary, blending poetic imagination and colloquial vigor; the frequent parodies of serious poetry; the deliberately shocking indecencies; the flexible and picturesque use of meter; the free and unconventional sentence-structure; but these and other such subordinate devices occur in many authors who are not always dead serious, and it would be a hard task to say who used them first, and in which type of literature.

Horace was right, then, to say that Lucilius "depended on" the Attic comedians. Take away the stage and the costumed chorus; keep the gaiety and the feigned inconsequence, the hiccupping rhythms and the indecorous words; allow a jester with a great heart to speak the truth directly to the people, naming names outright and mocking knaves and fools, and you will have Roman satire as Lucilius wrote it. Horace followed Lucilius, and from him that tradition (although interrupted in the Dark Age) has survived for two thousand years.[9]

When Horace said that Lucilius depended on Aristophanic comedy, he was new at his job: a keen young satirist, just graduated from the lampoon, and eager to criticize his most eminent predecessor. He himself never claimed to be following the genius of Old Comedy, although he read masterpieces both of Old Comedy and of New.[10] For his own work he named quite a different prototype. In a poetic letter composed toward the end of his life, he complained that it was difficult to please everybody.

> Lyrics appeal to A, lampoons are B's delight,
> while C loves talks in Bion's manner, coarsely spiced.[11]

These are three types of poetry which Horace himself had written: lyrics (we miscall them the Odes); lampoons or iambics, the Epodes; and talks, *sermones*, chats, informal discourses, a word that covers both his satires and his poetic letters. "Coarsely spiced" is a rendering of what Horace calls "black salt": for the Greeks and Romans "salt" in a literary context meant wit and humor, and black salt was therefore crude pungent humor.[12] But Bion—who was he, and why did Horace call his satires (and letters) "talks in the manner of Bion"?

Greek philosophy began with a few austere and arduous thinkers, "voyaging through strange seas of thought alone." They set down their doctrines in books as obscure as oracles, or entrusted them by word of mouth to a select few pupils. After them came the sophists. They claimed to be able to teach wisdom to anyone, but in practice they taught only members of the middle and upper classes. Next, the great schools of philosophy were formed: Plato's Academy, Aristotle's Lyceum, the Stoics, the Epicureans. On the whole, they too confined most of their teaching to pupils who were already prepared for theoretical discussions, and who sought them out because they were already interested. Yet any philosophical creed risks becoming sterile or esoterically mystical if it gets out of touch with ordinary men and their problems. (We have seen this recently with Wittgenstein and his followers.) Therefore, in the fourth stage of Greek philosophy, missionaries began to go out to teach and preach philosophy, not among leisured and receptive hearers in the great cultural centers of Greece, but to the crowds in the streets, to the inhabitants of smaller and remoter regions, and to the dynasts and officials of petty courts throughout the Greek-speaking world. That world had been vastly enlarged when Alexander the Great destroyed the Persian Empire and brought most of its countries under Greek dominion. During the three centuries before the birth of Jesus and for long afterward, the Hellenistic lands were crisscrossed by wandering philosophical preachers, whose aim was to awaken men from their sensual slumbers and to give them a set of firm principles by which to live. This missionary traffic was made necessary partly by the sterility of Greek education, and partly by the breakdown of the old Olympian religion and the collapse of the little local cults. Across the paths of the philosophers moved others, the emissaries of weird mystical creeds, driving their donkeys laden with sacred trumpery, preaching and performing miracles and collecting money.[13] When St. Paul started on the journeys described in The Acts of the Apostles, he was part of a tradition which was already three hundred years old, and more.[14]

One of the most famous of these philosophical missionaries was a remarkable man called Bion. He was born about 325 B.C. in the remote and isolated Greek settlement called Olbia, or Borysthenes, far away on the Black Sea, near the site of modern Odessa. His father had been a slave, who won freedom, and his mother a prostitute. Because of a fraud committed by his father the entire family (though free) was sold into slavery again. But the boy was bought by an intellectual, a teacher of rhetoric, who left him, at his death, a small fortune and his liberty. He went to Athens and studied in the best philosophical schools; then devoted his life to traveling and preaching philosophy. But "preaching" is the wrong word; and so is "lecturing." Bion worked out a style of his own which was designed to capture and hold the attention of audiences who hated preaching and would never have gone to a lecture, people who were ill educated and uninterested in philosophy and inapt for systematic thought, yet still capable of understanding moral problems and of changing their own lives.[15]

His message was realistic. Despising both naive religion and idealistic philosophy, illusionless as a Cynic and voluptuous as a Cyrenaic, he was a moral nihilist.

His style was lively, but not simple. He told jokes. He made puns. He used plain language, popular slang, coarse words, obscenities, Doric dialect. He brought in flowers of rhetoric. He quoted famous poets—particularly Homer and the favorite tragedian Euripides—although he usually made fun of them, using their verses incongruously or distorting them into parody. He illustrated his talks with fables, and anecdotes, and bits of folk-wisdom. It was said of him that he was the first to dress philosophy in the flowery clothes of a prostitute.[16] And, what is perhaps the most important thing of all, he did not deliver regularly planned discourses in which point five was inevitably followed by point six, and point six, at an equal distance, by point seven. Instead, he appeared to be improvising. He would start with a casual remark or an arresting quip; he would approach his subject tangentially; he would hold an argument between himself and an imaginary opponent; and his audience, never knowing what he was going to say next, hung on his words. It may sound like a silly way to teach philosophy. Certainly it would be quite inappropriate for serious students. But it was effective in attracting and impressing hearers who would otherwise never have opened their minds to a single general idea.

Furthermore, Bion's teaching was well within one great tradition of philosophical method: the tradition of Socrates. Again and again in the dialogues of Socrates' pupil Plato we see that other thinkers (the "sophists") are denigrated because they teach by delivering formal lectures, neatly arranged and tightly packaged. Socrates declares that such a lecture may make its hearers admire the speaker's verbal agility and marvel at his apparent control of his subject, but that it cannot teach them anything. He himself rarely delivered a continuous discourse. Instead, he began with a casual incident, or a remark dropped by an acquaintance; he asked for an explanation of the incident or the remark; then he slipped almost imperceptibly from question to objection to renewed interrogation, and so into the dialectic process. Repeatedly he explained that he was not setting out a doctrine which he had already thought through, or delivering a speech which he had already composed and polished and memorized, but was simply following "wherever the argument led." A formal discourse, according to Socrates, was limited, static, moribund; true wisdom lives, and moves in ways which are unpredictable. It is extremely difficult to take any of the large Platonic dialogues in which Socrates appears, and to reduce it to the skeleton of a philosophical treatise in the traditional shape. What Bion did, then, was to follow Socrates rather than the sophists and the systematic teachers who succeeded them.[17]

Bion had another model, scarcely less famous. This was the Cynic philosopher Diogenes, the beggar, the "dog." Diogenes is supposed to have written both philosophical dialogues and poetic dramas to carry his teaching, but even in his lifetime they were insignificant. What made him famous in his lifetime, and what has perpetuated his memory to this day, was his bold vivid method of teaching through pithy unconventional remarks and drastic anti-social acts. One of his central principles was absolute frankness (παρρησία): he observed no conventions of speech, always spoke his mind, and shrank from no crude words. This frankness is characteristic of the best satire. Everyone knows, too, how he lived in an empty cask, to show that most people thought far too much about unnecessary comfort, and how he walked through the market-place at high noon with a lighted lamp, looking for an honest man. A single memorable gesture, one meaty remark seasoned with black salt, can often teach more effectively than a skillfully articulated discourse on the principles of ethics.

The ethical themes used in Bion's informal discourses were repeated by generations of moralists, Greek, Roman, and Jewish. Philo, Dio Chrysostom, Musonius, Epictetus, Seneca never tire of reproaching and deriding their contemporaries for misunderstanding the true standards of life. One of their favorite topics, for example, is the concept of hereditary nobility: they point out that, as a blind man cannot benefit from the sharp sight of his parents, so a vicious man or a fool cannot be called noble because his ancestors were distinguished: nobility is nothing but wisdom and virtue. And they frequently attack the luxurious extravagance of the Greco-Roman world. How perverse, they cry, to search the seas from end to end for delicate fish, when we can live on bread and salt; how absurd to have cups of embossed silver when cups of clay will quench our thirst; and why drape the walls with crimson hangings and cover them with rare marbles brought from distant lands, when a simple house will give us warmth and shelter?[18] Not only themes such as these but illustrative anecdotes and memorable apophthegms were part of the continuous tradition of popular philosophical preaching. It was apparently Bion who stood out as the most brilliant stylist in that tradition.

Therefore, when Horace calls his own conversational satires and letters "discourses in the manner of Bion," he means that they are light monologues with a serious content, decorated with witticisms and other attractive devices; that they are apparently haphazard in structure; and that their humor is rather rough than delicate. He means also that they deal with important ethical and social problems, which concern every thinking man; but which he will not discuss in a complex argument filled with technical jargon. Rather, even at the risk of over-simplifying them, he will make them plain to understand and easy to remember, so that they may bridge the gulf between philosophy and the general public.[19]

Horace mentions Bion because he was the best known and the most extreme of the philosophical preachers. Yet in fact there was a large tradition of Greek satirical writing and talking, both in verse and in prose, which existed before the first Roman satirist began his work; and although Bion, accurately speaking, was scarcely a satirist, he did use many of the devices worked out by the genuine Greek satiric writers. Their books have almost wholly disappeared. They were not often imitated by Roman authors, and many of the Romans who imitated them have, in turn, been lost. Therefore they do not regularly appear in histories of Greek and Roman literature. Most of us are apt to think that the history of satire begins with the Romans of the Republic, continues in Latin for three centuries, and diverges into Greek only with Lucian. This is an over-simplification.

Outside the drama, there were three chief kinds of Greek satirical writing.

One was philosophical criticism. This began with the brilliant Ionian Xenophanes (c. 570–c. 475 B.C.), who wrote a lively hexameter poem called *Leers* or *Looking*

Askance (Σίλλοι). Among other things, it criticized popular anthropomorphic religion:

> Now, if hands were possessed by oxen, by horses and lions,
> and they could paint with their hands, and carve them-
> selves statues as men do,
> then they would picture the gods like themselves with
> similar bodies:
> horses would make them like horses, and oxen exactly
> like oxen.[20]

This poem seems to have been in the shape of a monologue, didactic, and yet evidently critical and humorous. After the philosophical schools were formed, this special type of satire was taken up enthusiastically by the Cynics and the Sceptics, who enjoyed pointing out the absurdities and inconsistencies of other sects. Diogenes himself seems to have written only serious poetry; but his pupil Crates (c. 365–285 B.C.) produced satiric poems against rival philosophers, in iambics, elegiac couplets, and hexameters, containing much parody.[21] Another Cynic, Cercidas (c. 290–c. 220 B.C.), wrote against wealth and luxury in the un-usual form of satiric lyrics. More famous and far more influ-ential was the Cynic Menippus (c. 340–c. 270 B.C.), a Syrian slave who won his freedom and eventually became a citizen of the noble Greek city of Thebes. He was ap-parently the first non-dramatic writer of satire to make his work continuously funny, instead of merely inserting gibes into it here and there. He is called the σπουδογέλοιος, "the joker about serious things" par excellence; and he surely modeled much of his work on Aristophanes.[22] He is also famous for inventing a new pattern for satire, prose mingled with snatches of verse—a pattern which may be Semitic in origin rather than Greek.[23] After him came the author of a mock epic in Homeric hexameters about the conflicts of the professional philosophers, the Sceptic Timon of Phlius (c. 320–c. 230 B.C.), who introduced

Xenophanes as his hero, and called his poem *Leers*, as Xenophanes had done.

From these men—particularly from the brilliant Menippus—a second tradition of satire flowed into Latin. The soldier, statesman, and polymath Varro wrote a large number of Menippean satires in prose interspersed with verse, which—to judge by their titles, their reputation, and the pitifully few fragments that have survived—were learned and original and witty. Many of the best of these, it would seem, were not discursive monologues, but narratives of fantastic adventure told in the first person. Their language was so rich in vulgarisms, archaisms, neologisms, and bold imagery, and their metrical interludes so skillful and so various, that they even make the straight verse satires of Horace and Juvenal look rather tame and monotonous. In the same line of development lie the *Apocolocyntosis* of Seneca, the *Satyrica* of Petronius (both fantastic narratives), some of the most ambitious satires of the Greek-speaking Lucian, and finally a satire by the last philosophical monarch of antiquity, Julian the Apostate.[24]

Outside the theatre, there were two other types of Greek poetry which were satirical in effect, or, without being truly satirical, used the weapons of satire.

The Greeks are proud, and therefore envious. They despise other nations, but they hate other Greeks. Hence their long tradition of self-seeking and treachery, which begins with the first book of the *Iliad* and is still active today. Just as sexual energy is the central reason of existence for many Italians, so rivalry with other Greeks is, for many Greeks, the motive force of all life. This impulse was vented by several powerful Greek poets in works which, because they expressed only their authors' own hatred for an enemy, lacked the judge's, or at least the policeman's, impersonality which could entitle them to the name of satire.

Archilochus (fl. 700 B.C.) was a soldier of fortune. He justified neither his loves nor his hates, but spoke them out boldly. For his hate-poems he chose the meter which, being closest to the rhythms of ordinary speech, is most effective: the iambic. Thenceforward abusive poems motivated by purely personal spite were usually written in this rhythm, and generically called "iambics." Even more bitter was Hipponax (fl. 540 B.C.), whose vituperations drove some of his victims to suicide, and who invented the ugliest of all Greek meters to express his hatred, the *scazon* or "limper," *choliambic* or "lame iambic," a line in which five iambic feet are succeeded by a spondee, so that its regular march slumps heavily in the last foot. Long afterward, in the Alexandrian era, the brilliant but cross-grained Callimachus (c. 305–c. 240 B.C.) published a book called *Iambics*, in which, posing as Hipponax reborn, he attacked his enemies with witty abuse. It is likely that the versatility and sophistication of this book helped to inspire Lucilius at the beginning of his career as a satirist; and Horace's early collection of *Epodes* cites Archilochus and Hipponax as his predecessors.[25] Still, satire in Rome rises higher and develops more boldly than the poems of this school in Greece.

The satiric impulse also cropped out among the Greeks in amusing or bitter poems on general themes. The Greeks admire cleverness, and have no pity for stupidity. The hero of the *Odyssey*, although brave and resolute, is preeminently clever, even to the point of devising unnecessary lies to tell those who love him. Therefore someone wrote a comic poem about the antithesis of Odysseus, a man so stupid that he could not count beyond five (the fingers of one hand) and was afraid to make love to his wife in case she complained to her mother.

Many skills he knew, and always got them wrong.

On the model of the bold upstart in the *Iliad*, Thersites, it was called *Margites*, "Madman."[26] The poem was in a lopsided rhythm, dactylic hexameters irregularly interspersed with iambics, which to Greek ears would sound awkward and preposterous like Margites himself. In antiquity it was usually ascribed to Homer, but nothing survives of it except broken lines and amputated jokes. We cannot even tell whether it was shaped as a narrative (a life-story, or a string of adventures) or as a character-portrait; certainly it was not considered to be a parody in the strict sense, but rather a protracted pleasantry.[27] Apart from setting the satiric model of the Perfect Fool (like Simplicissimus and Candide) it had little direct influence on literature. More important and more durable was a mock epic satirizing military glory and epic grandiloquence by describing in Homeric terms a one-day conflict between tiny animals, *The Battle of Frogs and Mice*. Men are never tired of criticizing women; and so (apparently from the seventh century B.C.) we have an iambic poem by Semonides of Amorgos surveying the different types of wives, comparing one to a yapping bitch, one to a lazy sow, and so forth; only one, the bee, is praised. This stands at the head of a long series of misogynistic satires, which still shows no sign of coming to an end. Another favorite topic for satirical treatment has always been food; and so in the fourth century we meet the first of many satires on dinners good, bad, and ridiculous. This theme was brought directly into Latin in a poem called *Hedyphagetica*, or *Delicatessen,* by the first great Latin poet, Ennius.[28]

However, we are considering satires in the form of monologue; and not all the Greek satires in verse, or in prose mingled with verse, were monologues. Whatever their shape, Horace, the first extant satiric monologist in Latin, never mentions them, although he may well have used material drawn from them.²⁹ Some he may have thought to be too special, too contentiously philosophical; some too rude and naive; and some (like Cercidas and Callimachus) too ambitious and recherché for the true impact of satire. The model whom he chose to name was the witty, unsystematic, free-spoken prose critic of society and of philosophy, Bion of Borysthenes.

Bion's discourses were called diatribes. The word has nowadays come to mean a bitter polemic, but in Greek and Latin it has no hint of bitterness or hostility. *Diatribé* in Greek is an absolutely neutral word, meaning "occupation." By Plato's time, when the occupations best worth mentioning were intellectual, it had come to mean both "study" and "discourse": in his defense speech at his trial Socrates says (according to Plato) that he used to give among the Athenians διατριβὰς καὶ λόγους, "discourses and talks."³⁰ The talks given by Bion, although in intention critical, were in this sense philosophical discussion; and when Horace called his own satires *sermones*, "talks," he meant to show that they were less haphazard than *saturae*, "medleys," and that, although informal in tone, they still had a purpose which was thoughtful and a meaning that was meant to be remembered.

These, then, are the origins of the first main type of satire. It is a monologue, usually in verse, but often also in prose or in prose mingled with verse, which is informal and is apparently improvised. It appears to be perfectly spontaneous and to have no set logical structure, but to spring from a momentary impulse, a casual occurrence, a passing remark. It is marked by constant variety of tone and shifts of subject-matter, and it is enlivened by wit, humor, parody, paradox, word-play, and other decorations. It is of course non-fictional, non-narrative. It deals with a theme of general interest, but it illustrates its subject by personal references, topical allusions, and character-sketches, and it introduces fiction in the form of anecdotes and fables. Its language is sometimes lofty, but is more usually prosaic and comic, generally colloquial, even obscene. Its tone is not serious, but flippant, sarcastic, ironic, shocking, and in general inappropriate to the full gravity of its subject. It is not a lecture. It is not a sermon. As soon as an author begins to arrange his thoughts under strictly logical headings, to cut away all irrelevancies, and to speak in a tone of unvarying seriousness, he is not writing satire. He may be creating something more important and more effective, but it will not reach the same audience as satire, and it will not produce the same result. The tone of improvisation—even if it be only a semblance—is essential to this type of satiric writing. It comes down from those vigorous ancestors, the Old Comedy of Aristophanes, with its chorus of masked revelers, and the free-wheeling philosophical conversations of Socrates. It is strange to look back and see how many of the thoughts that move us today and have moved generations of our ancestors, and how many of the artistic forms we love, in stone and in poetry, in drama and in thought, came from that little republic of Athens during a few decades of its life, when taste, and intellect, and freedom, and careless gaiety were all at play together.

It has a long and splendid history, monologue satire.[31] In verse it was introduced into Latin by Ennius, and elaborated by Lucilius. Horace, a kindlier man, made it milder, refined its style, and infused into it a richer ethical content. Persius took it over from Horace, filled it with Stoical propaganda, and developed for it a strange, wry, contracted style, which grimaces like the mask of a satyr: this is particularly odd for a Stoic, since Stoics do not care much about the powers of style, and never grimace. Juvenal enlarged its size and scope, endeavored to make it rival epic and tragedy, and spoke of vices and sins viler than any touched by his predecessors; but by his time it was too dangerous, under an absolute monarch, for a satirist to speak out freely.[32] We hear of other verse satirists in Latin after Juvenal, but their work has practically vanished. Yet, as the western Roman Empire was falling into anarchy and chaos, there emerged a surprisingly strong and spirited satiric monologist, Claudian. This man was the poet laureate of Stilicho, the half-barbarian marshal of the western empire; and he wrote two invectives against Stilicho's political opponents, Rufinus and Eutropius, which, although predominantly serious in tone, still mock their victims with enough energy and enough sense of incongruity to be close to satire. In this, their ancestor is Juvenal's fourth, the satire on the Emperor Domitian and his subservient court; but they carry Juvenal's blend of satire and epic upward to a new height.[33]

In Greece under the Roman Empire a milder and gentler satirist was writing in prose: fairly good prose, considering that his native tongue was not Greek. This was Lucian (fl. A.D. 160), a Syrian (or Assyrian?) born on the banks of the Euphrates. I confess that I always feel foreignness in his work, and that I can never quite do him justice. When I try to read those satires in which, with the same subtlety as a freshman preaching atheism, he deflates the ancient Bronze-Age myths of Zeus and the Olympians and lards his thin dictionary-Attic prose with cultured quotations from the correct classics, I feel as though I were trying to savor a satire on the medieval Christian cult of relics, written in Chaucerian verse by an intelligent Hindu of the present day. To put it bluntly, most of Lucian's problems are dead, and were dead when he wrote about them; his language is a colorless pastiche; and he has almost wholly abandoned one of the essential virtues of satire, which is to be topical in subject and realistic, urgent, combative in style. As a foreigner, he wished to be more Greek than the Greeks themselves. Therefore he modeled his satirical dialogues and comedies on the work of Greek authors of the long-departed classical age, filling his prose with obsolescent idioms and citations borrowed from the most approved sources.

A few of his satires, however, have some contemporaneity and some bite: his monologues on that familiar subject, the misery of the intellectual. In his time most of the poor intellectuals were Greeks and most of the brainless taste-less rich were Romans, so that these are in effect anti-Roman polemics. Such are his *Professor of Oratory*, his denunciation of an *Ignorant Book-Collector*, his account of the humiliations of *Paid Companions*, and his *Nigrinus*, a description of Roman multimillionaires and their toadies, put in the mouth of a beggar-philosopher who lives in Rome but thinks in Greek. These and a few other mono-logues of Lucian are pictures of contemporary life which—but for their rather desiccated prose style and their reluc-tance to name names—could stand beside the satires of Juvenal. Lucian and Juvenal, the anti-Roman Greek and the anti-Greek Roman, they make a splendid pair of satiric opponents, they would have cordially detested each other, and anyone who wants to understand imperial Rome of the second century must read them together.[34]

The line of classical satirists ends with a surprising figure: the Emperor Julian, called the Apostate because, although baptized as a Christian, he reverted to paganism. An attack on Christianity which he published has long ago disappeared, and we cannot surely tell whether it was satirical. But we have one curious and rather good mono-logue satire addressed by him to the people of Antioch. It was in Antioch that "the disciples were called Christians first," so that its people can have had no love for the pagan emperor. They had mocked Julian for wearing the simple clothes and rough beard of a professional philosopher; and in an amusing diatribe called *The Beard-Hater* (A.D. 361-362) he defended himself and counter-attacked his proud and unruly subjects.

But with the coming of Christianity, monologue satire virtually died away. Many monologues were still delivered, to denounce the wicked and berate the foolish, but none had the smile of satire, none had the bold personal structure of satire, none had its variety and its joy in incongruity and its cheerful or contemptuous independence. In the world where Christianity had to make its way, fighting incessantly against paganism and heresy, no believer could jest about truth, since truth was divinely revealed; and no churchman could be content to smile, or even to sneer, at sinners. Among the polemical writings of Tertullian and St. Jerome and other Christian apologists there are many passages which are satirical in feeling, but as the argument proceeds it always changes into loud-mouthed oratory or embittered invective.[35] Throughout the long centuries when the church was converting the western world, we find scarcely a single monologue satire, either in prose or in verse.

In the Middle Ages also, there were not many satires in this particular form. Medieval authors who wished to write satirical attacks on anomalies and abuses usually selected other patterns than the monologue. When they did attempt a monologue, they were often so grimly serious, so passionately sincere, that they could not make it various enough and grotesque enough to be a true satire. They wrote what in effect were invectives, or sermons. Such is *On the Contempt of the World*, by Bernard of Morval (fl. A.D. 1150) a furious and brilliant poem written in Latin verse so passionate, so flexible, and sometimes so insanely ingenious that it would have astounded the classical Romans. But instead of the photographic precision of satire, it gives us broad generalizations repeated and elaborated with obsessive passion. Instead of wit, it has rage. Instead of variety and realism, it has the glum intensity of an ascetic preacher.[36] There are, however, a few medieval satirists who know classical Latin and have divined, from reading the Romans, enough of the essence of satire to write good satirical monologues. The eldest, and perhaps the best, of these is an enigmatic fellow from the Rhineland who wrote, about A.D. 1044, four books of *Sermones* on moral topics in a lively conversational tone, with many quotations from the Roman satirists, particularly Horace. (He burdened himself with the name of Sextus Amarcius Gallus Piosistratus, no one can imagine why.)

There are even a few lyrical poems in the vernacular languages which have the form of monologues. From England, in the early fourteenth century, we hear one of the innumerable echoes of man's complaint against woman's finery:

> In pride
> every shrew will her shroud
> though she has not a smock her foul ers to hide. . . .
> in hell
> with devils they shall dwell
> for the jewels that hang by their jowls.[37]

A song of complaint, if it is grotesquely amusing like this, and has an edge of bitterness, may be called a satire.

Of course the satiric impulse did not die away. It was simply directed into channels other than monologue satire. Material for satiric treatment existed then almost as plentifully as it exists now. In a learned, if sometimes testy, book called *Literature and Pulpit in Medieval England* (Cambridge, 1933) Dr. G. R. Owst gives many specimens of the sermons rebuking sin and folly which were preached, both in Latin and in vernacular English, during the centuries immediately preceding the Reformation. But although the priests and the friars were undoubtedly earnest in their struggle to warn mankind against its own corruption, it was their very earnestness that prevented them from making their sermons into satires. Most of those cited by Dr. Owst are unremittingly serious and doggedly systematic. We can, however, trace certain devices which often recur in them and which can be called satirical. One is the illustrative anecdote, an odd or amusing tale (be it fiction or fact, it scarcely matters) used to point a moral. Another is the fable. Another is the vivid character-sketch tinged with amusement and contempt. And, just now and then, we see a short passage of true satire in which, for a moment, the author actually ventures to play with a serious idea: as when St. Bernard produces a series of sharp-edged criticisms made pointed by puns, about clerical dignitaries who care more for roast pasty than for Christ's Passion and study more in salmon than in Solomon; or when the Dominican John Bromyard, in savage and paradoxical irony, calls money a divinity more potent than God, because it can make the lame walk, set captives free, cause the deaf judge to hear and the dumb advocate to speak.[38]

The moral themes and examples used by medieval preachers were (as Dr. Owst shows) often taken over by poets outside the church. Among the social and ecclesiastical satires of Walter Map, Walter of Châtillon, Gilles de Corbeil, and Gillebertus, there are some short and amusing monologues, occasionally even called *sermones* and written as parodies of pulpit oratory. One of the most striking of the poems by the rebellious "Goliards" is *Golias Against Marriage*, a group of misogynistic monologues put into the mouths of three saints of the church.[39] And we sometimes find satirical monologues embedded in the solider material of larger works, like frail fossils in carboniferous stone. Such is that delightful satire on marriage seen from

Devils packing monks, ladies, bishops, princes, and princesses
into the boiling caldron of hell.

Gothic sculpture, the Cathedral of Bourges
Photograph by Giraudon, Paris

the woman's point of view, the *Wife of Bath's Prologue* in Chaucer's *Canterbury Tales*;[40] here and there in the rambling half-mystical half-realist preachments of *Piers Plowman* there are sharp little sallies of satire; and, like gargoyles in a vast and intricate Gothic cathedral, we can find several satiric diatribes crouching among the flying buttresses and crocketed pinnacles of *The Romance of the Rose*.

With the Renaissance, strong individuals felt more free to assert themselves and declare their personal opinions, in protest, or in derision, or both: the art of "telling the truth in a jest" was once more explored. The Roman satirists were more closely studied and understood; the work of the Greek satirical writers became known. Eventually (after Casaubon published his illuminating essay on satire in 1605) the full power and meaning of the genus satire was understood. Many good satirists now appeared, and a few geniuses. In Italian there were Vinciguerra and Berni and Ariosto; in French, Vauquelin de la Fresnaye and Régnier; in English, Skelton and Wyatt and Donne and Hall and Marston. All these men preferred the monologue form—which also emerged triumphantly in the prefaces of Rabelais and in some of his long speeches. In this age, too, the very type of the satirical observer appeared in drama and in real life—the lonely individual, standing at one side of that stage which is the world, observing the actors though taking none of them quite seriously, and commenting with wry humor on the fantastic drama of life. Such is Jaques in Shakespeare's *As You Like It*, who, like a true (though optimistic) satirist, says

> They that are most galled with my folly,
> They most must laugh.[41]

In the baroque age, these men were followed by greater satirists who used, although they did not always prefer, the monologue form: Boileau, Oldham, Young, Pope. The court preacher to the Holy Roman Emperor from 1677 to 1709, Abraham a Sancta Clara, although filled with deep religious emotion and inspired by unmistakably sincere moral feeling, still wrote sermons which are often indistinguishable from satiric diatribes in the spirit of Bion, so full are they of witticisms, parodies, proverbs, anecdotes, puns, and other diversions, and so unpredictable is their rapid explosive tempo. He specialized in humorous attacks on the follies and frailties of mankind. His most famous predecessors (in comparatively modern times) were Brant with his *Ship of Fools* and Erasmus with his *Praise of Folly*. His closest successor was Joseph Stranitzky, who opened the first Punch and Judy show in Vienna. Stranitzky quoted freely from Abraham's sermons and books, and one of his chief characters, the Jack Pudding or Hanswurst, used the freedom traditionally given to fools to criticize the Austrians as boldly from the puppet-stage as Abraham had criticized them from the pulpit.[42]

It was right that Lord Byron should begin his serious career as a poet with a satiric monologue, for he was an embittered cynic, a relentless humorist, and a rapid improviser. Infuriated by the *Edinburgh Review*'s hostile criticism of his *Hours of Idleness*, he turned from mild lyric to the strong satire of Juvenal, whose first poem he imitated in *English Bards and Scotch Reviewers* (1809).

> Still must I hear?—shall hoarse Fitzgerald bawl
> His creaking couplets in a tavern hall,
> And I not sing?

In verse satire of this kind Byron's most eminent modern successor was Victor Hugo, with his attacks on the monarch whom he called Napoleon the Little. He was admirably suited for it, since almost all he wrote sounded like an enormous monologue. After Hugo there is a gap in the history of this particular type. However, it was revived after the First World War, by the South African poet Roy Campbell, with splendid energy and sovereign contempt. His most ambitious poem in this vein, *The Georgiad* (1931), is only partly indignant monologue, and slips now and then into parody: this mixture of tones is one reason why it is not wholly successful; but it has some fine passages. Here is his description of the English literary scene in the late 1920's.

> Now Spring, sweet laxative of Georgian strains,
> Quickens the ink in literary veins,
> The Stately Homes of England ope their doors
> To piping Nancy-boys and crashing Bores,
> Where for week-ends the scavengers of letters
> Convene to chew the fat about their betters—
> Over the soup, Shakespeare is put in place,
> Wordsworth is mangled with the sole and plaice,
> And Milton's glory that once shone so clear
> Now with the gravy seems to disappear,
> Here Shelley with the orange peel is torn
> And Byron's gored by a tame cuckold's horn.

And his evocation of the lanky and lugubrious form of Lytton Strachey, whose reputation was established at the opening of the decade with his biography of the good Queen Victoria.

> While here ungainly monarchy, annexed
> By more ungainly Somebody, is vexed
> And turning in her grave exclaims, "What next!
> In life did fat and asthma scant my breath,
> Then spare me from the Tape-worm, Lord, in death."[43]

Two years later, in 1933, Wyndham Lewis, whose ambitious satiric novels had made less impact and earned him less fame than he hoped, published his only verse satire, a series of monologues called *One-Way Song*. In this he boasted of some of his ideals, complained bitterly of the conspiracy to boycott and impoverish him, and put some of the charges against him into the mouth of "the Enemy." It is a vigorous poem, but too full of the cheap old-fashioned slang he affected, and sometimes obscured by his devotion to private fads and feuds. In 1934, a far more drastic satirist working in prose issued the first of his monologues. This was Henry Miller, whose *Tropic of Cancer* was followed in 1939 by *Tropic of Capricorn*. In form these are autobiographical novels: both follow a certain time-sequence and contain certain characters who reappear and may be said to develop.[44] But Miller is, or was, an incessant talker and letter-writer. The most powerful and durable parts of these books are the meditations and manifestoes in which, with hideous violence and shocking foulness of language, he denounces the whole world of his time and most of its component parts. His passion for obscenity is like that of Aristophanes and Rabelais; and indeed many of the exploits of which he boasts resemble those of Panurge. The difference is that in spite of its absurdities and hypocrisies they love mankind. Miller, like Swift, believes that humanity is a filthy crime.

In the modern United States the satiric monologue struck new roots, and had a vigorous, although not always graceful, growth. Americans have always enjoyed listening to the humorous disillusioned observer who, from the side-lines, watches the parade of the rich and the mighty and with a few biting words converts them into thieves and clowns. Finley Peter Dunne not only amused the public for twenty years with the dialect monologues of "Mr. Dooley," but did something to influence public opinion on serious questions: at least as much as he could have done by earnest unsmiling propaganda. A generation later came another monologist, Philip Wylie, whose *Generation of Vipers*, published in 1942, has sold over two hundred thousand copies. It is a commentary on American delusions and vices (in particular, "Momism"), written with passionate intensity but also with bold and acid humor. Its free and easy language and its gleeful confrontation of harsh facts with much-advertised ideals make much of it excellent satire.

Toward the end of the 1950's satirists of a type both very old and very new began to appear in American night-clubs and theatres, and—greatly to their own surprise—to be listened to with delight and admiration. These men publish nothing, but deliver monologues which are usually in fact and always in appearance improvised. Although it is fairly certain that none of them know anything about the Greek diatribe and the Roman ancestors of modern satire, they nevertheless use many of the same devices: topical references, shocking words, weird paradoxes, cruel parodies, snatches of foreign languages (in particular, Yiddish and Italian), an easy conversational tone with much up-to-date slang, and a loose apparently planless format. The most famous, Mort Sahl, usually works with the symbol of im-permanence, today's newspaper, in his hand;[45] another, Shelley Berman, improvises long and grotesque telephone conversations with an imaginary interlocutor. Although, like the masters of Greek diatribe, they all have certain favorite themes of satiric commentary which recur again and again in their work (for instance, they all detest children), still, the best of them never deliver the same monologue twice, and all of them will improvise large passages and bold humorous developments on the spur of the moment. Vulgar and garrulous, insecure and opulent, sensitive and brash, they are the modern descendants of Bion, and the latest members of those powerful sects, the Sceptics and the Cynics. The closest coincidence between the modern and the ancient diatribists is their hatred of materialism; but the moderns are far more frank about politics than their forerunners dared to be. Thus, dis-cussing the publication of the Yalta papers, Mort Sahl suggested that they "should be put out in a loose-leaf binder so you can add new betrayals as they come along." Of the American turncoats in Korea, he said "They were steadfast: they refused to give anything except their name, their rank, and the exact position of their unit." When Eisenhower was first elected, Sahl commented that the country needed a man on a white horse: "We got the horse, but there's nobody on him." And when Kennedy was nominated, he said the committee sent a wire to Kennedy's multimillionaire father saying, "You haven't lost a son, you've gained a country."

2. VARIATIONS OF THE SATIRICAL MONOLOGUE

This is not a history of satire. Although that would be an attractive enterprise, it would require three large volumes at least. This is an essay in morphology. We must now look, therefore, at some important variations on the first main type of satire, the monologue.

Far back among the earliest beginnings of verse satire, we find one important subspecies. This is the monologue which is delivered, not by the satirist in his own person, but by the satirist's victim. The poet makes a man whom he despises and hates stand up and speak his whole soul, boast of his evil talents, display his shameful faults, glory in his outrageous vices. Ultimately this is a trick of the theatre. It appears in the opening speech of Shakespeare's *Richard III*:

> I, that am rudely stamped, and want love's majesty
> To strut before a wanton ambling nymph;
> I, that am curtailed of this fair proportion,
> Cheated of feature by dissembling nature,
> Deformed, unfinished, sent before my time
> Into this breathing world, scarce half made up,

And that so lamely and unfashionable
That dogs bark at me, as I halt by them, . . .
I am determined to prove a villain.

The Greeks and Romans knew and enjoyed this trick, from hearing the boastful speeches of parasites, chefs, and soldiers of fortune in their comedies. From comedy, Ennius, the first poet to call his works "satires," transferred it into a monologue, in which, boasting and belching, a parasite explained what a rich and easy life he led by gorging other men's victuals, and thus (without realizing it) attracted scorn and hatred upon himself from all normal men.[46] This particular type of self-exposure is difficult to bring off, and must be written by a man who is both a skillful poet and a subtle psychologist; but when it succeeds the resulting self-portrait is immortal. Two good Latin satires (both shaped as dialogues, but mainly spoken by the men satirized) belong to this type: Horace's satire on the gourmet who is compiling a manual of exquisite living (*Serm.* 2.4), and Juvenal's portrait of the professional pervert who is growing old and starting to worry about the future (Juvenal 9). The Wife of Bath's monologue is another famous member of this group. Its most illustrious example is one of the master satires of the Renaissance: *The Praise of Folly* by Erasmus of Rotterdam (1509).[47] At first sight this might seem to be more correctly classified as a parody: a parody of an encomium. One of its chief models was the epideictic speech—the "display" oration in which divinities or great men or famous cities were praised, and which ingenious Greeks sometimes perverted to paradoxical praise of comical or repulsive things, such as baldness or flies. (They were followed in Erasmus' own time by Francesco Berni, encomiast of eels, debt, etc.) But, since this is *self*-praise, in which Folly herself speaks as the ruler of much of the world, glorifying her all but omnipotent domination, it is better described as a mighty mono-

logue satire, spoken not by the satirist but by his victim—
his collective victim, the fools of this world represented by
their presiding deity.

In modern times Robert Browning was the master of
this particular kind of satire. Most notable are his bitter
exposure of a "spiritualist," *Mr. Sludge, "The Medium"*—
which was very topical, being based on the career of a real
medium, whom Browning profoundly distrusted and despised, Daniel Dunglas Home—and the suave confession
he wrote for an ambitious worldly churchman, *Bishop
Blougram's Apology.* (The vein of satire is evident in the
grotesque names: for the bishop's interlocutor, Gigadibs,
and for the medium, Sludge.) Among my own favorites are
the bitter tirade of a hate-maddened monk, *Soliloquy of
the Spanish Cloister* ("G-r-r-r, there go, my heart's ab-
horrence! Water your damned flower-pots, do!"), and the
frivolous self-revelation of a lazy aimless Italian gentleman:
*Up at a Villa—Down in the City (As Distinguished by an
Italian Person of Quality).* In this poem, which rattles along
with a gay flimsy rhythm like the clatter of tambourines
and the jangle of mandolins, an Italian gentleman, too
noble to work but too poor to enjoy himself, laments that
his poverty forces him to stay on his estate in the country—
where there is nothing but scenery, olive-trees and oxen,
fireflies and tulips—when he would far rather live in the
city to enjoy its noise and bustle.

Had I but plenty of money, money enough and to spare,
The house for me, no doubt, were a house in the city-square;
Ah, such a life, such a life, as one leads at the window there!
Noon strikes.—Here sweeps the procession!
    Our Lady borne smiling and smart
With a pink gauze gown all spangles,
      and seven swords stuck in her heart!
Bang-whang-whang goes the drum, *tootle-te-tootle* the fife;
No keeping one's haunches still: it's the greatest pleasure in life.

The humorous incongruity of these sentiments, and the speaker's complete lack of self-criticism, assure us that we are right in calling it satire. Browning's graver monologues, which contain no bitter wit and no satiric distortion (*My Last Duchess, Saul, Cleon*) are varieties of drama.[48]

In another, a more subtle variant of the satirical monologue, we hear not the tirade of the satirist himself, nor the brag of his victim, but the voice of the satirist speaking out of a mask. Behind the mask his face may be dark with fury or writhing with contempt. But the voice is calm, sometimes soberly earnest, sometimes lightly amused. The lips of the mask and its features are persuasive, almost real, perfectly controlled. Some of those who hear the voice, and see the suave lips from which it issues, are persuaded that it is the utterance of truth and that the speaker believes everything he says.

This mask is Irony. The voice speaks a gross exaggeration or a falsehood, knowing it to be exaggerated or false, but announcing it as serious truth. Listening to it, intelligent men think, "That cannot be true. He cannot possibly mean that." They realize that he means the reverse of what he says. For the truth is sometimes so contemptible, sometimes so silly, sometimes so outrageous, and sometimes, unhappily, so familiar that people disregard it. Only when the reverse of such a truth is displayed as though it were veridical, can they be shocked into understanding it. Sometimes even then they are not convinced. They attack the satirist as a provocator, a liar. That is the penalty of being a satirist who uses irony.

Aristotle, who knew men and liked neat definitions, said that irony was the opposite of boasting: it was mock-modesty, dissimulation, self-depreciation.[49] The best known example of its practice is Socrates. After being pronounced by a sovereign authority (the Delphic oracle) the wisest man in the world, he went about asking people questions. To justify his interrogations, he explained that he himself knew nothing: he wanted therefore, to learn from others who were eminent men in their professions or convinced believers in their own knowledge. Surely they knew more than he. Surely they understood what they were doing and why they were doing it. Yet under Socrates' mild but searching cross-examination it usually transpired that they did not. Although they were experts and he posed as an ignoramus, his questioning proved that they knew nothing and did not even know they knew nothing.

This "irony" of Socrates produced divergent effects on the Athenians. Some admired it, and became his pupils. Others detested it, and condemned him to death.

In his time the word irony with its cognates was uncomplimentary. In Aristophanes (who is the first we know to have used it—in his satire against Socrates, *The Clouds*) and later in Demosthenes it is a harsh word, connoting sly cleverness. The type of irony is the fox; the user of irony is something very like a hypocrite. Socrates himself is never recorded as saying that "irony" defined his method of philosophizing; in the works of his pupil Plato the word is used (whether of Socrates or of others) as a joke or a reproach. It was Plato's pupil Aristotle who used irony in a good sense, to describe the gentle assumption of weakness and ignorance, coupled with a polite desire to be enlightened, which was the characteristic dialectic technique of Socrates; and he passed on the concept of Socratic irony through the Romans to us. Yet it was more than a technique of philosophical investigation: it was also a weapon of satire. Again and again in Plato's polemical dialogues we see Socrates using irony to satirize people and beliefs that he distrusts. Sometimes it is so gentle that it may have puzzled them, but could scarcely wound them. Starting his interrogation of the brilliantly versatile intellectual

Gorgias, he does not raise an abstruse metaphysical problem, but says to a pupil, "Ask him who he is." Sometimes it appears so sincere that the unwary reader may believe it the utterance of truth: as when, at the opening of *Menexenus*, he eulogizes the Athenian democratic orators, saying that after he listens to their patriotic speeches, their voices keep echoing in his mind, and that it is four or five days before he recovers and realizes he is not in heaven but in Athens.

The word "sarcasm" is often associated with irony. By derivation it means only cruel and biting speech of any kind. But no one would now think of calling the curses of Timon sarcasm. In general usage the word means irony whose true underlying meaning is both so obvious that it cannot be misunderstood and so wounding that it cannot be dismissed with a smile. Many of Hamlet's bitterest remarks are of this kind. "Vouchsafe me a word with you," says his false friend Guildenstern, and he replies, "Sir, a whole history." Attempting politeness, the king asks, "How fares our cousin Hamlet?" and Hamlet answers, "Excellent, i' faith; of the chameleon's dish: I eat the air."[50]

"Dramatic irony" is a particular type of theatrical effect which has no inherent connection with satire and is not relevant here.[51]

Gentle irony and wounding sarcastic irony can be used as weapons in all types of satire. They are, however, most effective in monologue, where a skillful satirist can, now and then, allow the real truth to flash through the mildly-colored cloud of dissimulation. The finest example of this in English is a prose pamphlet published by Jonathan Swift in 1729. Even in its title we see the touch of the ironist: *A Modest Proposal for Preventing the Children of Poor People in Ireland from Being a Burden to Their*

Parents or Country, and for Making Them Beneficial to the Public. It did not purport to be by Swift himself, but by an anonymous Irish patriot, whose motive in writing it was to benefit the kingdom of Ireland by solving one of its chief problems. The problem was that, under English domination, the population of Ireland was starving to death. One radical solution, Irish independence, could not then be considered. Other measures of complete social, financial, and moral reform were obviously right, and therefore (Swift thought) would never be initiated. So, behind the ironic mask of a philanthropist, he proposed a solution which was couched in terms of blandly persuasive logic, but was so atrocious that no one could possibly take it as serious.

This solution is that, since too many Irish babies are being born, they should be treated, not as human beings, but as animals. They should be slaughtered and eaten. The best age at which to eat them (from the point of view of the consumers) would be one year, when, having been nursed by their mothers, they would be healthiest, and their flesh tenderest. There is, Swift remarks, a supplementary suggestion, to let the children grow to the age of twelve or thirteen and then serve them in place of venison, which is becoming unhappily scarce; but to this proposal he objects, on the ground that the meat would, at least in the males, be lean and tough. "And besides, it is not improbable that some scrupulous people might be apt to censure such a practice (although indeed very unjustly) as a little bordering upon cruelty; which, I confess, has always been with me the strongest objection against any project, how well soever intended." Gravely, with a sweetly reasonable manner and an appearance of earnest concern for a miserable down-trodden population, Swift enumerates the advantages of his modest proposal. It will diminish the number of papists, increase the annual income of the coun-

try, and raise the general standard of living. Even in outline, this idea is horrible; the supporting arguments are
revolting; but Swift, who was long and deeply lacerated
by the restless ulcer of indignation, excels himself when
he goes into the practical details.

Cooking and serving. "A child will make two dishes [i.e.
two separate courses, for instance chops and a roast] at an
entertainment for friends; and when the family dines alone,
the fore or hind quarter will make a reasonable dish, and,
seasoned with a little pepper or salt, will be very good
boiled on the fourth day, especially in winter."

Other uses. "Those who are more thrifty (as I must
confess the times require) may flay the carcase; the skin
of which, artificially dressed, will make admirable gloves
for ladies, and summer boots for fine gentlemen."

And the most difficult problem of all, *the method of
slaughter.* "As to our city of Dublin, shambles may be
appointed for this purpose in the most convenient parts
of it, and butchers, we may be assured, will not be wanting;
although I rather recommend buying the children alive
and dressing them [i.e. cooking them] hot from the knife,
as we do roasting pigs."

In a dozen pages, Swift has written a perfect satire. After
going over the various advantages of this terrible scheme,
he briefly considers and contemptuously dismisses other
solutions for the Irish problem: what we should call sensi-
ble reforms, such as taxing absentee property-owners, cutting off expensive imports, and "teaching landlords to have
at least one degree of mercy toward their tenants." "Let
no man," he says with bitterness flashing out, "talk to me
of these and the like expedients, till he has at least some
glimpse of hope that there will ever be some hearty and
sincere attempt to put them in practice." The irony, the
scorn, and the despair of the satirist can go no further.
He has attacked the demoralized Irish poor, the dishonest

Irish middle-class, the luxurious and indifferent ruling group, the petty factionalism of all together, and the callous greedy English. "We can incur no danger," he says reassuringly, "in disobliging England. For this kind of commodity [infants' meat] will not bear exportation, the flesh being of too tender a consistence to admit a long continuance in salt; although perhaps I could name a country which would be glad to eat up our whole nation without it." Has satire ever had any immediate and visible effect? Certainly Swift's modest proposal had none. The rulers of Ireland did not think for a moment of eating the Irish children. They merely went on letting them starve to death.

Yet, fantastic as the proposal was, it could not be called wholly unthinkable. Another plan to solve the problem of Ireland, a plan which approached this in boldness and actually outdid it in finality, was seriously put forward by an Irish patriot. The unhappy Colonel Edward Despard (one of the last men to be hanged, drawn, and quartered for treason in England) told a friend that he had discovered an infallible remedy for the miseries of his country: "viz., a voluntary separation of the sexes, so as to leave no future generation obnoxious to oppression. This plan of cure would, he said, defy the machinations of the enemies of Ireland to interrupt its complete success."[52] Swift proposed regulated cannibalism, which would have kept the Irish people alive although lowering their rate of increase. Despard proposed racial suicide, which would have extinguished the suffering nation forever in three generations. Which was more extreme? If Swift, instead of recommending the sale, slaughter, cooking, and eating of babies, had written a Modest Proposal suggesting that the Irish should liberate themselves from servitude by refusing to have children altogether, would that pamphlet not have seemed to be a perfect satire on a hopeless situation?

We said that irony was stating the reverse of truth as though it were clear truth. In Colonel Despard's suggestion, what had been irony in Swift became theoretical truth, for it was seriously intended. And in our own day, with Adolf Hitler's "final solution to the Jewish problem" we have seen Swift's outrageous fantasy almost rivaled by reality. The heaps of gold teeth extracted from the mouths of corpses, the hair clipped from cadavers to be used as stuffing, the lampshades made of human skin, the medical experiments on living victims—do these not seem like the crazy imaginings of some perverse satirist, rather than part of the history of our own times?

Another mutant of the satirical monologue is that which was apparently invented by Horace: the letter, in verse, or even in prose. This is sometimes in danger of losing the full energy of satire, by becoming calm, suave, easy-going, or else by being purely personal and avoiding public problems and general moral judgments. Even so, some of Horace's *Letters* are in part satirical, and so are those of his closest modern counterparts, Boileau and Pope.[53] Among the earliest integral satires in French are the comic letters called *coqs-à-l'âne*, written by Clément Marot in the early sixteenth century. They are in one of the favorite meters of light easy satire, octosyllabic couplets; they contain rather too many personal touches and transient lampoons to be successful satire: still, they were popular in their day.[54] Several good scorners and haters have addressed their enemies in prose letters which contained enough good wit, variety, and venom to be called satirical. St. Jerome's bitter humorless nature and his intense seriousness kept him from being a true satirist: yet his letters often approach the vivacity and never lack the vigor of satire.[55] The famous letters in which "Junius" attacked George III and his government are surely among the masterpieces of satirical prose. There is something (as Pepys would say) mighty pleasant in watching the continuity of satire, seeing satirists admire one another, quote one another, even use one another as characters. It is particularly delightful to find, at the climax of Byron's *Vision of Judgment*, Junius himself appearing, and described in such a way as to be a very personification of satire.

> The shadow came—a tall, thin, grey-haired figure,
>   That looked as it had been a shade on earth;
> Quick in its motions, with an air of vigour. . . ;
> Now it waxed little, then again grew bigger,
>   With now an air of gloom, or savage mirth;
>   But as you gazed upon its features, they
> Changed every instant. . . .
>
> The moment that you had pronounced him *one*,
>   Presto! his face changed, and he was another;
> And when that change was hardly well put on,
>   It varied, till I don't think his own mother
> (If that he had a mother) would her son
> Have known, he shifted so from one to t'other.[56]

Yet another variant of the simple monologue is the pre-arranged dialogue. During the growth period of the Communist party in the West, this was one of its favorite techniques. The Communist department called Agitprop (for Agitation and Propaganda) used to send its agents out in teams, into areas where conditions were favorable for provoking "revolutionary action." An "activist" or a "cadre" would call a meeting outside a factory at the noon hour, and make a brief powerful militant speech. Before any of the ordinary audience could raise awkward objections to his statements, or voice opposition to his assumptions, a member of his team, posing as a simple man in the crowd, would ask a pointed question, for which the speaker was already prepared with a convincing answer. After that exchange another notional heckler would intervene with another problem, which the speaker would again solve effectively, and so on until it was nearly time for the meeting to close. Then the questioners would proclaim their complete satisfaction: "You're right, brother," they would cry, "I see the tricks of the exploiters now! Where do I sign up? Right here? Good! Come on, now, friend, you heard all that too, didn't you?"

In philosophy this particular trick goes back to the technique of Socrates, as represented by Plato. In the earliest Platonic dialogues, Socrates is shown as questioning, arguing, and meeting difficult and stubborn opposition. But in the dialogues which Plato wrote later, Socrates puts out his theories in a flow of talk which is virtually continuous, broken only by enquiries from his hearers which make part of the stream of his thought ("Why do you say that?" "So it would appear, Socrates") and encourage him to go on explaining in detail. In the same way, the popular teachers of philosophy such as Bion used to interrupt their own discourses to conjure up an imaginary opponent—a member of a rival school of philosophy or a hostile member of the crowd—whose objections they would state, and then ridicule, and then destroy.

Such a conversation, although it contains questions and replies, is not a true dialogue, because it is not the spontaneous talk of two people who are genuinely exchanging their thoughts on an equal basis. It is a monologue, disguised, and punctuated by pre-set questions. But because it is sometimes livelier than a continuous monologue, it makes good reading; and, in the hands of a poet who can write brisk colloquial exchanges, it can be truly dramatic. Here is Pope, justifying his own satire and defending himself against the charge of libeling his victims.

P. Who starved a sister, who forswore a debt,
I never named; the town's inquiring yet.
The poisoning dame—
                    F. You mean—
                            P. I don't.
                                        F. You do.
P. See, now I keep the secret, and not you!
The bribing statesman—
                    F. Hold, too high you go.
P. The bribed elector—
                    F. There you stoop too low.[57]

In such conversations the satirist himself is usually the principal speaker. He addresses a friend, or a critic. Often he opens his satire with a protest, as though he were in the middle of a heated discussion; or he starts by uttering, or by answering, a provocative remark; then he continues until he silences his interlocutor and wins his point. For example, the first satire in the first book of Horace is a diatribe against the accumulation of wealth, punctuated by objections from a miser. (It is introduced by a short discourse on human discontent, addressed to Maecenas, Horace's friend and patron; but that is merely a gesture of politeness. Maecenas himself was so rich that he had no need to worry about making money, and so indolent that he would never have dreamed, like the objects of Horace's satirical attack, of risking his life for it.)

Sometimes, in the technique of the Agitprop speakers, the satirist pretends to be answering various objections from different sides, voiced by faceless people who emerge from the crowd, each with his own question, and then vanish again.

Sometimes, again, he himself is the "straight man" and asks the questions. The protagonist of the satire, or a witness to the scene described, or some other talkative interlocutor, replies, at length and in detail. This is the method of Horace 2.8, an account of a pretentious dinner. Here the technique once again reminds us of Plato, who sometimes makes a man who was present at an important discussion repeat it in complete detail to someone who missed it.

In another variation, the satirist himself is questioned or criticized, and replies; but most of the satire is put into the mouth of his critic. That means that the satire is a sustained scolding, which the satirist apparently tries to answer, but without success. Horace, typically elusive and ironical, wrote this unusual and difficult type of satire beautifully. Such is the seventh satire of his second book, in which his own slave—relying on the traditional freedom of speech granted to servants at the Saturnalian holiday—addresses him with a string of severe reproaches on the inconsistencies of his behavior and the weaknesses of his character. The reproaches are perfectly true, as Horace admits by becoming furious and driving his candid servant out of the room; and, what is quite as amusing, they are couched in exactly the same tone as Horace's admonitory satires addressed by himself to others.

Satiric monologues cover almost every theme which has evoked derision and provoked protest, so that it would be unprofitable to try to classify their subjects. But we can say that they and their variants fall into two chief patterns: introvert and extravert. The introvert monologues (with their variants, the letter and the dialogue) are usually quiet talks delivered to a single individual or to a small group of friends: we are permitted to overhear them. The extravert monologues, on the other hand, are vigorous protests, aimed at awakening and instructing the mindless public, which has hitherto been terrified into silence or sunk in lethargy. Some monologists in satire use the concealed microphone; others the loud-speaker. Whatever the instrument, the satirist's own voice is nearly always heard through it.

But sometimes the satirist hides. He speaks, but in a disguised voice. He wears a mask, through which we see only a pair of bright sharp eyes. Of the antithetical pair of precepts given in the Book of Proverbs, he follows the second: *Answer a fool according to his folly, lest he be wise in his own conceit.* He is the satirist who works through parody.

III PARODY

1. PARODY AND MIMICRY

ARODY is one of the most delightful forms of satire, one of the most natural, perhaps the most satisfying, and often the most effective. It springs from the very heart of our sense of comedy, which is the happy perception of incongruity. A little boy and a little girl sitting at the head and foot of the dining-table, gazing gravely at each other, talking with exaggerated seriousness in adult phrases, saying "Hush, dear" to their parents, and wearing, one a false moustache and the other a spangled evening bonnet, are parodying, and thereby satirizing, the solemnity of all grown-ups and in particular the portentous authority of their mother and father. A great clown such as Grock laboriously shifting the piano toward the piano-stool, setting the height of the seat with microscopic precision, rolling up his sleeves, arching his eyebrows, gazing upward in anguished concentration, and then playing one brief two-note discord, is a criticism of all the romantic musicians who ever paraded their sensibilities on the concert platform. (I once saw Vladimir de Pachmann stop before attacking a group of Chopin pieces, and refuse to continue until a red-haired lady wearing a purple hat was removed from his line of vision.)

Nevertheless, parody is not merely distortion; and mere distortion is not satire. The underprivileged adolescent who pencils a beard on the face of the pretty model's photograph in the subway station is not indulging in parody, but simply in deliberate disfigurement, the envious destruction of the unattainable. When Marcel Duchamp exhibited a reproduction of the Mona Lisa to which he had attached a moustache, a goatee, and an opprobrious title, he was scarcely satirizing academic art: he was merely insulting it.[1] Consider also the numerous paintings by serious modern artists which are adaptations or travesties of "classical" pictures: Picasso's variations on Velazquez' "Las Meninas," Manet's "Picnic on the Grass."[2] Their divergence from their models we find interesting and lively: if it is sometimes a little grotesque, it is surely not insulting, and it carries no implication of contempt or hostility. Not all distortion, then, is parody.

And parody is not simply imitation. The mocking-bird is not a mocker: he imitates the songs of other birds through honest pleasure in their beauty and in his own agility. If a copy amuses its hearers and readers, and pleases them with the accuracy of its imitation, but leaves them quite unshaken in their admiration of the original, feeling no scorn for it and seeing no weakness they had not seen before, then it is no parody, and it is not satirical. But if it wounds the original (however slightly), pointing out faults, revealing hidden affectations, emphasizing weaknesses and diminishing strengths, then it is satiric parody. There have been many famous mimics who could copy to perfection the voices and manners of eminent men and women. When such a mime reproduces the speech and gait of his original with photographic precision, the audience cries out, in admiration of his skill, "Marvelous! Exactly like!" and its attention is centered on the magical ability of a good actor to change himself into a different personality. But when he exaggerates the faults and underscores the foibles of his victim, so that the audience sees something new and ridiculous, or contemptible, or hateful, in the character of the person mimicked, and laughs with a certain malicious delight, and thereafter admires the original a little less than it did before seeing that cruel portrait—then the act is parody, and the effect it produces is the effect of satire.

It is the difference between a portrait-sketch and a carica-ture. Both resemble the subject; but one is intended to reproduce the most central and typical features of its model, and the other (however delicately) to distort, to belittle, to wound.

Parody, then, is one of the chief shapes which satire assumes. We may define it as imitation which, through distortion and exaggeration, evokes amusement, derision, and sometimes scorn.[3]

It is tempting to divide parodies into two main types: formal and material. When we think of parody, we are apt to think first of all of an *external* resemblance between the original and its parodic copy. For instance, A. E. Hous-man's *Fragment of a Greek Tragedy* is a brilliant parody, primarily of the affectations of style which appear in nearly all Greek tragedies and of the over-scrupulously exact English translations which were current in the later nine-teenth century; and, secondarily, of the peculiar Greek dramatic convention which demands that the climactic acts of violence be committed off stage, while the chorus remains in full view of the audience, uttering helpless protests and solemn generalizations. Yet what is actually *done* in Housman's parodic tragedy is not far out of line with the average Greek tragic drama. It is the fantastic lan-guage which starts us laughing, and—although the crime of matricide is being committed—keeps us laughing to the end: for although every single idiom and image in the parody can be paralleled from one or more of the Greek tragedians, none of them ever heaped up so many bold metaphors and odd locutions within such a close compass as Housman does. He takes only the extremes and the eccentricities, and groups them into a montage which is cumulatively absurd.

Chorus:	O suitably-attired-in-leather-boots
	Head of a traveller,[4] wherefore seeking whom
	Whence by what way how purposed art thou
	come
	To this well-nightingaled vicinity?
	My object in enquiring is to know.
	But if you happen to be deaf and dumb
	And do not understand a word I say,
	Then wave your hand to signify as much.[5]
Alcmaeon:	I journeyed hither a Boeotian road.
Chorus:	Sailing on horseback, or with feet for oars?
Alcmaeon:	Plying with speed my partnership of legs.
Chorus:	Beneath a shining or a rainy Zeus?
Alcmaeon:	Mud's sister, not himself, adorns my shoes.
Chorus:	To learn your name would not displease me much.
Alcmaeon:	Not all that men desire do they obtain.
Chorus:	Might I then hear at what your presence shoots?
Alcmaeon:	A shepherd's questioned mouth informed me that—
Chorus:	What? For I know not yet what you will say.[6]
Alcmaeon:	Nor will you ever, if you interrupt.
Chorus:	Proceed, and I will hold my speechless tongue.
Alcmaeon:	—This house was Eriphyla's, no one's else.
Chorus:	Nor did he shame his throat with hateful lies.
Alcmaeon:	May I then enter, passing through the door?
Chorus:	Go, chase into the house a lucky foot,
	And, O my son, be, on the one hand, good,
	And do not, on the other hand, be bad,
	For that is very much the safest plan.

In all this, and in the rest of the *Fragment*, the thought is normal for Greek tragedy. The stress is on the massed absurdities of its expression.

Yet there are other satiric parodies in which the form is maintained virtually unaltered, without exaggeration, without distortion, while the thought within it is made hideously inappropriate to the form, or inwardly distorted, or comically expanded. These might be called material parodies. Many religious satires are of this nature. In them, a ritual pattern is preserved unaltered, but the thought within it is coarsened, made crueller or more violent, altered into selfishness or absurdity; and so, by contrast with the pious words and reverent formulae which carry it, is satirized. Robert Burns has a fine poem called *Holy Willie's Prayer*, which, except that it is in verse, is a perfectly regular and sincere prayer addressed to the Calvinist deity worshipped by many of Burns's Scottish contemporaries. (When I was a young Scottish churchgoer, brought up in doctrines not too far removed from Calvinism, and perfectly unable to conceive that they might be open to intelligent criticism, I was incapable of understanding why the poem was so much disliked by my elders and betters.) It is couched in the ritually correct form, opening with an invocation to the divinity and a statement of his power, proceeding to his special relation to the worshipper, then moving through a series of petitions, and concluding with an ascription of glory to his name. Its shape—apart from the verse-form, which is conventional and far from jocular—is correct. What makes it a parody is the distortion and exaggeration, the brutal frankness and the unctuous hypocrisy, which mould its thought.

> O Thou that in the heavens does dwell!
> Wha, as it pleases best Thysel,
> Sends ane to heaven and ten to hell,
>   A' for Thy glory;
> And no for ony guid or ill
>   They've done before Thee!
>
> I bless and praise thy matchless might,
> When thousands Thou hast left in night,
> That I am here before Thy sight,
>   For gifts and grace
> A burning and a shining light,
>   To a' this place.

Now, this is what many have thought, but few have said. (In essence, it is an expansion of the prayer of the Pharisee in Luke 18.11—a prayer which is itself fictional, and even satirical, being part of a bold and derisive contrast in one of Jesus' parables.) It is through its improbable frankness, its self-adoration disguised as awestruck humility, and its loving multiplicity of detail that *Holy Willie's Prayer* acquires the exaggeration and distortion characteristic of parody. And yet many of its separate sections look quite serious and authentic. Only two generations before Burns wrote it, the famous English hymnist Isaac Watts, in his "Praise for the Gospel," was singing:

> Lord, I ascribe it to Thy grace,
> And not to chance, as others do,
> That I was born of Christian race,
> And not a Heathen, or a Jew.

Holy Willie's final petition is so close to the thought of many genuine supplications to the Almighty that it almost ceases to be amusing.

> But, Lord, remember me and mine
> Wi' mercies temporal and divine;
> That I for grace and gear* may shine,
> Excelled by nane!
> And a' the glory shall be Thine,
> AMEN! AMEN!

At this point parody almost coincides with reality. Indeed, some of the best material parodies are those which might, by the unwary, be accepted as genuine work of the original author or style parodied. I believe, although I do not know for certain, that one example of this is the question which everyone nowadays believes was actually discussed by medieval scholars:

How many angels can dance on the point of a needle?

* property

St. Thomas Aquinas and other scholastic philosophers were indeed deeply interested in angels, and in the peculiar problems presented by the corporeal nature of angels, which must logically be less subordinate to gross physical laws than the bodies of human beings. They asked, for example, whether an angel could be in two places simultaneously; whether an angel could move from one point to another in space, without traversing the intermediate points; and whether two or more angels could occupy the same space. The schoolmen's discussions of some of these problems do appear nowadays to be strangely subtle, but they were framed seriously and they were seriously discussed. But the question about angels dancing on a needle's point is not framed seriously. It is therefore a satirical parody of medieval angelology. A moment's reflection will show that the form of the question is wrong. A medieval philosopher would not picture a group of angels as dancing, nor conceive them so small as to be associated with a needle, nor imagine them in such a paradoxical act as dancing on a tiny steel point. I feel sure, therefore, that this is a parody; but I have not been able to discover who first created it. There are some things like it in the annals of the Scriblerus Club; but perhaps the likeliest author of the hoax is Voltaire. Whoever invented it, the problem is now accepted as genuine. It is not thought to be an absurd parodic exaggeration, but a typical and authentic instance of the superfine ratiocination of medieval thinkers.

I once had the pleasure of actually seeing a new parody impose itself on the public, at least for a time, as the genuine article. On July 13th, 1942, southbound on a train for Washington, I opened the *New York World-Telegram* at the page then occupied by its chief columnists and commentators. In those days the bitter and vindictive Westbrook Pegler used to fill the top of the page with rancorous comment on his thousands of victims and enemies, while the bland and saccharine Eleanor Roosevelt, with a naïve and warm-hearted chronicle of her doings day by day, appeared at the foot. On this particular afternoon the piece under Westbrook Pegler's name opened like this:

> Yesterday morning I took a train to New York and sat beside a gentleman who was reading the 1937 Report of the International Recording Secretary of the World Home Economics and Children's Aptitude and Recreation Foundation, of which my very good friend, Dr. Mary McTwaddle, formerly of Vassar, is the American delegate. This aroused my interest and I ventured to remark that I had once had the pleasure of entertaining a group of young people who were deeply concerned with the neglected problem of the Unmarried Father. It turned out that the gentleman himself was an unmarried father so we had a very interesting chat until he got off at Metuchen.
>
> In the afternoon a group of young people came in for tea and we had a discussion of the effect of early environment on the efficiency of war workers. I am afraid environment is more important than many of us think and I have asked the Department of Agriculture to make a survey. Of course some people have more than others but then, I am afraid, very often the reverse is true and that is something that one cannot dismiss lightly these days.

After some further paragraphs in this vein, the piece ended with a frank and clear-eyed vision of a profound truth.

> In bed I read Ludwig Donnervetter's All Is Everything. It is very beautiful and brings out powerfully the struggle of the young people to organize their world through student collaboration and discussion. I sometimes think we seem to miss many opportunities for better understanding because peoples are set apart by differences in language.

The entire article was a very close imitation of Mrs. Roosevelt's intimately personal style, her idealistic outlook, and her infinite capacity for generalization. (Like the ship's captain in one of Joseph Conrad's novels, Mrs. Roosevelt tends to "enunciate platitudes, not with the desire to dazzle, but from honest conviction.") There were no introductory remarks, no cautionary footnotes, nothing but the signature of Mr. Pegler to indicate that the piece did not come from Mrs. Roosevelt's well-lubricated typewriter. For a moment, I hesitated. Could the article actually be by Mrs. Roosevelt, and had it been misplaced by a careless printer? But no, it was too absurd, and besides, there was Mrs. R. herself, chatting away in her accustomed place at the foot of the page. I reread the parody, and then looked round the lounge-car. Eight other men were reading the *World-Telegram*. One by one, I saw them all go through the same experience. They started to read Pegler's parodic "My Day." They stopped. They glanced down the page in puzzlement, to see whether Mrs. Roosevelt had slipped, or been pushed, upstairs. They found her. They looked back at Mr. Pegler's piece; and then, at varying speeds and with varying degrees of amusement (depending on their intelligence and their political sympathies), they began to savor the peculiar pleasure of satiric parody.

The same newspaper published, in 1960, another admirably close travesty, a *Standard Speech to the United Nations Organization*, suitable for all occasions. Although it is a parody, yet the speech could, with very little modification, be seriously delivered and seriously heard.

Mr. Chairman:
    On behalf of my delegation, my government, and the people of my country, I wish to congratulate you and your distinguished colleagues on
    (a) election
    (b) re-election
    (c) national independence day
    (d) successful survival of earthquake, revolution, &c.
        (*Choose one as appropriate.*)
    This being the first occasion during this session on which I have had the honor to address this distinguished committee, I would like to offer my sincerest congratulations also to

    (a) the Secretary-General
    (b) the Assistant Secretary-General
    (c) the secretary of the committee, &c. (*Choose one.*)
on (*See above, and choose one.*)

    There is a proverb in my country (*quote in original language*).

To turn now to the subject-matter of our debate, I wish to state briefly the views of my government on those vital issues which are involved. It is not necessary to repeat in this connection what was said

    (a) last year
    (b) a year ago
    (c) two, three, four, &c. years ago
by
    (a) my minister of foreign affairs
    (b) my prime minister
    (c) the head of my delegation
    (d) my colleague
    (e) myself
in this very
    (a) room
    (b) Assembly hall
    (c) corridor
    (d) bar
    (e) washroom, &c.

I need not do so for two reasons. The first is that I am sure the words spoken then are still as pertinent today as they were then. The second reason is that nothing that has occurred in the interval makes it possible for me to hope that more attention will be paid to our statements in the future than they have received in the past.[7]

Many of the finest political and religious satires are material parodies. They preserve the form of the original almost inviolate, and merely distort the content a little— usually making it franker and more realistic. Burns set down in his *Prayer* the secret thoughts of a stern self-righteous Calvinist. So Abraham a Sancta Clara says that the world is a theatre, in which the part of Mammon is acted by Praenobilis Dominus Aurelius Goldacker. A worshipper sings to him this litany:

> Silver have mercy on us
> Gold have mercy on us
> Silver hear us
> Gold hear us
> Silver, Father of Turmoil, have pity on us
> Gold, Consoler of the World, have pity on us.[8]

Blending political with religious satire, the British radical Henry Labouchere produced a parody of the national anthem, which kept the meter, the rhyme-scheme, and the refrain of the original unaltered, but changed the subject-matter to a realistic statement of fact about the prolific and profligate family of Queen Victoria.

> Grandchildren not a few,
> With great-grandchildren too,
>   She blest has been.
> We've been their sureties,
> Paid them gratuities,
> Pensions, annuities.
>   God Save the Queen.[9]

On hearing of this, Her Majesty was not amused. Yet the facts were unimpeachable, and the final sentiment unobjectionable. The good Queen would surely have been even less amused if she had foreseen that Max Beerbohm would not only cherish with mock reverence a copy of her diary, *Leaves from the Journal of our Life in the Highlands*, but embellish it with comments whose style equals the platitudinous viscidity of the original, actually written in a close imitation of her own imperial and royal handwriting.[10]

For there is a point at which, in order to satirize certain authors or artists or personalities, it almost becomes superfluous to parody them. The unfortunate young courtier who ventured to imitate Queen Victoria, in (if the expression is permissible) the flesh, may not have been cari-

caturing her at all. Certainly Max Beerbohm did nothing
more than write appropriately Victorian comments in Victoria's own published diary; and yet both mimicries had
the effect of satire. Perhaps we naturally enjoy the incongruity which ensues when anyone comparatively unimportant copies the manners of someone majestic and awesome. But perhaps also certain very grand people, and
grave books, and ambitious works of art, are already very
close to being absurd, so that they are apt, with the slightest
aberration in their taste or the slightest deviation of public
opinion, to become exquisitely ridiculous. We do not laugh
at Queen Victoria as a monarch. Although she was self-
willed about the duties she conceived to be hers, she performed them, or most of them, faithfully and efficiently.
We laugh at her as a person, because she was shallow and
pompous, and because she insisted, through obtruding her
private emotional life on the notice of the public, on being
observed as an individual, and therefore on subjecting
herself to personal criticism which she was ill-equipped
to sustain.

Since Queen Victoria lacked the power of self-criticism,
it was scarcely necessary for anyone to parody her. So also,
if, without excessive reverence and with our sense of the
absurd alert and lively, we examine the works of many
distinguished authors, we shall find them studded with
genuine passages which equal and sometimes excel the
burlesques of the most gifted parodist. In the same year,
1798, as Wordsworth composed his beautiful *Lines above
Tintern Abbey*, he produced a ballad which opens thus:

> Oh! what's the matter? what's the matter?
> What is't that ails young Harry Gill?
> That evermore his teeth they chatter,
> Chatter, chatter, chatter still?[11]

In that year also Wordsworth described a case of edema,
in verses almost as painful as the disease:

Few months of life has he in store,
　　As he to you will tell,
For still, the more he works, the more
　　Do his weak ankles swell.[12]

To anyone who is sufficiently interested to pursue the
subject into the more rarefied air of self-parody, I recommend an anthology of such delicate monsters drawn from
the works of many famous English bards. It was edited by
D. B. Wyndham Lewis and Charles Lee, and published in
1930. Its title, *The Stuffed Owl*, comes from a sonnet by
Wordsworth, little known but full of deep emotion. Miss
Anne Jewsbury, it seems, had been ill for a long time, and
her only constant companion had been (in Wordsworth's
phrase) "the inanimate object on which this Sonnet turns."
Friends, as the Poet Laureate observed, too rarely prop the
languid head.

Yet, helped by Genius—untired Comforter,
The presence even of a stuffed Owl for her
Can cheat the time; sending her fancy out
To ivied castles and to moonlight skies,
Though he can neither stir a plume, nor shout;
Nor veil, with restless film, his staring eyes.[13]

It is difficult to avoid the thought that Wordsworth, although he felt a deep and true sympathy for poor sickly
Miss Jewsbury, had more in common, by that time, with
the stuffed owl. In all English poetry there is no self-
parodist to equal William Wordsworth, although Ezra
Pound runs him very close. His peculiar achievement was
admirably summed up in a parodic sonnet by J. K. Stephen:

Two voices are there: one is of the deep;
It learns the storm cloud's thunderous melody,
Now roars, now murmurs with the changing sea,
Now bird-like pipes, now closes soft in sleep:
And one is of an old half-witted sheep
Which bleats articulate monotony,
And indicates that two and one are three,

That grass is green, lakes damp, and mountains steep:
And, Wordsworth, both are thine; at certain times
Forth from the heart of thy melodious rhymes
The form and pressure of high thoughts will burst:
At other times—good Lord! I'd rather be
Quite unacquainted with the A.B.C.
Than write such hopeless rubbish as thy worst.[14]

2. PARODY OF FORM AND
PARODY OF CONTENT

It is sometimes possible to classify satiric parodies as we have done, distinguishing those which are chiefly material parodies (like the religious and political satires) from those which (like Housman's skit on Greek tragedy) are mainly concerned with form. Yet form and matter are so closely connected in literature that it is often difficult and unwise to dissociate them.

For an example, let us take two famous poetic parodies which appear at first sight to be diametrically opposite to each other in purpose. One is a miniature Greek epic poem called *The Battle of Frogs and Mice*, apparently written in the fifth century B.C. by an author now unknown.[15] The other is a satirical narrative in English verse called *The Vision of Judgment*, written by Lord Byron in 1821. One is light and flimsy, the other rich and thoughtful. They both have one virtue which is not common among parodies: they are amusing even if you do not know the originals which they are satirizing.

Now, *The Battle of Frogs and Mice* is a careful and clever travesty of the style of Homeric epic poetry. It is in strong and melodious hexameter verse, full of traditional epithets and lofty words and bardic turns of phrase. It describes a savage war, which rages so violently that the gods themselves are compelled to intervene. Its heroes have noble compound names. Thus, the herald of the mice is introduced in a long-resounding hexameter:

Son of the proud Cheese-scooper was he,
named Saucepan-invader.[16]

The champions do deeds of prowess and deal mighty wounds and slay their opponents with the same high élan as the princes who fought on the ringing plains of windy Troy. They address one another in haughty chivalrous speeches, like the Achaeans and the Trojans; and the poet narrates their exploits with the same grave dedicated energy as Homer in the *Iliad*. In fact, the main difference between *The Battle of Frogs and Mice* and the *Iliad* is a matter of scale. The heroes of the *Iliad* are mighty men. The heroes of *The Battle* are vermin, whose one-day war is broken up by an incursion of miniature monsters, grandly and grotesquely described:

THE BATTLE OF FROGS AND MICE

Then Lord Lickplatter fell to the gallant Couch-in-the-Mudhole, crushed in the head by a vast boulder: out from his brainpan ran his brain through his nostrils; the earth was bespattered with blood-drops.

Then there came suddenly on, crook-claws and carapace-
  armored,
slantwise-walking and nipper-bejawed and bandy, the
  skew folk,
notch-in-the-arm, every one, eight-footed, with eyes in the
  bosom,
double of horn and tireless of body, the people whom men
  call
crabs.[17]

At first sight, we should judge that this was a satire on
the style of Homer, and of the poets who followed him in
epic. Homer is devoted to the sublime. In the *Iliad* particularly, nearly everything is over life-size, emotions are
intense, acts are superb and dramatic, the language is
fierce and haughty. Surely, then, *The Conflict of the Well-
Greaved Batrachia and the Swift-footed Rodents* is intended to satirize the old-fashioned, periphrastic, inflated
style of the Homeric epics. It does so through a favorite
device of stylistic parody. By applying Homer's manner to
subjects smaller and meaner than his own, it makes us feel
that the Homeric style is, even when applied to men, exaggerated, theatrical, and bogus.

There is a pleasant parallel in modern orchestral music:
Erno von Dóhnanyi's *Variations for Piano and Orchestra*.
As the piece opens, the piano remains silent, while the
orchestra plays an impressive introduction in the late
romantic style, something which might be the overture to
a tragic opera by Richard Strauss. Ominous chords rise
slowly, groping like blinded giants. The most formidable
sounds of the full orchestra mass themselves more and more
thickly: cumulonimbus gathering before a tempest. Somber
and menacing blasts from horns and trombones fill the air
like the groans of a Titan tormented. Crescendo, sforzando,
the music towers up to an awesome fortissimo, and then
stops. We await some tremendous utterance. The piano
enters. With one finger, the pianist plays the simple tune

which we know as "Baa, baa, black sheep, have you any wool?"

No doubt, then, the chief emphasis in *The Battle of Frogs and Mice* lies on the archaisms and exaggerations of the Homeric style of poetry. Yet after we finish reading the little poem, we see that its satire extends also to the subject-matter of the Homeric epics. The Olympian gods, who are often rather irreverently treated in Homer, are here mocked far more boldly—just as daringly as they were on the Athenian comic stage. Athena declares that she will not try to help the embattled mice, because they have spoiled the garlands and lamps in her temple by nibbling the wreaths and drinking up the oil; and, worse still, they have gnawed holes in her great ceremonial Panathenaic robe. At the end, when the other gods implore Zeus to stop the war, he takes his terrible swift lightning, utters a peal of thunder, and hurls the bolt down to earth with a fearsome crash. The mice pay no attention to it. Then again, as we watch the dauntless frogs and the magnanimous mice battling one another with iron will-power and unquenchable courage, and as we see them finally driven into rout only by a swarm of armored monsters with eyes in their breasts, we inevitably think of human wars; and we conclude that war itself, when seen in proper proportion, is essentially ridiculous, that human warriors are comparable to squabbling vermin, and that the poets who glorify their prowess are exalting the absurd, the animal side of human nature. Therefore *The Battle of Frogs and Mice*, although it appears to be a parody of a special poetic style, is also a parody of an important subject.[18]

Let us turn now to Byron's *Vision of Judgment*. It is a mistake to think that satire, or its masked servant parody, is purely negative and necessarily ephemeral. Satires often

live longer than their victims; and here is a parody which
has far outsoared its leaden-winged original.

King George III became insane at the age of fifty. He
recovered, and lapsed again, and at last crossed the frontier
permanently into the realm of darkness. When he died
at the age of eighty-two, he had been a burden to himself
and others for many years. Never a good king, he had been
neither popular nor successful, and it would have been best
to allow him to be forgotten. But the Poet Laureate,
Robert Southey, had a strong sense of duty, a passionate
devotion to the ideal of monarchy, and a high-ranging
poetic ambition. Since his appointment to the Laureate-
ship, he felt that far too few opportunities for writing
ambitious ceremonial poetry had presented themselves.
Among the living members of the royal house of Hanover,
not many were worth glorifying. This did not discourage
Southey. To celebrate the death of George III, he composed a poetic apocalypse in which he personally raised
George from the grave, escorted him up to the gates of
heaven, saw him examined, with witnesses for and against,
on his fitness to enter the hosts of the blessed, beheld the
king's triumphant entry into paradise, and returned home
again to that earthly paradise, Cumberland. This is not an
exaggeration. Southey's *Vision of Judgment* is actually a
vision of the resurrection, trial, and beatification of King
George III, written in a tone which the author himself
explicitly compares to that of Dante, and in English hexameters which were clearly intended to rival the verse of
Vergil.

The subject is one at which we are all reluctant to scoff,
for we should think seriously of death and the judgment;
but poor old George was too weak to support its weight,
and it became, even in Southey's reverent hands, absurd.
As the poet's own son put it, "It must be allowed that to
speculate upon the condition of the departed, especially

when under the influence of strong political feelings, is a
bold, if not a presumptuous, undertaking."[19] Even apart
from George's own narrow character and eccentric manners, his blindness and his insanity made him quite unfit
to be the central figure of a mighty cosmic event involving
God Almighty, the archangels and the angels, the souls of
the blessed, George Washington, Charles I, Queen Elizabeth, Richard Lionheart, Alfred the Great, Chaucer, Spenser, Shakespeare, Milton, Marlborough, Handel, Hogarth,
Warren Hastings, Cowper, Chatterton, Wilkes, Junius, and
Satan—all of whom, in the *Vision*, are concerned with his
admission to, or exclusion from, heaven. Southey could
scarcely ignore the unhappy disabilities under which the
deceased monarch had long labored: so he cured him of
them by a pair of miracles. Through the first miracle, King
George, having been resurrected, regained his reasoning
faculties. (Then, in a passage of exquisite absurdity, he
got a complete report of all that had happened while he
was out of touch. The report was rendered to him by
Spencer Perceval, once Prime Minister of England, who
had been murdered in 1812 and was restored to life by
Southey for this purpose.) Through the second miracle,
George regained his youthful appearance, and the mortal
put off mortality: not that any of the house of Hanover
were particularly handsome. The welcome given to King
George at heaven's portals, the unsuccessful attempt of the
Archfiend, supported by those minor devils, Wilkes and
Junius, to keep him out, and his triumphant entry into
the realm of eternal bliss are too ridiculous to describe
in detail. Were it not for a certain fluency in the verse and
a certain unmistakable conviction in the tone, they would
be irresistibly comical self-parody. Southey's *Vision of Judgment* reminds us, both of the huge baroque tombs of noble
nonentities which clog the churches of western and central
Europe, and of the elaborate floral tributes and family

tive and such a Laureate that, for him, any British monarch must be a good monarch. Even to criticize would be blasphemy against that divinity that doth hedge a king. Therefore his trial of George III was not a fair trial. He made Satan produce two of George's enemies: Wilkes and Junius. They were so overwhelmed by the pure light from George's fair white soul that they could offer no evidence. Disgusted, the devil threw them back into hell and joined them there. But Byron makes it a real trial, with the archangel Michael as defender, Satan as prosecutor, and a great cloud of witnesses. Byron's climax is the same conception as Southey's but better handled. Wilkes is called to the bar (that bar over which the blessed damozel was later to be seen leaning), and, with his typical contemptuous humor, says

> For me, I have forgiven
> And vote his habeas corpus into heaven.

But when Junius, a man of principle, is summoned, he will not forgive. In one of those deadly serious, profoundly true utterances which often come in the middle of the gayest satire, he accuses George III of injuring Britain.

> I loved my country, and I hated him.

And then—but before the verdict can be rendered, the case is blown up and whirled away in the fireworks of laughter. As a character-witness for George, Southey himself is miraculously wafted up to the judgment seat, and begins, inevitably, to read his *Vision of Judgment*. This is too much. It terminates the proceedings. Not even the austere court of heaven can remain in session and listen to Southey's poetry, unmoved.

> Those grand heroics acted as a spell;
>   The Angels stopped their ears and plied their pinions;
> The Devils ran howling, deafened, down to Hell;
>   The ghosts fled, gibbering, for their own dominions. . . .

Michael took refuge in his trump—but, lo!
His teeth were set on edge, he could not blow!

Saint Peter, who has hitherto been known
For an impetuous saint, upraised his keys,
And at the fifth line knocked the poet down—

—into his own favorite lake, Derwentwater. But how about
George III? Is he to be damned, or saved? Is he a sinner,
or a potential saint? Neither, says Byron. He is not a super-
nal being (as Southey made him) or a great evildoer: he
is a nincompoop, misplaced both on the throne of Great
Britain and in Southey's laureate vision. What does he
matter? Heaven is full of blameless idiots.

All I saw farther, in the last confusion,
Was, that King George slipped into Heaven for one;
And when the tumult dwindled to a calm,
I left him practising the hundredth psalm.

This satire might appear to be a parody of Southey's
poem which concentrates entirely on subject-matter. It
tells the same story, merely altering its tone and its out-
come: the setting, the problem, and most of the characters
are the same in the original and the parody. Yet in fact
Byron is also satirizing Southey's poetic form. Southey
chose hexameters for his *Vision*. But they never feel right
in English—unless perhaps for light gay subjects such as
Clough's *Bothie of Tober-na-Vuolich* or soft romantic subjects such as Longfellow's *Evangeline*. Usually they sound
forced and unnatural; Byron called them "spavined
dactyls." Byron himself chose a flexible eight-line stanza
which could carry both light humor and serious thought
equally well; and thus he criticized the medium of his
rival's poem. Furthermore, he produced a work which had
a far better structural pattern, more energy and variety,
and more psychological finesse. Although Southey compared his own work with that of Dante, Byron actually

From Byron's *Vision of Judgment*. Engraving by
Henry Fuseli. Photograph by Giraudon, Paris

comes closer to the bold clear-eyed realism of Dante, while Southey reads more like the slow processions of Petrarch's *Triumphs*. Byron's Satan is certainly worthy of Dante, or of Milton, or of his own soul at its blackest.

> Fierce and unfathomable thoughts engraved
> Eternal wrath on his immortal face,
> And *where* he gazed a gloom pervaded space.

Finally, Byron writes better poetry. In spite of his jocular damn-it-all amateurish manner, in spite of his pitying contempt for his central subject, the "old, blind, mad, helpless, weak, poor worm," and even although he thinks the trial itself as imagined by Southey is a ridiculous fantasy, he does it justice, he makes it dramatic, and he compels his readers to take sides and to feel the conflict.

So then, if we consider these two famous parodic poems, *The Battle of Frogs and Mice* and Byron's *Vision of Judgment*, and ask how they do their work, we shall find that at first sight one appears to be a parody of form, and the other a parody of matter; but that in fact the *Battle* also satirizes subject-matter and the *Vision* criticizes and ridicules form. It is therefore always difficult and sometimes impossible to distinguish between formal and material parodies. A parody which appears to concentrate entirely on mocking the outward semblance of some pretentious work of art may at the same time be gnawing at its inwards; and a parody which appears to neglect the problem of form and go straight to the heart of the subject may, either directly or by implication, carry a satiric criticism of the shape and outwardness of its victim.

Satiric parody is not confined to literature. In the plastic arts there are thousands of parodies, some satirizing a special style or an individual artist, some a particular theme. When the Laocoon group was rediscovered in 1506, it fascinated most contemporary artists. Michelangelo adapted the pose of one of its figures for an athlete on the Sistine ceiling and for the statue of a dying captive; Titian borrowed it for a painting of the martyred Saint Sebastian.[21] But some artists also felt what is indubitably true: that, in spite of the amazing technical and psychological skill of the sculptors, there is something hateful about the group. It is repulsive that the death agonies of a father and his children should be represented with such morbid realism. The Laocoon is an atrocity. Titian himself felt this, and indicated it clearly by executing a bitter parody of the group. Instead of being a man in the prime of life with his two young sons, the victims in his picture were a giant ape and two cubs. The grotesque poses and agonizing grimaces of the original were only slightly exaggerated. It was legitimate satire.[22]

In music there are many ingenious and delightful parodies. William Walton's *Façade*—which is now famous while the Edith Sitwell poems it was written to accompany are forgotten—parodies popular and sentimental songs of the early twentieth century. Stravinsky's ballet *The Fairy's Kiss* is a parody of Tchaikovsky, with the sugar content of that eminent sentimentalist raised to an almost diabetic level. There are some pleasant things in a set of piano pieces published in 1914 by Alfredo Casella, with two contributions from Maurice Ravel. This is called *À la manière de* . . . (doubtless after the famous collection of literary pastiches by Paul Reboux and Charles Muller) and contains satiric parodies of Brahms, Debussy, d'Indy, Chabrier, and even Ravel himself. The parody of d'Indy is charmingly called *Prélude à l'Après-midi d'un Ascète*; while Ravel takes one of the most banal of Gounod's melodies, "Gentle flowers, lie ye there," from *Faust*, and converts it into something dashingly Spanish in the manner of Chabrier. In 1926 the brilliant and opinionated composer

Titian's satirical parody of the Laocoon

Woodcut by Boldrini, after Titian. New York Public Library Prints Division

Arnold Schönberg, "to warn off some younger contemporaries who had been attacking him," published *Three Satires for Mixed Chorus* (op. 28), with bitter, contemptuous, but amusing texts by himself:

> What genuine false hair!
> What a periwig!
> Exactly (the little Modernsky thinks of himself)
> exactly like Papa Bach!

The music, of course deliberately grotesque, is parodically contrapuntal.

More recently, a brief but amusing satirical criticism was levelled at a famous orchestral piece. Everyone knows Tchaikovsky's overture *1812*, which depicts Napoleon's invasion of Mother Russia, and describes the conflict by alternating Russian themes and French themes until the Russian melodies swell out in victory. It is a grandiose piece, rather too simple-minded for refined musical taste, rather too Russian in its determined repetition of simple motives. At the end Tchaikovsky abandons the attempt to express his ideas in music,[23] and resorts to sheer noise. The overture concludes with a salvo of heavy guns. (It was originally designed to be performed out of doors in a Moscow square, with real cannon.) In recent years this effect has been successfully satirized. In February 1952 the Rochester Philharmonic Orchestra performed *1812* in the Eastman Theatre at Rochester, New York. Galloping cavalry and marching infantry, gay defiant trumpets and rolling obstinate drums, on they surged to the climax—"La Marseillaise" triumphantly overborne by Slav church-bells and the majestic Russian hymn "God the All-Terrible"; and then, as sensitive ears shrank from the uproar, the final explosion of cannon was set off behind the stage. While its echoes still reverberated around the theatre, a shower of white duck-feathers was released from the ceiling and floated slowly down through the throbbing air, covering the audience with a delicate satirical anticlimax.[24]

3. THE HOAX AS SATIRE

At this point satiric parody begins to pass out of the arts into action. In action, its most famous and representative product is the hoax. As far as I know, there is as yet no good analysis of this branch of satire. There are amusing descriptions of individual hoaxes, and occasionally a distinguished hoaxer such as Hugh Troy has his biography written; but most of the anthologies of hoaxes fail to define the hoax with any accuracy. It is really quite mistaken to discuss a vile propaganda fabrication such as the "Protocols of the Elders of Zion," a greedy swindle such as the financial career of Ivar Kreuger, and a harmless joke such as a news-photograph of a newly captured pterodactyl published on April Fool's Day, as though they were all inspired by the same impulse and produced the same effect.[25] Hoaxes are lies or exaggerations intended to deceive. Swindles are lies or exaggerations intended to deceive. The purpose, it is the purpose that defines them. The hoaxer wants to prove something. The swindler wants to get something. The swindler wants to deceive everyone permanently (or at least until he has died in triumph). The hoaxer wishes at some time to be exposed, or to reveal his own jest. The result of a successful swindle is gain for the swindler. The result of a successful hoax is hearty laughter —although it is the laughter of satire, in which the victim rarely joins.

To clarify the nature of the satiric hoax, let us look at three famous impersonations. They all took place within the present century, and all involved the same type of deceit practiced on the same type of victim. One was carried out in 1944, one in 1910, and one in 1906.

In 1944 an elderly British lieutenant called Clifton

James, who had been an actor in civilian life, was picked out of a desk-bound job in the Army Pay Corps, and given a special mission. He was to impersonate General Bernard Montgomery. Physically he looked very much like his model: spare frame, keen birdlike face, brisk nervous manner. Spiritually, he was almost the exact reverse of that harsh little martinet. But he was shown motion-pictures of Montgomery, he was seconded to Montgomery's personal staff so that he might learn the timbres of his voice and observe his mannerisms, he was given an exact replica of Montgomery's highly individual uniform, and finally he talked with Montgomery himself face to face. After this training, he was briefed, and converted into Montgomery. He was flown to Gibraltar, where he was received by the Governor with a guard of honor, and observed by a number of German agents operating under Spanish cover. Next, he proceeded to Allied HQ in North Africa, where he was seen in public for an entire week. Then he returned to Britain in utter secrecy. This impersonation was so successful that it deceived the German intelligence organization led by Admiral Canaris. It was one part of the stupendous deception worked out by Allied intelligence officers in order to conceal from the Germans the time and place of the D-Day landings—and in particular to make them believe that a massive blow was to be delivered across the Mediterranean from North Africa into southern France. This, like the rest of the great D-Day deception, was brilliantly successful. Was it a hoax?[26]

Two wars earlier, in 1906, a middle-aged German workman called Voigt, who had spent fifteen years of his life in prison for minor offenses (except that the Germans do not consider any offense unimportant), found that it was impossible for him to get regular employment. He was a shoe-machinist, but whenever he got a job, the police told the factory manager he was an ex-convict and moved him on. He determined to leave Prussia for good and go south, but he could not travel without a passport, and the police would not let him have one. Unable to loosen the chains of authority by persuasion, he determined to break them by superior force. In his memoirs he says that he recalled how the Great Elector imprisoned the mayor of Königsberg and Philip Kohlhaas defied the authorities of Saxony. So he procured the uniform of a captain in the Prussian army, took command of a squad of soldiers he met in a Berlin street, transported them by train to the quiet suburb of Köpenick, posted them with fixed bayonets outside the town hall, sent the chief of police home to take a bath, and arrested the mayor and the treasurer, saying "The administration of the town is now in my hands. For all that happens I am responsible!" Only then did he realize that the intricacies of the German administrative machine had thwarted him once again. Passports were not issued by local police stations, but by the regional Landratsamt, which had no office in Köpenick. Taking four thousand marks from the treasurer's office (and giving a receipt for it), he went back to Berlin in mingled triumph and despair. A few days later he was caught, and sentenced to four years' imprisonment in a fortress. Rather unexpectedly, he was later pardoned by Kaiser Wilhelm II (perhaps because the Kaiser was, like him, a fraud), and, with a hundred thousand marks which were collected for him by German sympathizers, disappeared from history. Most Germans thought that the Captain of Köpenick was a criminal. Outside Germany, people laughed. Was his masquerade a hoax?[27]

The third of these adventures ascended to a higher level. Whereas Clifton James deceived one section of the German intelligence, and poor Voigt the municipal administration of a Berlin suburb, this group hoodwinked the Royal Navy. About 1910, the famous English joker Horace de Vere Cole collected a small group of friends, had them made up with

Oriental robes, dark faces, and beards, and converted them into the Emperor of Abyssinia with his imperial retinue. Preceded by a forged telegram from the British Foreign Office, the group traveled down to Weymouth, were taken aboard H.M.S. "Dreadnought," the flagship of the British Channel Fleet, reviewed the Admiral's guard of honor, inspected the ship, talking to one another in Abyssinian, and returned in safety and secrecy to London. There were several awkward moments—for instance, in the British cold and rain the moustache of one member of the imperial suite began to peel off, and another of the participants, who was difficult to disguise because he stood six feet five, recognized his own cousin on the quarterdeck. Three members of the group later became well-known in Bloomsbury: the artist Duncan Grant, Adrian Stephen, and his sister Virginia. Stephen wrote a little book on the adventure, which contains some delightful details.[28] Since he had to pose as the interpreter, he had to pretend to turn his hosts' English into long paragraphs in a foreign language. He tried Swahili, which he had attempted to learn during the train journey in a grammar produced by the Society for the Propagation of the Gospel; but his Swahili soon gave out. Rather than remain speechless, he went on:

Tahli bussor ahbat tahl aesque miss. Erraema, fleet use. . . .

which is the opening of a sad and passionate passage in Vergil's *Aeneid*, but so distorted in word-division and accentuation that only a very alert classicist, and certainly no preoccupied naval officer, would ever detect it.[29] Throughout the remainder of the visit Stephen spoke in a mixture of Homer's Greek and Vergil's Latin, blessing the fact that he had had a good classical education. Amusing as this is, perhaps the most charming thing about the little adventure is to see, in the photograph of the masqueraders, peering out below a turban, from a heavily bearded and moustached brown face, the high slender nose and large sensitive eyes of the future Virginia Woolf.

Now, a hoax is correctly defined by the Oxford Dictionary as "a humorous or mischievous deception with which the credulity of the victim is imposed upon." It is clear therefore that the element of pure amusement and pure mischief in a deception determines whether or not it is satire. Thus, the impersonation of General Montgomery by Lieutenant James was in deadly earnest, and was aimed at fulfilling a highly important purpose. Similarly, when Hannibal drove herds of cattle along a mountainside in the darkness, with burning torches tied to their horns, in order to make the Romans believe his entire army was shifting ground and escaping from a trap, he was not hoaxing the enemy: he was practicing a serious military deception, setting up a moving decoy. The case of the Captain of Köpenick is more complex. Although most of the Germans took it seriously, hardly anyone else did. Therefore, within Germany it was a criminal fraud; but—because it displayed in full efflorescence certain German characteristics which members of other nations find unadmirable and ludicrous —for the rest of the world it was a hoax: it was the equivalent of a satire on German militarism, German discipline, German accuracy, all those painful German virtues.

And what of the Emperor of Abyssinia? Does that impersonation contain satire? One might perhaps dismiss it as a prank, like putting a cow into the chapel tower. But Adrian Stephen's book shows that it cut deep. The Admiral of the Channel Fleet and his officers were laughed at. When they went ashore, little boys followed them, shouting "Bunga bunga!" in imitation of the "Abyssinians." Questions were asked in Parliament. The Navy grew very bitter. In the wardroom, Virginia Stephen was called "a common woman of the town"—no doubt because she had disguised herself as a man and made an unchaperoned excursion into male territory. Finally, Horace Cole and Duncan Grant were sought out by groups of officers who intended to thrash them. These vengeful warriors were at last contented with administering a few symbolic taps with a cane, but it was clear they felt their honor had been wounded and needed some repair. The hoax, therefore, was felt to be meaningful: it was critical; it was satiric. It exposed the bland readiness of the British government and the Royal Navy to entertain any distinguished foreigner, however odd-looking, without enquiring closely into his bona fides, and to do him the honors so thoroughly that he went away awed and flattered. That kind of diplomatic courtesy helped to build up a gigantic empire. The "Dreadnought" hoax was a mocking exposure of its flimsiness and insincerity. Thus, the light-hearted little impersonation carried out by half a dozen youngsters in their twenties was a satire on the entire British imperial system.

At least two of the world's most famous satiric writers were responsible for elaborate hoaxes, which were essentially parodic satires. In the year 1532—the same year which brought forth *Pantagruel*—Rabelais published two forecasts of the future. One was an *Almanac for 1532, Calculated on the Meridian of the Noble City of Lyons and on the Climate of the Kingdom of France*. On its title-page he described himself as a doctor of medicine, which he was not yet, and a professor of astrology, which he would never be. This spoof delighted Rabelais and he kept it going for nearly twenty years; but almost every copy has now disappeared. The other was a *Pantagrueline Prognostification* signed Maistre Alcofribas Nasier. (The pseudonym is an anagram on his own name, but, like the word "almanac," it looks and sounds Arabian.) The book is an amusing parody of the vague predictions of the usual popular almanac: "This year the blind will see very little, and the deaf will hear poorly. . . . Old age will be incurable this year, because of the years past. . . . According to the calculations of Albumazar, this will be a plentiful year for those that have enough. . . . In winter wise men will not sell their fur coats to buy firewood."

Nearly two centuries later a crueler satirist produced a deadlier hoax. A self-educated English cobbler, using the name of John Partridge, had made a good living for many years by writing and publishing a yearly almanac of forecasts for the coming twelvemonth, called *Merlinus Liberatus*, "Merlin Set Free." This in itself would scarcely have been objectionable; but the danger with all this kind of forecasting is that the unscrupulous can use it to prey upon the unwary by slipping in propaganda, and Partridge so used it. He was an out-and-out Whig, an enemy of the Established Church, and an ardent foe of the Papists: he saw danger to British liberties everywhere, and frequently influenced the public mind by the gravity of his prophecies. He caught the sharp cold eye of Jonathan Swift, who resolved to destroy him. Partridge had repeatedly challenged rival astrologers to compete with him in foretelling the future. Under a fictitious name, Swift accepted the challenge. At the end of 1707, as usual, Partridge published his *Merlinus Liberatus* for 1708. A little later Swift published a collection of *Predictions for the Year 1708, by Isaac Bickerstaff*. Most of the Bickerstaff forecasts were harmless, but the one which really told was the prognostication that John Partridge, almanac-maker, would die of a raging fever about 11 p.m. on March 29, 1708. Then, on March 30, Swift brought out a little book portentously entitled *The Accomplishment of the First of Mr. Bickerstaff's Predictions. Being an Account of the Death of Mr. Partridge, the Almanack-maker*. It described the last illness and death of Partridge, exactly as foretold—except for the minor fact that Isaac Bickerstaff's calculations had been wrong by nearly four hours. Shortly afterward, having killed Partridge, Swift nailed down his coffin by publishing a funeral *Elegy on Mr. Partridge.* The wretched man was now so generally believed to be dead that the publishers' guild, the Company of Stationers, took him off its roll of living members; and a copy of Bickerstaff's *Predictions* which reached Portugal was solemnly burnt by the Holy Inquisition, on the ground that a forecast so terrifyingly accurate could only have been made by direct inspiration from the devil. Meanwhile, Partridge himself was protesting that he was not dead. He even advertised in the newspapers that he was alive and well, and issued an almanac for 1709 repeating the fact and attacking "Bickerstaff" as an impudent lying fellow. But this simply evoked from Swift a *Vindication of Isaac Bickerstaff*, pointing out that the supposed Partridge's denials of well-established facts were absurd. Seldom has there been a more keenly conceived and efficiently executed hoax. Partridge actually died. At least, he issued no annual almanac for 1710, 1711, 1712, or 1713; and though he plucked up courage and produced one for 1714, he was, like his own Merlin, "overtalked and overworn" and expired in real earnest the following year.[30]

Purely literary hoaxes are rather difficult to execute, but if successful can give rare delight. Prosper Mérimée in 1827 satirized the romantic cult of unknown and exotic countries by creating a non-existent "Illyrian" poet called Hyacinthe Maglanovitch. He translated his poems into French (calling the collection *La Guzla*), gave him an imaginary biography, and published a portrait of him—which was in fact a portrait of Mérimée himself wearing Balkan costume and a huge false moustache. For a time, he had Maglanovitch accepted by historians of European literature. Germans wrote serious studies of his folkish poetry. The young savant Ranke cited him in a history of the Serbian revolution. Several critics translated them into English, and Pushkin, enthusiastically greeting a Slavic brother, turned a dozen of them into Russian. They inspired the Polish poet Mickiewicz to lecture on Serbian poetry at the Collège de France, and Gérard de Nerval used them for the libretto of a romantic opera called *The Montenegrins*. Once again a satire had found acceptance as the truth.[31]

There was a powerful expansion of literary production and appreciation in the United States between 1900 and 1920. In 1916, the existing Americo-European schools called Imagism and Vorticism and Chorism were joined by a new one called Spectrism. It was represented by some fifty lyrics in more or less free verse, by Emanuel Morgan and Anne Knish. Their volume, *Spectra: A Book of Poetic Experiments*, had a sympathetic title and "intriguing" contents. For instance—

> Despair comes when all comedy
>   Is tame
> And there is left no tragedy
>   In any name,
> When the round and wounded breathing
>   Of love upon the breast
> Is not so glad a sheathing
>   As an old brown vest.
>
> Asparagus is feathery and tall,
> And the hose lies rotting by the garden-wall.

This book was welcomed by some American critics and disparaged by others, taken seriously by almost all. It was a hoax. The Spectrists were invented by a real poet, Witter Bynner. Their poems were composed in ten days, with the help of ten quarts of whisky, by Bynner and his friend Arthur Davison Ficke. The two hoaxers sent the collection to a reputable publisher, who accepted it as a bona fide manuscript. *The New Republic*, always looking for a better future, helped the spoof by asking Witter Bynner himself to review *Spectra* in its columns—which he did with gusto. ("It takes a challenging place," he wrote, "among current literary impressionistic phenomena.") Reporters tried to interview Miss Knish and Mr. Morgan; magazines of poetry asked eagerly for more of their poems; a group of Wisconsin undergraduates parodied their work by inventing the Ultra-Violet School, headed by Manual Organ and Nanne Pish (these subtle student jokes!); and an officer in the American army, talking to Ficke, actually claimed that he himself was Anne Knish and had written the poems published under her name. Intellectuals were much too ready in those days to give serious attention to anyone who claimed to have a new theory of poetry, and to accept flimsy little strings of words as genuinely powerful or perceptive lyrical poems. The *Spectra* hoax was legitimate satire.

Satirists are always in danger. Witter Bynner revealed the masquerade in April 1918, in response to a direct challenge delivered in public. Before the laughter had died away, he himself was hoaxed. He was sent a sheaf of untutored but strangely sincere poems by a farmer, Earl Roppel, of Candor, N.Y. He admired them. He showed them to his friends, one of whom set a Roppel lyric to music and had it sung by a choir of three thousand voices. (It was a patriotic poem, and this was 1918.) Both Roppel and his poems were the creation of two young sceptics, Malcolm Cowley and S. Foster Damon, who wanted to see if the hoaxer could himself be hoaxed.

Earl Roppel and the Spectrists have been followed by others: Fern Gravel, the child poetess of Iowa, author of *Oh Millersville!* (Muscatine, Iowa, 1940); and Ern Malley, the imaginary mechanic doomed by Graves' disease, who was given thirty pages by the leading Australian literary magazine. At this point truth and satire, reality and hoax, begin to interpenetrate. The poems of "Ern Malley," when prosecuted for obscenity, were defended by T. S. Eliot and Herbert Read. The name of the leading Australian literary magazine is said to be *Angry Penguins*. Can this be true? Can there ever have been a real person called Ezra Pound, who named his son Omar Shakespear Pound?[32]

It would be wrong to leave this part of the subject without praise for one of the deftest and funniest satires in modern literature. This is a short book by the eminent French novelist Jules Romains, called *The Pals* (*Les Copains*): an account of three major and several minor hoaxes. (Romains himself, as a student at the École Normale Supérieure, is said to have originated several superb hoaxes. The special word at the Normale for a hoax is *canular*; and not long ago Romains, now seventy years old and a member of the Academy, procured the admittance of *canular* to the august Dictionary of the French Language.) His novel tells how a group of practical jokers from Paris invaded two of the dullest and quietest towns in the provinces: how, in one, disguised as government officials, they turned out the entire garrison and made it repel an imaginary guerrilla attack at half-past two in the morning, to the great inconvenience of the soldiery and the terror of the citizenry; how one of their group entered the pulpit in the church, posing as an eminent priest lately returned from a visit to the Pope, to deliver a sermon on the texts *Love one another* and *Be fruitful and multiply*, which had the most potently protreptic effect on the congregation; and how, in the other town, they erected an equestrian statue, classically nude, of the local Gallic hero Vercingetorix, which, after being unveiled and addressed in passionate rhetorical apostrophes, silenced the orator and put the audience to flight with a shower of baked potatoes. As you read, these appear to be merely practical jokes; but on reflection it becomes clear that Romains is writing a satire on certain ingrained traits of the French provincial: respect for the army, regional patriotism, ceremonial oratory, arid piety, devoted self-admiration, and lack of humor. All these qualities are vulnerable to the finest of all French arts. Great are the French in Amour; greater still in Cuisine; greatest of all in Wit.

4. TYPES OF LITERARY PARODY

Satirists have taken all the famous patterns of literature and distorted them. The most important have naturally evoked the most energetic and penetrating parodies. We must, however, be careful to differentiate two principal methods of satirizing serious literary forms such as epic, drama, and romance. One may be called mock-heroic, the other burlesque.

A mock-heroic parodist pretends to be serious. His vocabulary is grand or delicate. His style is lofty, full of fine rhetorical devices and noble images. If he speaks in prose, his sentences are long and orotund; if in poetry, he uses a dignified meter. He is ambitious, and pretends to rival the mightiest achievements of serious literature— Homer, Vergil, Cicero, Livy, Dante, Shakespeare. He strikes Apollo's lyre. He calls on the Muses.

The writer of burlesque is a vulgarian. He likes low words. (This is one of the surest tests for determining a literary genre, particularly in Latin and in modern literatures influenced by Latin standards. In the noble style, flat ordinary words are kept to a minimum, diminutives are eschewed, and vulgar words prohibited, unless on rare occasions for special purposes. Thus, there are two words for "tired" in Latin, which have the same rhythmical pattern and sound much alike: *lassus* and *fessus*. Of these, one, *fessus*, is "noble"; the other is ordinary, with overtones of colloquialism—*lassus*, which was naturally carried over into some of the Romance languages, *las, lasso*. Therefore

Vergil in the *Aeneid* uses *fessus* many times, but *lassus* only twice, both times in contexts of tender emotion.[33] The word *puella*, "girl," is a diminutive, common in love poetry, and comedy, and satire. Vergil prefers *uirgo*, and uses *puella* only twice in his epic, both times in pathetic passages.[34] In Latin and in later Greek history, oratory, and serious drama, as in epic, the choice of words is carefully and strictly limited.) The habitual use of common or vulgar words and ignoble images always stamps low comedy, epigram, and certain types of satire; and it is typical of burlesque. The writer of burlesque in prose or poetry also likes a simple colloquial style, avoids solemn rhetoric, tries to sound natural. His sentences are short and easy; if he writes verse, his meter is jogtrot (octosyllables are a favorite) or clumsily comical. His poetry is often like prose, and his prose like conversation. Or else he may turn all his poetic art into laughable ingenuity, rhyming "Peri Hupsous" to "dupes us" and "veni, vidi, vici" to "twice I";[35] he may coin a new language, hybridized from dignified Latin and colloquial Italian, called "macaronic" after the coarse mixed peasant dish.[36] He eschews artifice and ambition, and tells the plain unvarnished truth. The mock-heroic parodist pretends to soar. Burlesque toddles, or limps, or squats. The inspiration of the burlesque writer is not Apollo, but Pan; not the Muses, but Momus.

The mock-heroic parodist loves to use quotations from high poetry, as nearly as possible in the original words; he gets his satiric effect by applying them to less serious themes than the original. The burlesquer, if he borrows from serious literature, debases his borrowing by translating it into lighter rhythms and coarser phrases. In mock-heroic, supernatural intervention, ostensibly serious, is frequent: Belinda is warned and defended by sylphs, Pallas delivers the debtor from jail, the goddess Dulness mounts the throne of the universe.[37] In burlesque, supernatural figures are made "human, all too human," talk coarsely, behave ridiculously, act ineffectively or absurdly. Vergil depicts Fame as a formidable monster, sister of the earth-born Giants; Butler makes her

> a tall long-sided dame,
> That like a thin camelion boards
> Herself on air, and eats her words.[38]

Reading mock-heroic poetry, we are often surprised by echoes of true nobility, glancing reflections of real beauty. Reading burlesque, we are often shocked by harsh words and vulgar pictures. Thus, in the mock-heroic games of Pope's *Dunciad* two publishers compete in urinating. Although the notion is disgusting, the description is actually graceful, the bodily fluid is never named, and the efforts of the contestants are compared to the noble classical rivers Maeander and Eridanus.[39] But coprologous Swift, depicting the Irish parliament as a house of bedlam, hails two of its members with revolting frankness:

> Dear companions hug and kiss,
> Toast old Glorious in your piss.[40]

The two types of humor are dissimilar in method and in effect. A mock-heroic parody takes a theme which is usually trivial or repellent, and treats it with elaboration, grandeur, and feigned solemnity. A burlesque treats its subject with ridicule, vulgarity, distortion, and contempt.

In mock-heroic parody, the actual story told may be interesting and important; it need not necessarily be mean; but it must be smaller than the pomp and circumstance surrounding it. The best example is the earliest. The battle between the mice and the frogs was, for them, a serious thing: they suffered; they bled; they died. But when the little creatures were given grand compound names resembling the ancestral appellations of ancient heroes, when their tiny bitings and scratchings were described with all the intensity of a Homeric battle, and when the Olympian gods watched their warfare with deep concern, then the whole thing became ludicrous. Similarly, there was nothing intrinsically base about the subject of Pope's little masterpiece. Lord Petre cut a lock of hair from the nape of Arabella Fermor's neck. She was beautiful, he was gallant, both were young, rich, and well-born. Treated as a piece of amorous play, the incident could have made a charming elegiac poem—and indeed Pope had in mind a famous love-elegy by Catullus, on a lock of hair cut off as a gage of fidelity.[41] But because Lord Petre's forwardness had incensed the Fermors and the two families had quarreled, Pope wished to "laugh them together again."[42] He chose therefore to show that the incident was not a serious outrage, by treating it with an exaggerated gravity which was in itself comical and made the offended dignity of the Fermors comical too.

A mock-heroic parody is like a laughing child or a grinning dwarf wearing a full-scale suit of majestic armor. A burlesque epic is like a powerfully muscled boor carrying a cudgel and riding a donkey. He is strong enough, perhaps, to accomplish bold deeds of derring-do, but he will not, because he has no style, no inner harmony, no ideals. Whatever he attempts will be graceless and absurd. In both senses, he is a clown.

Satirists do not always observe these critical distinctions. Occasionally an author will pass from mock-heroic to burlesque within the same work, or the reverse. Cervantes sometimes does so in *Don Quixote*, and Tassoni constantly does it in *The Rape of the Bucket*. But on the whole, most mock epics and parodies of drama and of other serious literary types fall pretty clearly into one class or the other: mock-heroic, where the treatment is grandiose; and burlesque, where the treatment is low. Don Quixote himself is mock-heroic; Sancho is burlesque. Pistol is mock-heroic; Falstaff, apart from one scene, is burlesque.

Although these two styles of satire are clearly different, it is not easy to find fully satisfactory names to distinguish them. Addison (in number 249 of *The Spectator*) made the distinction fairly clear, but did not name the two types. "Burlesque is therefore of two kinds: the first represents mean persons in the accoutrements of heroes, the other describes great persons acting and speaking like the basest among the people. Don Quixote is an instance of the first, and Lucian's gods of the second. It is a dispute among the critics whether burlesque poetry runs best in heroic verse, like that of the Dispensary [Garth's poem on a squabble among doctors]; or in doggerel, like that of *Hudibras*. I think when the low character is to be raised, the heroic is the proper measure; but when a hero is to be pulled down and degraded, it is done best in doggerel." Since "mock-heroic" does contain the idea of grandeur and nobility, while "burlesque" (from the Italian *burla*, "jest") makes us think of guffaws of laughter, "mock-heroic" seems appropriate for *The Battle of Frogs and Mice* and all its successors, "burlesque" for *Hudibras* and all its tribe.

EPIC

Many successful satires have been couched in the form of epic parody. The first satire of Lucilius showed the gods in council, determining to save Rome from destruction by killing off one of its most obnoxious politicians, and was apparently a close parody of the epic *Annals* of Ennius. Juvenal's fourth satire, on the terrifying trivialities of the tyrant Domitian's court, is a travesty of the laureate poet Statius's epic on Domitian's German wars.[43] There are a number of pleasant satires on human derring-do, in the form of parodic epics about animals, all more or less indebted to *The Battle of Frogs and Mice*: a *Battle of Flies* by the macaronic poet Folengo; Lope de Vega's delightful *Battle of Cats* (1618), whose chief characters have sinuous feline names—Mizifuf, Marramaquiz, and the heroine, silky Zapaquilda; a short *Battle of Donkeys*, by Gabriel Álvarez de Toledo y Pellicer (1662-1714), who later repented of writing it; and perhaps we should include an elegant *Battle of Cranes and Pygmies*, in Latin verse, based on a hint in the *Iliad*, by Joseph Addison.[44]

The Lectern, by Nicolas Boileau (Books 1-4, 1672; Books 5-6, 1683), is an ironically mock-heroic account of a trivial dispute between two ecclesiastical officials of the Sainte Chapelle in Paris: it begins with a fairly close imitation of the opening passages of the first and seventh books of Vergil's *Aeneid*.[45] Dryden, in *Absalom and Achitophel* (1681), carried out with triumphant success the bold idea of taking an episode from Hebrew history, turning it with apparent seriousness into heroic poetry, and thereby satirizing certain prominent politicians. The theme was Shaftesbury's attempt to make Monmouth (an illegitimate son of Charles II) the accepted heir to the throne. Shaftesbury and Monmouth and their supporters are keenly characterized and slashingly satirized; but only a very daring satirist would have ventured "upon the desire of King Charles the Second" to write a poem in which the monarch

> His vigorous warmth did variously impart
> To wives and slaves; and, wide as his command,
> Scattered his Maker's image through the land.[46]

Next year, in a sharper, coarser, funnier, but smaller satire, *Mac Flecknoe*, Dryden attacked a Protestant poet. This also is a parody of a heroic theme: the coronation and consecration, by his predecessor, of a mighty king and prophet, Thomas Shadwell, who is gravely compared with Ascanius the heir of Aeneas, Hannibal following Hamilcar Barca, Romulus attaining the kingship of new-founded Rome, and Elisha receiving the mantle of Elijah, as he becomes [the] last great Prophet of Tautology.

It is curious, but perhaps attributable to Dryden's vanity, that he should have forgotten not only Tassoni's *Rape of the Bucket* and Boileau's *Lectern* but his own *Absalom and Achitophel* (which is undoubtedly mock-heroic, and which he himself in the preface called a satire), and have described his *Mac Flecknoe* as "the first piece of ridicule written in heroics." However, Alexander Pope, aged seventeen, corrected him. (" 'Tis true," said Dryden, "I had forgot them.")[47]

Pope's own *Rape of the Lock* is a graceful, and his *Dunciad* a graceless, parody of Homer. When working on a translation, writers often have a strong desire to assert their own independence by satirizing their author; and such was Pope's case.[48] His friend Swift, after several disappointments in serious poetry, would never attempt it again; but in his prose *Battle of the Books* he wrote a parody of Homer—inspired, although he denied it, by the much richer and wittier parody by François de Callières, *Poetic History of the War Recently Declared between the Ancients and the Moderns*, and dealing with the same subject transferred to England.[49] Henry Fielding declared that his *Tom Jones* was a comic epic, and spent much energy on trying to prove it, in his disquisitions scattered through the novel. It is not. It is essentially a comic romance, with the essential emphasis on love and the final revelation of a concealed identity; but it does contain some passages which parody the grand effects of heroic poetry.

The most famous modern distortion of a heroic poem is Joyce's *Ulysses*, which is based on the *Odyssey*.[50] Since most of it is low in emotional tone, vulgar in expression, and trivial in subject, it is mainly a burlesque. Still, it contains passages of lofty parody, particularly the big chapter about the birth of the Purefoy baby, where the processes of conception, maturation, and parturition are paralleled by a series of parodies covering many types of literature, from the most primitive to what was in Joyce's day fully contemporaneous. The satiric purpose of *Ulysses* (insofar as it is a satire, for the book is many other things as well) is to make mockery of the notion that modern Ireland is a heroic country nourished by noble epic traditions, and to show it as a comical province on the outer fringes of the world of true civilization.

The poem which for long was the most famous of all mock epics, *The Rape of the Bucket* by Alessandro Tassoni (1622), is an amusing and confusing blend of nobility and power on the one hand with humor and vulgarity on the other. It tells, in twelve cantos of light and fluent stanzaic verse, the story of a medieval war between two Italian cities, Bologna and Modena—a war which, since it was part of the rivalry of Guelphs and Ghibellines, involved large forces and caused great bloodshed. It was a grave conflict. It could easily have been described in serious epic poetry; and in fact Tassoni built his poem on a recognizably epic plan: initial clashes, failure of an attempt at peacemaking, council in heaven ending with a dispute among the gods, marshaling of the opposed contingents, renewed attack, etc. But he wished to treat the theme satirically. He believed that all wars were rather absurd; that the conventions of epic poetry were silly; and—as others since his time have thought—that among the Italians magnificent gestures easily become ridiculous. (Was Benito Mussolini a heroic or a comic figure?) Therefore he opened the poem by describing a raid on Bologna in which the Modenese carried off, not an ancient and venerable banner, not a treasure of immense worth, not a woman as fair as Helen, but a wellbucket from which the exhausted Bolognese fugitives had been drinking. To match this trivial trophy, he made most

of his poem anti-heroic. The men of Modena are led by
their Potta (an undignified dialectal shortening of Podesta,
or Mayor), and the Bolognese are addressed (in their own
dialect) as "breadbaskets full of broth."[51] Juno absents
herself from the heavenly council because she wants to
wash her hair; Saturn makes a speech expressing divine
scorn of mankind, and starts it by breaking wind; Jupiter
is attended by Mercury carrying his hat and his eyeglasses;
and when we learn that the superintendent of Jove's
kitchen is Menippus, we see that the main ancestry of this
gay poem goes straight back to Greek Cynicism.[52] On the
other hand, Tassoni does not make all his actions and
artistic devices absurd, without exception. The war, in its
time, was a serious affair. Powerful figures were involved
in it: the diabolical Ezzelino of Padua, the gallant Manfred;
and the Pope himself had to intervene and settle it. Therefore Tassoni's narrative is sometimes grave and sometimes
comic. Sometimes he shows us a siege-engineer employing
grim machines of destruction, and sometimes a cook hitting
his opponent with a sausage-mixing pestle.[53] Sunset is the
chariot of Night wheeling beyond the straits that divide
Africa from Spain; and in the same canto dawn is Aurora,
blushing to be caught naked with Tithonus, and jumping
out of bed clutching her shift.[54] The historical events and
personages look authentic enough, but they are fantastically
confused: men who lived generations apart are portrayed
as contemporaries. Finally, some of the most important
characters are cruelly amusing portraits of Tassoni's own
enemies. *The Rape of the Bucket* is therefore a very unusual, perhaps unique, poem: a bewildering blend of the
heroic and the burlesque and the satiric. It has an absurd
opening and a smilingly domestic close. Most of its incidents are serious in substance or in implication, but at
some point they nearly all become comical; and in it there
are enough parody of grand literary devices and enough

rhetoric, which creep rather shyly into view during the early years of the Roman Empire, and to the long stories of chivalry, adventure, love, and enchantment which flourished in the late Middle Ages and the Renaissance. *Amadis of Gaul* is typical of the latter, and the *Ethiopian Adventures* by Heliodorus of the former. The Greek romances which have survived are long and intricate, ineffably high-minded, loftily artificial in style, wildly improbable in incident. A good way to parody such a thing is to turn the original emotions upside down and inside out. Thus, one explanation of that fragmentary work of genius, the *Satyrica*[58] of Petronius, is that it is a parody of the romance of love, travel, and adventure. It is a long narrative in prose mixed with poetry, told in the first person, of the picaresque adventures of three intelligent young scoundrels traveling through certain luxurious cities of the western Mediterranean. (Some readers have thought it might be a parody of the *Odyssey*, with the wrath of the sex deity Priapus pursuing the narrator [139.2] as the wrath of Poseidon pursued Odysseus; but this theme appears too seldom to make that notion convincing, and the book has few other traits which can be referred to epic.) In the romances, everything turns out for the best in the end: the hero preserves his courage and his devotion, if not always his chastity, and the heroine miraculously maintains her virginity. Their adventures, although painful, are all trials which they surmount with triumph, steps toward their eventual happiness. In the end they are reunited, and are usually discovered to be, not foundlings or commoners as they had believed, but rich and nobly born. The *Satyrica* has a plan exactly opposite to this. Instead of being naive and faithful lovers, the chief characters are intelligent crooks and debauchees. Their very names have disreputable meanings, and their morals are unspeakable. Instead of being put through trials which test their fiber and prove their fidelity, they have to endure a series of ordeals which befool and befoul them, although they amuse the reader. Whereas in the sentimental romances there is always tension between the innocent lovers and the cruel irrational outside world of pirates and savages and bandits, in the *Satyrica* we see a higher contrast (which Petronius himself perhaps felt deeply), the contrast between an intelligent Epicurean observer and a world packed to overflowing with stupidity, superstition, and bad taste. It is possible that Petronius wrote the book in order to discourage Nero from becoming a beatnik.[59] In any case, it is a cynically anti-idealistic work. Whenever I read something naive and optimistic like Walt Whitman's

> Afoot and light-hearted I take to the open road,
> Healthy, free, the world before me,

I think how Petronius could have written a spirited chapter about the Camerado's adventures in a hobo jungle full of syphilitic degenerates who had taken to the open road for totally different reasons. And yet, because he was a satirical genius, the chapter would be ironically amusing.

The Middle Ages were devoted to romance; and therefore the wits of the Renaissance made fun of romance. The whole of Rabelais' great work is in form a parody of the adventures of mighty giants and heroic kings which were told in the many cycles of medieval imaginative fiction; and its climax, the search for the oracle of the Holy Bottle, is a parody of the quest of King Arthur's knights for the Holy Cup or Grail. Count Matteo Maria Boiardo was no doubt serious in intention when he wrote *Roland in Love*, but the brilliant satirist Berni revised it so as to make it humorous and parodic; and throughout its continuation, *The Madness of Roland*, by Ariosto, we can expect parody to be blended with serious romantic feeling on every page.

The most illustrious of all modern satires on romance is Cervantes' *Don Quixote* (Part 1, 1605; Part 2, 1615). The hero of this marvelous book and his squire Sancho are so intensely and convincingly alive, and their adventures so engaging, that most readers nowadays are content to overlook the mistakes and inconsistencies of its creator. Many of these errors are relatively unimportant. But one at least is so considerable that it damages the impact of the satire. When I first read *Don Quixote* I was a schoolboy, and although I could see that the Don was eccentric, I could not be sure what his eccentricity was. Is he a contemporary eccentric, who is crackbrained because he wants to live in the past? or is he a knight who lived several centuries in the past and was at that time eccentric and ineffective? Is he a modern who makes a fool of himself by putting on obsolete armor and upholding obsolete ideals, or an antique man who fought the fights of his own time very badly? Is he someone like Villiers de L'Isle-Adam, who merely wanted to live in the Middle Ages, or a silly knight like Sir Pellinore in Malory who really did live in the Middle Ages? In fact, did Quixote live in the year 1600 or the year 1300?

Anyone who reads the book straight through will find it a little difficult to decide. Perhaps this is part of its charm. Certainly it makes clear one of the most interesting things about narrative satire: that, even if it is parodic, it is apt to pass into reality and to move out into fantasy again, sometimes escaping from the control of its author.

Cervantes began the work as a burlesque. In its opening pages, vulgar words and crude things and base people are frequent: whores, codfish, a pig-gelder, a caravan of mule-drivers. Most of its characters talk plainly and some coarsely.[60] The narrative style, although sympathetic enough, makes no attempt to disguise the fact that Quixote is an absurd lunatic. He himself usually talks in lofty

rhetorical tones: at the opening of his adventures he improvises an elaborate exordium for the future historian
who will write his exploits. But the narrative is couched
in the plain earthy comic realistic style of burlesque.

> At a place in La Mancha whose name I do not care to recall,
> there lived not long ago one of those gentlemen who keep a
> lance in the rack, an old shield, a lean horse, and a fast grey-
> hound. Stew with more beef than mutton in it, cold hash
> most evenings, bones and braxy on Saturday, lentil-soup on
> Friday, a young pigeon as a treat on Sunday, cost him three-
> quarters of his income.[61]

Quixada, or Quesada, lived "not long ago." Soon he is
dated more exactly. While he is recovering from his first
adventure, his friends the priest and the barber throw out
most of the books in his library. A few are spared. One of
them is *Galatea*, published in 1585 by Miguel de Cervantes
himself. As he sets it aside, the priest remarks, "This Cervantes has been a great friend of mine for many years."[62]
Therefore Quixada, who was "about fifty" when his adventures began "not long ago," is an exact contemporary
of Cervantes, who was fifty-eight when the first part of
Don Quixote was published. In some ways he was a projection of Cervantes himself. And as conceived in fiction he
was a contemporary monomaniac, whose sad but funny
adventures belonged to the present-day world in which
Cervantes was writing, and were described as though they
had occurred very recently and very near by.

Several scholars, notably Don Salvador de Madariaga,
have pointed out how, during their errant career, Sancho
comes to resemble Quixote and Quixote in some respects
grows Sanchified. It is even more touching to observe how
Don Quixote and his creator come by degrees to resemble
each other. One aspect of this is that Cervantes changes his
conception and treatment of the fake knight's adventures.
In the ninth chapter he says that in Toledo he discovered

a manuscript containing the history of Don Quixote, written in Arabic by someone called Cid Hamet Benengeli. A history of a Spanish hidalgo, written in Arabic: therefore before the expulsion of the Moorish dogs in 1492, and probably long before. With this change in conception, the style begins to change from plain eggs-and-bacon prose into a white-plumed imitation of a lofty chivalric history. A fight between the absurd Quixote and a comic Basque who no speak so good Spanish is described in the purest mock-heroic prose:

> Poised and raised aloft, the keen swords of the two valiant and infuriated combatants seemed to threaten heaven and earth and the depths beneath.[63]

By the end of the first part, Don Quixote himself has been pushed back from the present day into the age of real romance. The knight has ceased to be a contemporary. His death and burial took place several centuries earlier: Cervantes says that they were described in parchment manuscripts containing poems written in "Gothic" characters, found in the ruins of an ancient hermitage and only partially decipherable. This means that Quixote was a remote half-mythical figure like the Cid Campeador.

No doubt the "Arabic historian" and the "ancient Spanish poems in Gothic lettering" are intended to ridicule the fantastic fictions of the romances which were contemporary with Cervantes. But by this change of conception Cervantes has abandoned realism for fantasy, and so has made himself into Don Quixote. By turning from contemporary burlesque to mock-heroic parody, he shifts the aim of his satire. He mocks the cheap modern romances and those who addle their brains by reading them; but he also affectionately mocks the ideal of knighthood even as it was in its full flower—the ideal which he himself had nobly tried to serve—by contrasting its impossible aspirations with the hard low comic facts of real life.

Quixote has had many imitators in many languages. In English the best-known is a smaller and wittier work, less tender and more sharply satirical, Samuel Butler's *Hudibras* (in three parts, 1663, 1664, 1678). (Besides *Don Quixote*, its chief models were Scarron's *Vergil Travestied* and Rabelais.) The hero of this poem, riding out "a-colonelling," is, like the original Quixote, a contemporary crackpot. As Quixote believed himself a medieval knight-errant, so Hudibras is a Puritan reformer. His name comes from a knight in Spenser's *Faerie Queene.* He has never fought a battle, and his weapons are obsolete.

> [His] trenchant blade, Toledo trusty,
> For want of fighting was grown rusty,
> And ate into itself, for lack
> Of somebody to hew and hack.[64]

He has a squire, Ralpho, who is just as incompetent as Sancho Panza: born a tailor, he had got religion in his poor cracked brain and was proud of having "the inward light." With him, Hudibras sets off on a quest almost as ill-conceived as that of Don Quixote. His aim is to prove his prowess. But everything he does and everyone he meets are low, vulgar, ludicrous. Just now and then, when the reader might find it tedious to meet a large rabble of nonentities, Butler moves from burlesque into parody, and describes them in terms of "high heroic fustian,"[65] but this mood never lasts for long: he soon reverts from the haughty metaphors and Cambyses vein of parody to the frank disillusioned gaze and brisk shocking vocabulary of burlesque. Sometimes Cervantes doubted whether he spoke for Quixote trying to change and amend the world, or for the world laughing at Quixote's useless efforts. But Butler always knew who was fooling whom, and never entertained the idea that madness might be a nobler thing than sanity. *Don Quixote* is a daring expedition on an imitation war-horse which keeps collapsing because it is asked to do more than it can; but throughout *Hudibras* we hear the clip-clop and hee-haw of the dogged humorous disillusioned donkey.

D R A M A

From romance we turn to drama. Serious drama can be satirized by the application of either of the two methods, mock-heroic parody and burlesque. In Greek literature and art we can see them both at work. From the tragedies of Euripides, Aristophanes takes the elaborate lyrical aria, appropriate for the agonies of a princess half-mad with despair, and uses it to express the grief of a housewife whose neighbor has stolen her pet rooster.[66] From a passage of profound meditation, he lifts a mystical question, gives it to a mocking speaker, and adds puns that turn it into nonsense:

> Who knows if life may not be really death?
> and breath be broth? and sleep a pillow-slip?[67]

Aristophanes can also burlesque a heroic theme, the journey of Hercules down to the land of death, by having it repeated by the gay god Dionysus, wearing Hercules' lion-skin and club but retaining his own silk robes, luxurious shoes, and sensitive nature.[68] In the Greek world there were many such dramatic burlesques of great myths, although their texts have now disappeared. We know them mainly by their name (*phlyakes*, which the Greeks translated as "fooleries") and by many ludicrous paintings on Greek vases. These pictures are the reverse of the conventional Gilbert Murray–Edith Hamilton idealistic view of the Greeks, and are cruder than the worst comic strip of today. For instance, there was a famous legend which said that Zeus, king of the gods, took on the exact semblance of King Amphitryon of Thebes so that he could possess Amphitryon's virtuous Queen Alcmena. On her, during a night miraculously prolonged, he begot Hercules. The vase-paintings, which seem to represent the myth as it was translated into burlesque for the stage, show a gross fat-bellied Zeus with goggling eyes, helped by an equally coarse and grotesque Hermes, carrying a precarious ladder to a second-story window, where sits Alcmena, looking out expectantly as though she were a cheap adulteress or a prostitute. The Roman comedian Plautus (working on a Greek original now lost) raised the story above that low level, in a comedy which is sometimes seriously romantic and sometimes coarsely comical. In one of his most richly pregnant sentences, Jung said "The gods are libido." Since it expresses the masculine desire to possess another man's virtuous and beautiful wife without offending her or killing him, *Amphitryon* is the perfectly libidinous burlesque comedy. It inspired many imitations—for instance by Dryden and Molière; and finally, in *Amphitryon 38* by Jean Giraudoux, it rose high above burlesque and satire into the heaven of pure comedy.

In English there are a number of famous parodies of serious drama. Beaumont and Fletcher's *Knight of the Burning Pestle* and Buckingham's *Rehearsal* are both plays within plays: in each case the device emphasizes the forced unnatural quality of the exaggeratedly heroic style they are parodying. One of our most versatile satirists, Henry Fielding, struck off *Tom Thumb the Great* at the age of twenty-three, and next year, in the mock-scholarly manner of the Scriblerus Club, added a number of notes, showing how widely he had ranged among the obsolescent heroic dramas of the high baroque period.[69] It was shortly outdone by Henry Carey (best remembered for the charming song, "Sally in our Alley") in a parodic drama whose opening exceeds in sonority even the most portentous effects of Aeschylus:

Aldiborontiphoscophornio!
Where left you Chrononhotonthologos?[70]

Shelley poured his hatred of the British ruling classes and
King George IV and his Queen Caroline into a mock
tragedy called *Oedipus Tyrannus, or Swellfoot the Tyrant.*
With its chorus of pigs, and its lyrics sung by a gadfly, a
leech, and a rat, it is intended to be a parody in the Aristophanic manner; but the plot is both so topical and so
fantastic that it can scarcely be understood, much less enjoyed, nowadays; much of the verse is so genuinely majestic
as to remind us uncomfortably of *Prometheus Unbound*;
and the jokes are painfully pedantic, as when the Ionian
Minotaur turns out to be Ion the Man-Bull, i.e. John Bull.
One of the most successful dramatic parodies of the present
century covers one of the most difficult, most revered, of
subjects. In a short story containing an ambitious unfinished verse tragedy, Max Beerbohm poked fun not only
at a splendid historical period and a somber theme, but
at a proud English heritage, the Shakespearean tradition.
Its very name embodies the contrast between two sides of
the English nature: one quiet, respectable, bowler-hatted,
imitative; the other romantic and antiquarian and quixotic.
He called it *"Savonarola" Brown.* Beerbohm, being an
elusive writer, does not aim at one individual satirical
target. Some elements of the play are parodies of Shakespeare—for instance the unintelligible witticisms of the
fool, which are permitted to interrupt a serious episode,
and the trick of closing a scene with a rhyming couplet:

> Tho' love be sweet, revenge is sweeter far.
> To the Piazza! Ha, ha, ha, ha, har!

But the absurdly lofty idealism of some of the speeches,
and the improbable multiplicity of historical characters
("Re-enter Guelfs and Ghibellines fighting. Enter Michael
Angelo. Andrea del Sarto appears for a moment at a

window. Pippa passes.") are closer to the blank-verse dramas of such authors as Tennyson, Browning, and Stephen Phillips; while the elaborate crowd-scenes and colossal stage-effects are probably parodies of the production techniques of Beerbohm's brother, Herbert Beerbohm Tree.[71]

Shakespeare himself enjoyed writing parodies. Falstaff, a burlesque knight, has an attendant who is a parody of a soldier. Scolded by Doll Tearsheet, Pistol discharges himself in Marlovian verse:

> Shall pack-horses,
> And hollow pampered jades of Asia,
> Which cannot go but thirty miles a day,
> Compare with Caesars, and with Cannibals,
> And Trojan Greeks?[72]

The strangest and least likable of his major plays, although not a parody, may well be called a satirical burlesque. *Troilus and Cressida* (produced soon after Chapman issued his translation of certain books of Homer) takes the greatest episodes from the *Iliad* and dramatizes them, partly with ferocious realism, partly with bitter and contemptuous distortion. Beginning with the duel of Menelaus and Paris and moving on to the slaying of the Trojan champion Hector, it frames the entire epic within a ruined love story—a story initially as passionate as that of Verona, but defiled throughout by the slimy character of its promoter Pandarus.[73] All the other persons and incidents are similarly distorted into cruel burlesque. In the *Iliad*, Achilles remains in his tent after suffering the insult to his honor, singing to his lyre "the glorious deeds of men"; but Shakespeare makes him loll on his bed and watch Patroclus travestying the speech and manners of the other Greek heroes.[74] Thersites speaks but once in the *Iliad* and is then silenced forever; but here he is tolerated, at least by one of the heroes, and continues to vent his spleen in coarse wit all through the play until the final battle, when he taunts the men who caused the war, Paris and Menelaus, and then runs off glorying in his own meanness and cowardice.[75] It has been suggested that the power of satire flowed into this repellent but memorable drama after the church had officially banned the writing of regular satires; certainly Prince Hamlet, who was reading satire during his fits of melancholy, would have enjoyed it.[76]

John Gay's *Beggar's Opera*, which proclaims itself a burlesque by its very title, and confirms the fact by the grace and nobility of the sentiments married to honestly charming music, but put in the mouths of whores and cutthroats, was popular for many years.[77] It has recently had a revival, now downgraded to burlesque social satire of the bitterest kind, in the work of two left-wing rebels, Bertold Brecht and Kurt Weill, produced in Germany as *Die Dreigroschenoper* (1928), and still running in New York (1961) as *The Three-Penny Opera*. Of operatic parodies, the most popular in the last three or four generations have been the operettas in which Gilbert and Sullivan carried to absurdity the theatrical devices of contemporary grand opera: the pompous choral processions:

> Bow, bow, ye lower middle classes!
> Bow, bow, ye tradesmen, bow, ye masses![78]

and

> When the foeman bares his steel,
>   Tarantara! tarantara!
> We uncomfortable feel,
>   Tarantara![79]

the soliloquies in recitative leading into a great solo:

> Am I alone,
>   And unobserved? I am![80]

the dynastic plots turning on the confusion of two babies:

> I mixed those children up,
>   And not a creature knew it![81]

the artificial nomenclature (Lady Sangazure, Little Butter-cup, the Duke of Plaza Toro, Ralph Rackstraw), the choral shouts of alarm ("Oh, horror!"), the family curse, and other conventions which often made even serious operas appear ridiculous. To us these Gilbert and Sullivan oper-ettas seem (apart from the few consistently romantic pieces such as *The Yeomen of the Guard*) to be little more than parodies of serious opera, as the gay frolics of Offenbach—*Orpheus in Hell, Beautiful Helen,* etc.—are burlesques of serious opera. But the Offenbach pieces also satirized con-temporary French morality, for Orpheus does not even want to recover his lost wife (what Frenchman wants to recover a lost wife?). And what seems to us a perfectly innocuous piece, *H.M.S. Pinafore,* was in its time a biting satire on that sensitive organism, the Royal Navy. One of its climaxes—the rebuke of Captain Corcoran for saying "damme"—satirizes the enlightened modern democratic principles of discipline which the innovators in the Navy were trying to introduce; and one of its chief characters, Sir Joseph Porter, K.C.B., satirizes William Henry Smith, who after a successful career as a bookseller moved into politics and became First Lord of the Admiralty in Dis-raeli's 1877 Cabinet, having never, or hardly ever, gone to sea. It stung Disraeli, for he said that *H.M.S. Pinafore* made him feel "quite sick." But the satiric part of the Gilbert and Sullivan operas has long evaporated, leaving something saccharine and conventional, so that, in their turn, they have been parodied and satirized by a brilliant British humorist, Sir Alan Herbert.[82]

In 1935 that restless innovator T. S. Eliot brought some-thing new into the theatre with his *Murder in the Cathe-dral.* In 1957, it was parodied, much of Eliot's lyrical poetry was travestied, and Eliot's entire life-work was satirized in a book called *The Sweeniad,* written by a Cambridge Uni-versity don under the cheap pseudonym of "Myra Buttle."

In form, *The Sweeniad* is a drama in a dream. As the central problem of *Murder in the Cathedral* is the temptation of Archbishop Thomas à Becket, so the central problem of *The Sweeniad* is the trial of T. S. Eliot—although the figure representing him is named after one of the characters whom Eliot himself created, Sweeney. He, his works, and his influence are examined before a court consisting of the Public, in the same way as the character and career of a dead Roman Catholic are examined to see whether he is worthy of being declared a saint.

The court is first addressed by a "Postulator," a critic who admires Eliot. In an eloquent speech interrupted from time to time by lyrical ejaculations from a supernatural chorus, he describes the spiritual crisis in which *The Waste Land* was written and published, its mythical content, and its peculiar allusive technique. He then outlines Eliot's later poems (though not his plays), and finally proposes that Eliot should be canonized as a saint of literature.

The opposing point of view is eloquently put by the "devil's advocate."

> I aim to prove that Sweeney, a minor poet who might otherwise have escaped extensive notice, has, for motives altogether hostile to the spirit of literature, been elevated by vested interest into his present exalted position.

With deadly earnestness, he castigates *The Waste Land* for being a howl of unimportant personal discomfort, which ignored the far greater issues of its day—greedy financiers and desperate unemployed, war and the after-agonies of war. He accuses Eliot of despising democracy, and (in a peculiarly revealing phrase) of having a "partiality for General Franco, Marshal Pétain, Charles Maurras, [and] the banker-priest oligarchy of Europe and America." Finally, he denounces him for pretending, although a foreigner, to be an Englishman; and the chorus sings:

> An alien who adopts the stance
> Of guileless English arrogance
> And gazes down his nose askance
> Is bound to overdo it.

After some further debate, during which the "devil's advocate" delivers a savage attack on the entire Christian tradition as the corrupter of civilization and of poetry, the judge dismisses Eliot's claim to beatification; and Eliot, with a few phrases parodied from his own lyrics—

> Between the mystification
> And the deception
> Between the multiplication
> And the division
> Falls the Tower of London—

blows up and disappears,

> Not with a curse but a mutter
> Not with a flight but a flutter
> Not with a song but a stutter.

The inspirations of *The Sweeniad* are three famous literary satires: Aristophanes' *Frogs*, which ends with a trial by which Euripides, hoping for immortality, is consigned to perpetual oblivion; Pope's *Dunciad*, concluding with the conquest of the world by universal Dulness; and Byron's *Vision of Judgment*, centered on George III's entrance into heaven. In bitterness of spirit, it is closest to *The Dunciad*, in versatility of parody, to *The Frogs*. But in effectiveness, it falls far behind all these, because of the technical and spiritual weaknesses of its author.

There are two chief reasons for its failure. One is that it is timid and indirect. The name of Eliot is never mentioned. The character who resembles him is called Sweeney, which is ridiculously inappropriate. Although Eliot did create Sweeney and wrote several poems about him, the poetic significance of Sweeney is that he is *not* T. S. Eliot. He is the antipode of Eliot: an ape-man who seduces girls and callously abandons them in brothels, who gets involved in gangster intrigues, who is fascinating because of his sub-human crudity and violence. "Myra Buttle," whose hatred of Eliot prevents her from comprehending this, uses Sweeney partly because to English ears it sounds alien and vulgar, and partly (as we see by her addition of the first name Loyola) because it sounds Roman Catholic. Far neater to have given Eliot the name of one of his own *personae*, Prufrock or Harcourt-Reilly; or even to call him Jargon, or Guru. Similarly, "Myra Buttle" blunts her attack on his poems by distorting their names: *The Waste Land* becomes *The Vacant Mind*, and *Ash Wednesday*, significantly, *The Blood Bath of the Mass*. To attack non-existent poems attributed to a fictitious character is not the best way to create literary satire.

The other weakness of *The Sweeniad* is that it is false to fact—even falser than the conclusion of *The Dunciad*. It attributes Eliot's influence to the power of organized Christianity, working through critics who are "clerics," and says explicitly that English poetry was destroyed, after "the twenties of last century," by religion, patriotism, imperialism, and capitalism. Neither of these assertions is true; neither is even plausible as an explanation of the extraordinary influence of T. S. Eliot; and, as we reflect on their erroneousness, we conclude that "Myra Buttle," who misunderstands her own subject, is a convinced hater but an unconvincing satirist.

DIDACTIC POETRY

Didactic poetry, which tends to be rather a solemn genre, can easily be mocked. It would not, I think, be right to call Ovid's *Art of Love* a satiric parody of a didactic poem: it is a didactic poem on a light subject, treated with the appropriate levity; although I have no doubt that he intended it to be a gay worldly counterpart to the thoughtful idealistic *Georgics* of Vergil.

However, one of the most pungent satires ever written is a mock-didactic poem in dignified and skillful blank verse on an utterly trivial subject. This is *The Day*, in four sections, *Morning, Midday, Evening,* and *Night,* by a wretchedly poor and highly gifted intellectual, Giuseppe Parini (1729-1799).[83] It is a detailed description of a day in the life of an indolent, conceited, and worthless young nobleman, set forth with every semblance of solemn wide-eyed admiration. Although the poem is far longer than Vergil's richly detailed description of the hard-working farmer's routine, almost nothing happens in it. His lordship leads the life of *dolce far niente* which is still the ideal of many Mediterranean men. He does not, like Oblomov, lie in bed most of the day.[84] But he rises late, assisted by deferential servants: it takes nine hundred lines to describe his elaborate toilet and the various stages of his costuming, until at last he sallies forth

to bless the eyes of his dear fatherland.[85]

He goes to a luncheon-party: the hostess is charming to him as being her cavalier, while the host, her husband (whose rights extend only through the hours of darkness), is ignored. He and his lady, in their magnificent coaches, pay a round of visits and attend an evening party, with conversation, gambling, and intrigues. It is a routine of inane trifling; but Parini makes it clear that this shiftless thriftless life is made possible only by the labor of hundreds of despised "plebeians" and the attention of scores of obsequious lackeys. This, he explains with calm irony, is exactly as it should be. The rich and noble are super-human. In the style of the tributes paid by baroque poets to their patrons, he calls his lordship with his friends "a council of demigods living on earth";[86] and, in one of his finest passages (reminiscent of Lucretius, with a quotation from Juvenal) he relates the myth that once upon a time, long ago, all men were equal: his lordship's ancestors and those of the proletariat ate the same food, drank the same water, and enjoyed the same shelter; but the spirit of Pleasure divided them, since when they have belonged to two different species. Happy those whom Prometheus made of finer clay! Happy the nobleman, who can enjoy life, while the others merely serve and work![87]

All this is froth as light as *oeufs à la neige*. The problem with such delicacies is to give them a shape which will not be crushingly complex. Such satires must be delicate, rather than brutal. Who breaks a butterfly upon a wheel?[88] Since Parini was himself a tutor in two ducal families, he chose the perfect form for his satire. He made it a didactic poem. With eloquent humility he teaches his young lordship how to waste his hours and his days and his life. The aristocrat will not serve Mars, who might require him to shed his precious blood, nor Minerva, whose arts and sciences are for whining students. Parini, "teacher of the rites of pleasure," will explain to him, minute by minute, how to live for himself.[89] In order to make these trivial lessons more dignified, more worthy of the upper class to whom they are addressed, Parini fills them with Greco-Roman supernatural apparatus (God and the Christian church are never mentioned) and punctuates them with heroic images, classical quotations, and mythical episodes, such as the tale of the irreconcilable rivalry of Cupid, god of love, and Hymen, god of marriage.[90] The medium is dignified blank verse, heavily decorated with the loftier devices of style: apostrophe, inversion, antithesis, hyperbaton. It is a splendid rococo satire, and (in its genre) it makes an excellent parallel to Pope's *Rape of the Lock*. Or rather an antithesis. Mr. Pope in his heart admired high society: the "fair nymphs and well-dressed youths" who shine in London.⁹¹ Parini, like Dr. Swift (whom he seems, judging from portraits, to have resembled in face as in intellect), despised the nobility and their titles of grandeur, by which (as we know from Gulliver's visit to Lilliput) a Nardac is superior to a Clumglum.⁹²

Have you ever gazed at the noblemen and princelings portrayed by artists of the eighteenth century, and observed, from the canvases of Goya and other percipient painters, what fools they were within their fine clothes, and their jeweled orders, and their armor of snobbery? They stare at the artist, and, from his canvas, at you and me, with ineffable hauteur, as though they were conferring a privilege upon posterity by permitting themselves to be immortalized; and in fact they are pompous nonentities. In the same way, Thomas Jefferson, in one of his letters, speaks with contempt of the hereditary monarchs of Europe.

> While in Europe, I often amused myself with contemplating the characters of the then reigning sovereigns. . . . Louis the XVI was a fool, of my knowledge, and in despite of the answers made for him at his trial. The King of Spain was a fool, and of Naples the same. They passed their lives in hunting, and dispatched two couriers a week, one thousand miles, to let each other know what game they had killed the preceding days. . . . These animals had become without mind and powerless; and so will every hereditary monarch be after a few generations.⁹³

Parini's satire on the young nobleman's day is inspired by the spirit of Goya's pictures and Jefferson's revolution.

L Y R I C

Lyric poetry is easy to parody, if the parodist has a good ear. Since it usually depends more on sound than on sense, it is usually sufficient to twist or diminish the meaning a little, and to emphasize the tricks of rhythm and melody, in order to change the original from sweetness and power into laughter. Aristophanes satirized the lyrical solos and choruses of Euripides merely by applying their passionate roulades and urgent repetitions to trivial subjects. Vergil's early poetry is described by Horace, in a phrase which has often puzzled scholars, as possessing *molle atque facetum*.[94] But it is true that his *Bucolics* (which only the uninformed call *Eclogues*) are characteristically "sensitive and sophisticated," even "witty"; and although we can scarcely avoid seeing him as the architect of the tragic *Aeneid*, we should remember that he started his poetic career with a few light lyrics, some in imitation and at least one in parody of Catullus. (This is a little metrical tour de force, an inscriptional poem in "pure" iambics—i.e., preserving the sequence of short and long syllables invariably without once substituting or resolving a long syllable.)[95]

In the Middle Ages, parody of serious lyrical poetry was one of the commonest forms of satire: the songs of the Goliards are full of distortions of Christian hymns and of poetic sections of Holy Scripture. That mild but penetrating humorist Geoffrey Chaucer shows himself, when asked by the innkeeper for "a tale of mirth," responding with the story of Sir Thopas, a good parody of the naive detail, worn clichés, fill-in phrases, and rocking-horse rhythm of medieval balladry:

> Sir Thopas wex a doghty swayn,
> Whyt was his face as payndemayn,
>   His lippes rede as rose;
> His rode is lyk scarlet in grayn,
> And I yow telle in good certayn,
>   He hadde a semely nose.

But after some thirty stanzas of this "rym dogerel" the host has had enough:

> No more of this, for goddes dignitee!

says he, in the very voice of the approaching Renaissance,

and adds in the very tone of Rabelais that such poetry "is nat worth a tord."[96]

With the revival of the classics, lyrics in imitation of the two great Greek and Roman masters became popular: heroic, irregular, passionate Pindaric outbursts, and cool, graceful, economical, allusive Horatian reflections. Both styles were parodied: the Pindaric, as more ambitious, more frequently and more effectively. Swift actually began his literary career by writing (under Cowley's influence) Pindaric poems which were seriously intended. By their fulsome flattery and inappropriate imagery they become self-parody, as in the lines describing how the Archbishop of Canterbury could be promoted to heaven without losing his ecclesiastical vestments:

> There are degrees above I know
> As well as here below,
> (The goddess Muse herself has told me so)
> Where high patrician souls dress'd heavenly gay
> Sit clad in lawn of purer woven day,
> There some high-spirited throne to Sancroft shall be given,
> In the metropolis of Heaven;
> Chief of the mitred saints, and from archprelate here,
> Translated to archangel there.[97]

But Swift knew such stuff was useless, and after Dryden confirmed it ("Cousin Swift, you will never be a poet"), he became an anti-poet, who preferred to mock and degrade the goddess Muse. For example, Dryden wrote two spirited Pindarics intended to evoke the various powers of music and to be sung by the St. Cecilia Society. Swift wrote *A Cantata* ridiculing the poetic and musical imitation of acts and emotions, which made Pegasus into a hack, "trolloping, lolloping, galloping," in 6/8 time.

In English the most famous Horatian parody is an ingenious little poem which appeared in *The Anti-Jacobin Review* in 1798. In subject, it satirizes the philanthropists who are full of generalized love of humanity but will not give a charitable coin to a peddler. In form it is a neat imitation of Horace's Sapphic metre as transferred to English by Southey and forced upon a recalcitrant non-quantitative language—so that, if it is to be read as true Sapphics, the normal English accentuation must be distorted.

> Needy Knife-grindér! whither áre you going?
> Rough is thé road, yoúr wheel is out of order—
> Bleak blows thé blast; yoúr hat has got a hole in't,
>   So have your breeches![98]

It was similarly in Regency England that one of the most brilliant groups of parodies in literature (most of them lyrical) was assembled. This was *Rejected Addresses,* by the brothers James and Horace Smith. In 1812 the new Drury Lane Theatre, rebuilt after a fire, was opened, and a prize was offered for the best dedicatory address. The Smiths' volume purports to be a collection of the entries which failed. They are truly delightful. Some of them have so much charm and life that they would not disgrace their putative authors. Tom Moore, for instance, is credited with a gay song in his own lilting anapaests carrying his own favorite sentiment.

> When woman's soft smile all our senses bewilders,
>   And gilds while it carves her dear form in the heart,
> What need has new Drury of carvers and gilders,
>   With Nature so bounteous why call upon Art?

> How well would our actors attend to their duties,
>   Our house save in oil and our authors in wit,
> In lieu of yon lamps if a row of young beauties
>   Glanced light from their eyes between us and the pit?

A perfect parody touches both style and content. The Smiths satirize not only Moore's characteristic rhythms and imagery, but his thought: his light frivolous sensuality, his glib Irish blarney. So their parody of Lord Byron attacks

both the melodramatic crescendo of his Spenserian stanza
and his characteristic spleen.

> Sated with home, of wife, of children tired,
>   The restless soul is driven abroad to roam;
> Sated abroad, all seen, yet nought admired,
>   The restless soul is driven to wander home.
>   Sated with both, beneath new Drury's dome
> The fiend Ennui awhile consents to pine,
>   There growls and curses, like a deadly Gnome,
> Scorning to view fantastic Columbine,
> Viewing with scorn and hate the nonsense of the Nine.

In comparison with this hypodermic satire, the wooden
lyrics of "Peter Pindar" and his coarse mock-epic *The
Lousiad* are artistically ineffective, although they were, in
their time, good political propaganda.[99]

The mid-nineteenth century produced one of the most
brilliant of all parodists in English literature: C. S. Calverley (1831-1884). His mock-Morris ballad, with the pastoral
refrain "Butter and eggs and a pound of cheese," is a small
gem, and (although it is not lyrical but dramatic) his *Cock
and the Bull*, satirizing Browning's *Ring and the Book*, is
a masterpiece.[100] With unexpected humor, Swinburne
parodied himself in a luxurious lyric intituled *Nephelidia,*
which is quasi-Greek for "Mistinesses." The lines wamble
and waver like long drifts of cloud.

> Mild is the mirk and monotonous music of memory,
>   melodiously mute as it may be,
>   While the hope in the heart of a hero is bruised by the
>   breach of men's rapiers, resigned to the rod;
> Made meek as a mother whose bosom-beats bound with
>   the bliss-bringing bulk of a balm-breathing baby,
>   As they grope through the graveyard of creeds, under
>   skies growing green at a groan for the grimness of God.

A contemporary critic has said that Swinburne was here
parodying only his own trick of mechanical alliteration;
but surely he was also satirizing the logorrhoea which, in

his lyrics, often conceals the juvenility of his thought; his
sentimental adoration of what he used to call "babbies";
and his petulant dislike of God.

In recent years certain poems by T. S. Eliot, Ezra Pound,
and other moderns—poems which may be defined as ex-
tended lyrics—have been frequently parodied. When
(possibly following Laforgue) Archibald MacLeish wrote
himself into a modern *Hamlet*, his product was peppered
and served up hot and scrambled by Edmund Wilson in
The Omelet of A. MacLeish.

> Eliot alarmed me at first: but my later abasement:
> And the clean sun of France: and the freakish but beautiful
> fashion:
> Striped bathhouses bright on the sand: Anabase and The
> Waste Land:
>
> These and the Cantos of Pound: O how they came pat!
> Nimble at other men's arts how I picked up the trick of it:
> Rode it reposed on it drifted away on it. . . .[101]

Eliot has rarely been parodied with much success. He himself says, in characteristic tones, "One is apt to think one
could parody oneself much better. (As a matter of fact
some critics have said that I have done so.)" But he has
praise for one parody of his own work, *Chard Whitlow* by
Henry Reed:

> As we get older we do not get any younger.
> Seasons return, and today I am fifty-five. . . .[102]

PROSE: NON-FICTION

Parodies of prose can be divided for convenience into
fictional and non-fictional. There are some fine prose parodies in classical antiquity. In particular, that marvelous
stylist Plato was one of the greatest parodists who ever
wrote. Delicately and not unkindly, he imitated and
slightly exaggerated the mannerisms of Gorgias and Protagoras and Prodicus and other sophists. Accurately and

venomously, he parodied the voices of democracy. He begins one of his noblest dialogues, *Phaedrus*, with a parody of Lysias stylistically so close that it has sometimes been printed among that orator's genuine works, but in subject-matter so vile and contemptible that it betrays a profound hatred. Most of one short dialogue, *Menexenus*, is occupied by Socrates' recital of a speech to be delivered on the day when Athens paid annual homage to her war dead. The structure and the sentiments of the speech are unimpeachably orthodox, just a little overdone here and just a little vapid there—so much so that many scholars, who cannot realize how deeply Plato despised and detested Athenian democracy, have taken it quite seriously. (Cicero actually says it was recited annually in Athens, which is unconfirmed and is almost surely rubbish.)[103] Yet Plato tried to make it perfectly clear even to such simple-hearted readers that the speech was a satire. He made Socrates declare that he had been taught the speech by a woman— Aspasia, the mistress of Pericles; and that she had composed it, partly extempore and partly by sticking together fragments of the funeral speech she wrote for Pericles to deliver. (This would be very suitable in a satiric comedy by Aristophanes, but is not meant to be taken seriously as historical truth.) Socrates then says he will repeat the speech if his friend Menexenus will not laugh at him for being an old man and still having fun: in fact, since they are alone, he will even strip off his clothes and dance. He starts with a sentence based on the antithesis "In fact . . . but in word . . ." which was a favorite of Thucydides: this and other details make it likely that he is satirizing the idealization of Pericles which is most nobly expressed in Thucydides' version of that statesman's funeral speech. And with a final gesture of contempt, Plato makes the speech contain an allusion to a famous political event of his own day, which happened many years after Socrates, and Pericles, and

as being opposed to Christianity. They were urged on by a converted Jew called Johann Pfefferkorn (here, even at this early stage, the spirit of satirical absurdity begins to twitch and sniff). They were opposed by Johann Reuchlin, a classical scholar who knew Hebrew, and who declared that, on the contrary, Hebrew ought to be taught on the university level for the better understanding of the Bible. Ultimately (although I do not believe it was ever explicitly stated) the conflict was between men who knew that Holy Scripture was written in Hebrew, Aramaic, and Greek, three difficult languages, and that its text in all three was full of problems both of stability and of interpretation; and, on the other side, men who believed that Holy Scripture was clear in structure and expression, and that the Latin Vulgate translation which the Western church had used for a thousand years was the central path to its understanding. Erasmus, who spent much effort on establishing a reliable text of the Greek New Testament, was a friend and sympathizer of Reuchlin.

The dispute grew hot. The Dominicans used the wealth of their mendicant order to influence the Papal Court. They had a large organization, a venerable name, and a popular cause. Reuchlin had few supporters, except the new generation of classical scholars, the "humanists," who were believed by churchmen and laity to be inclined toward heresy. However, in 1514 he published a collection of their correspondence with him, written in Latin, Greek, and Hebrew, and called *Letters of Distinguished Men*. To this his opponents did not reply; but someone replied for them. In the winter of 1515-1516 there appeared a volume of forty-one *Letters of Obscure Men* addressed to an eminent member of the Faculty of Theology at Cologne, Ortwin von Graes. They are, it would appear, letters from earnest supporters of Master Ortwin, and Pfefferkorn, and the Dominican order. But they are not merely eulogies of

Reuchlin's opponents and invectives against Reuchlin. They are more. They are a series of satirical pictures of small minds naïvely expressing their ignorance, of pedants boasting of their misbegotten and misapplied knowledge, and, though indirectly, of coarse sensualists disguising their sins in priestly robes. Each of Master Conrad's correspondents pours out his mind with enthusiastic candor— usually in very bad medieval Latin which (as Milton says) "would have made Quintilian stare and gasp"—so that it is difficult to believe that the letters are parodies, or forgeries. The Germans have a sad tendency to choose clumsy personal names: this too is satirized, for the first time, perhaps, though not for the last. So Mammotrectus Buntemantellus writes to Master Ortwin explaining that, though he is in holy orders, he is in love, and asking for advice. (His name expresses his character: it means Bosom-handler Brightcoat.) Conrad Dollenkopf boasts that he knows all the myths in Ovid's *Metamorphoses* by heart, and can analyze them in four ways, naturally, literally, historically, and spiritually, with illustrative quotations from the Bible. There are letters from Lyra Buntschuch-macherius, Cunradus Unckebunck, Henrichus Cribelinio-niacius, and Magister Noster Bartholomaeus Kuckuk.

The *Letters of Obscure Men* immediately became popular and went into a second and a third edition; a new series with sixty-two additional letters came out in 1517; and the entire work was condemned by the Medici Pope Leo X in a Bull. The authors are not certainly known, but are believed to be Johann Jäger and Ulrich von Hutten, with assistance from Hermann von den Busche. Six months after the appearance of the second series, Martin Luther posted the manifesto which started the Reformation; and it is not a coincidence that Hutten was one of his chief supporters.[105]

The second of these famous satires is impossible to

understand without knowing the history of the wars of religion in France during the sixteenth century. The main conflict was between Catholics and Protestants; but there was also a struggle between moderate Catholics (who were also patriotic Frenchmen) and extremist Catholics (who were strongly supported by the Papacy in Italy and by the power of Spain). The *Menippean Satire*, which appeared in 1593 and was later reissued in a larger form, is a parody of a council held by the extremists.[106] Its title is not quite right: a Menippean satire is a mixture of prose and verse, while this is a mixture of French, Italian, and Latin prose. Its epigraph is Horace's phrase, "telling the truth with a laugh," and one of its contributors was Pierre Pithou, owner of the only good manuscript of Juvenal.[107] It describes with apparent gravity the opening procession of the council, the symbolic pictures on the tapestries in the hall, and the members of the assembly; then it goes on to give the chief speeches, and closes with the council's resolutions. The orations are, of course, impossibly frank: the Duc de Mayenne compares himself to a bloody-handed Roman dictator, saying that he was "a good Catholic Sulla"; and the papal legate ends with a benediction (in Italian), "God and war be with you!" It is an amusing, but a cutting satire; and although now scarcely readable except by specialists, it did in its time help to change history.

Both the *Letters of Obscure Men* and the *Menippean Satire* attacked the emotional and intellectual attitude of a group. Later, the art of prose became more complex. The subtleties of Greek and Roman rhetoric were rediscovered and adapted. Individual writers developed their special styles; affectations—such as the tight arabesques of Euphuism—became fashionable; and both were parodied. Satiric mimicry, delicate in the eighteenth century, became more energetic in the nineteenth. There are two fine prose parodies in the Smith brothers' *Rejected Addresses*: a rough, slangy, bare-fisted, boiled-beef-and-turnips speech by William Cobbett, and an engagingly sesquipedalian address by the ghost of Dr. Johnson.

> Parturient mountains have ere now produced muscipular abortions, and the auditor who compares incipient grandeur with final vulgarity, is reminded of the pious hawkers of Constantinople, who solemnly perambulate her streets, exclaiming, "In the name of the Prophet—figs!"

In our own day amateurs of parody have received particular pleasure from two minor masterpieces in this area. Several cryptographers have extracted sentences from the work of Shakespeare, anagrammatized them, and discovered them to contain assertions that the plays were really written by Lord Bacon or the Earl of Oxford or some other dark star. Ronald Knox applied the same methods to Tennyson's *In Memoriam*, and extracted from it a group of cryptograms quite as eloquent as those of the Shakespearean heretics. The first line of the poem

> I held it truth, with him who sings

becomes

> Who is writing this? H. M. luteth hid.

Similarly,

> O priestess in the vaults of death

can be interpreted as

> V.R.I. the poetess. Alf T. has no duties.

Thus Knox "proved" that *In Memoriam* was written by Queen Victoria to enshrine her affection for Lord Melbourne, but, to shield the dignity of a monarch and the emotions of a lady, published under Tennyson's name. In the same volume, *Essays in Satire* (1930), he ridiculed the critical dissections of the Bible, the *Iliad*, and similar works of venerable antiquity, by using the same techniques of "scholarly analysis" to show that the second part of Bunyan's *Pilgrim's Progress* was a forgery composed by a

woman, and an Anglo-Catholic to boot; and that three
different authors created Boswell's *Life of Johnson*.

Of all the American Presidents, Dwight D. Eisenhower
was perhaps the least eloquent and the most garrulous.
Frankness was there. Honesty shone through. There was no
artifice. There was no grandeur. Sometimes there was not
even grammar. His tongue-tied forthrightness, and the
mental fatigue which relied, for support, on clichés thick
as concrete, were handsomely satirized by Oliver Jensen,
who rewrote Lincoln's Gettysburg Address as Eisenhower
might have spoken it.

> I haven't checked these figures but 87 years ago, I think it
> was, a number of individuals organized a governmental
> set-up here in this country, I believe it covered certain East-
> ern areas, with this idea they were following up based on a
> sort of national independence arrangement and the pro-
> gram that every individual is just as good as every other
> individual. Well, now, of course, we are dealing with this
> big difference of opinion, civil disturbance you might say,
> although I don't like to appear to take sides or name any
> individuals, and the point is naturally to check up, by actual
> experience in the field, to see whether any governmental
> set-up with a basis like the one I was mentioning has any
> validity and find out whether that dedication by those early
> individuals will pay off in lasting values and things of that
> kind.[108]

PROSE: FICTION

Prose fiction, if intensely written, often parodies itself.
If popular, it always asks to be parodied. The modern
novel was no sooner born, in tears and vapors, than it was
parodied, in humors and leers. Samuel Richardson's
Pamela: or Virtue Rewarded (1740) tells how a servant-girl
with a noble heart resists the efforts of her master to make
her his mistress, and is rewarded by becoming his legal
wife. Henry Fielding's *Joseph Andrews* (1742) tells how her
brother, a footman with a noble heart, resists the efforts

of Lady Booby, his employer, to seduce him, and is rewarded far more reasonably by being discharged and finding a girl of his own. Since then, every eminent novelist has been parodied, and the work still goes on.[109]

Many of these parodies can be enjoyed for themselves alone, as pure comedy. While I was still a junior schoolboy, and long before I had even heard of most of the authors involved, I shouted with laughter over a clever collection of travesties by Bret Harte called *Condensed Novels*. It was easy to recognize the satire on Fenimore Cooper in *Muck-a-Muck*; but who was Miss Mix, the new governess at Blunderbore Hall?

> Drawing a chair into a recess, I sat down with folded hands, calmly awaiting the arrival of my master. Once or twice a fearful yell rang through the house, or the rattling of chains, and curses uttered in a deep, manly voice, broke upon the oppressive stillness. I began to feel my soul rising with the emergency of the moment.
> "You look alarmed, miss. You don't hear anything, my dear, do you?" asked the housekeeper nervously.
> "Nothing whatever," I remarked calmly, as a terrific scream, followed by the dragging of chairs and tables in the room above, drowned for a moment my reply. "It is the silence, on the contrary, which has made me foolishly nervous."

And who was the French author who told of Jean Valjean stealing the Bishop's candlesticks and then proved him innocent?

> Let us consider: candlesticks were stolen; that was evident. Society put Jean Valjean in prison; that was evident, too. In prison, Society took away his refinement; that is evident, likewise.
> Who is Society?
> You and I are Society.
> My friend, you and I stole those candlesticks!

When in time I read the originals, I was still amused,

without feeling that Bret Harte had diminished their intrinsic value as literature. Far different, however, is Max Beerbohm's *A Christmas Garland* (1912). This is one of the most brilliant achievements of parodic satire in any language; but its intent is destructive. It contains eighteen little tales about Christmas. Each is placed in the favorite setting, told in the preferred language and rhythm, and infused with the characteristic emotional color of a contemporary novelist. Examples:

> The hut in which slept the white man was on a clearing between the forest and the river.

One of Conrad's traders in a dark continent hears the aborigines approaching for a feast on Christmas Day, and finds that the feast is he.

> It was with a sense of a, for him, very memorable something that he peered now into the immediate future, and tried, not without compunction, to take that period up where he had, prospectively, left it.

Keith Tantalus attempts, with the convoluted cerebration of many Henry James characters, to determine whether he should, or, alternatively, should not look into his Christmas stocking to discover what, if any, gifts have been left for him by Santa Claus.

> I had spent Christmas Eve at the Club, listening to a grand pow-wow between certain of the choicer sons of Adam.

And thereafter Kipling, his own narrator, leaves to watch with sadistic delight P.C., X,36 arresting and bullying a suspicious "airman" with a white beard, a red ulster, and what looks like a sack over his shoulder. Beerbohm's parodies were intended to wound. As we know from his biography, he had a streak of feline cruelty. He liked making quiet little forgeries, and altering smooth pictures, and destroying rich reputations. He always loathed Kipling;

he drew harsh and wounding caricatures of Kipling; and no one who knows his parody of Kipling can ever read without disgust certain short stories which make up a large proportion of Kipling's work. As for Arnold Bennett, after he read Beerbohm's story in his manner—about the strong-willed girl who gave her lover a Christmas pudding full of broken pottery scraps (or "scruts," which sounds more authentically provincial) to test his love—he was paralyzed: he, who habitually turned out thousands of words every day, was inhibited from writing, until the shock of this operation wore off, and the scar of Max's cautery ceased to throb. Bret Harte parodied his novelists with hearty amusement; Max Beerbohm, though politely, with contempt, and at least once with delicately controlled hatred. Both hatred and amusement are impulses which move the satirist.

The same dual motivation appears in the work of the parodic satirists of our own generation.

> Amid this phantasmagoric chaos, in a thousand little sleeping towns built across the land (O my America! O my!) I have pursued my soul's desire, looking for a stone, a leaf, a door we never found, feeling my Faustian life intolerably in my entrails. I have quivered a thousand times in sensual terror and ecstatic joy as the 5:07 pulled in. I have felt a wild and mournful sorrow at the thought, the wonderful thought, that everything I have seen and known (and have I not known and seen all that is to be seen and known upon this dark, brooding continent?) has come out of my own life, is indeed I, or me, the youth eternal, many-visaged and many-volumed. Whatever it may be, I have sought it through my kaleidoscopic days and velvet-and-duvetyn-breasted nights, and in my dark, illimitable madness, in my insatiate and huge unrest, in my appalling and obscene fancies, in my haunting and lonely memories (for we are all lonely), in my grotesque, abominable and frenzied prodigalities, I have always cried aloud. . . .[110]

This lyrical monologue out of the cradle endlessly leaking,

these cloudbursts of adolescent emotion releasing deluges of sound uncontaminated by sense, the trumpet-shouts and drum-beats, the humorless urgency of a naïve idealist who is always chasing Rimbaud: these make up a picture of an ass in Wolfe's clothing. Clifton Fadiman's aim in writing it was to deflate what he saw as an enormous balloon full of stomach gas; to display a portrait of the artist as a fat greedy bawling baby. Its ruthless energy places this parody in the long powerful line of destructive satires.

But consider this.

> The cold Brussels sprout rolled off the page of the book I was reading and lay inert and defunctive in my lap. Turning my head with a leisure at least three fourths impotent rage, I saw him standing there holding the toy with which he had catapulted the vegetable, or rather the reverse, the toy first then the fat insolent fist clutching it and then above that the bland defiant face beneath the shock of black hair like tangible gas.[111]

An act of violence offered by a son to his father; the sudden realization of a dangerously dislocated relationship; sensitive and flexuous syntax, uniquely appropriate to the involuted psychical processes it is employed to image; a passion for unusual words ("defunctive" was invented by Shakespeare and is rarely used) and for striking even if almost meaningless images ("hair like *tangible* gas"): all this is William Faulkner rendered by Peter de Vries with the same reverential amusement as Saul Steinberg might employ in drawing a Confederate cavalryman eternally immobilized in his granitic caracol.

IV   THE DISTORTING MIRROR

1. SATIRE AND TRUTH

E HAVE looked at two of the chief forms
that satire assumes: the droll or scornful
monologue, which can be disguised in many
ways, but is usually the utterance of the satirist in his own
person; and the parody, which takes something real and
respected and, by using exaggeration and incongruity,
converts it into mockery of itself. If we examine the books
which are called satirical, we find a third main pattern,
which is nowadays the most popular and has always been
the most widely appreciated. This is a story. Just as the
satirist can preach an unconventional and grotesque sermon, just as he can take a traditional literary form, turn
it upside down, and grin through it, so he can tell a story
which carries his message. The narrative must be interesting, and it must be well told. But for the satirist the
narrative is not the end: it is the means. Sometimes he
conceals this fact, and pretends that he is concentrating on
reporting actual occurrences "just as they happened." So
Rabelais at the beginning of *Pantagruel* offers himself
"body and soul, tripe and bowels, to a myriad of devils"
if he tells a single word of falsehood in the whole of his
history. Sometimes, though less often, the satirist openly
admits his purpose in telling a story. So, in the prologue
to *Gargantua*, Rabelais reminds us that Alcibiades, the
most impudent pupil of Socrates, once compared his master
to a grotesque casket full of rare and precious drugs and
spices; and he tells us that, in the same way, his story is not
merely an amusing piece of fiction, but contains much
important truth about religion and life.

There are scores of different types of fiction. How can we

say which of them are satirical? Is it possible to examine a novel, or a play, or a narrative poem, and to say unequivocally that it is a satire? If so, how can we distinguish it from other pieces of fiction, externally similar to it in most respects, which are not satirical? Obviously a mock epic, describing the deeds of petty or ignoble people in grandiose or ludicrous terms, will be a satire; but these and similar narratives have already been discussed under parody and burlesque. However, there are many famous pieces of fiction which are accepted as being wholly or mainly satirical, and are not parodies at all.

One of the most famous is Swift's *Gulliver's Travels*. This is not a parody. It is a close imitation of contemporary tales of travel and exploration; but it does not, either in manner or in intention, imply that such tales are ridiculous, and that neither it nor they are worthy of belief. Some story-tellers do this—for instance, Lucian in his *True History*—but Swift does not. On the contrary, he tries very hard to make the book seem authentic, by inserting intelligible and credible details which a real voyager would record (weather, ship's course, latitude, longitude, etc.), by adding maps, by transcribing at least one passage verbatim from a genuine sailor's log, and by placing his imaginary countries in little-known parts of the world, where there is, so to speak, room for them. Thus, Lilliput is out in the Indian Ocean, south-west of Sumatra. The land of the Houyhnhnms is in the same region, within sailing distance of Australia, whose original inhabitants were so primitive as to resemble Yahoos. Laputa, which has an Oriental feel about it, is in the Pacific Ocean toward Japan. Brobdingnag is in the north-eastern Pacific: with uncommon serendipity Swift located it somewhere between the Kodiak islands, where the enormous bears live, and the area of Oregon and northern California, where the magnificent sequoias make us all feel as Gulliver did among the giants. Thus, *Gulliver's Travels*, although it is unquestionably a satire and although there is a sneer in its name, is by no means a parody. It is presented as a serious and veridical narrative. It may best be compared with two pieces of realistic fiction which, like *Gulliver*, were wholly due to their author's reading and imagination: Daniel Defoe's *Robinson Crusoe*, published in 1719, and the same writer's *New Voyage Round the World*, published in 1725, just one year before Swift brought out *Gulliver's Travels*.

What is the difference between these two narratives? What makes *Gulliver* a satirical story, and the *New Voyage* straightforward non-satirical fiction? The cardinal test is the effect on the reader. The *New Voyage*, like other adventure stories, can be read with interest and excitement: it awakens few other emotions. But it is impossible for an adult to read *Gulliver's Travels* without feeling, as the most potent part of his experience, a complex emotion which is compounded of amusement, contempt, disgust, and hatred, and whose effect is generally negative and destructive. A story which successfully produces and sustains this emotion is a successful satiric narrative. A story which merely amuses us or thrills us, with no aftertaste of derisive bitterness, is a comedy, or a tale of adventure, or a romance, or, to use the vaguest term, a novel. Hatred which is not simply shocked revulsion but is based on a moral judgment, together with a degree of amusement which may range anywhere between a sour grin at the incongruity of the human condition and a delighted roar of laughter at the exposure of an absurd fraud—such are, in varying proportions, the effects of satire. When they are absent from a piece of fiction, it is not satirical.

If a story or a play produces feelings of pure hatred and revulsion, without a trace of scornful amusement or regretful contempt, it is not a satire. It is a negative novel, an anti-romance. Such books are as yet uncommon, though more are being written in our generation. The best examples which occur to me are the novels of the Marquis de Sade, and certain recent tales of brutality and degradation, such as Mirbeau's *Torture Garden*, Bowles's *Sheltering Sky*, Faulkner's *Sanctuary*, and the works of Genêt. These black books lack nearly all the central purpose and underlying idealism of satire, and although the nausea which they induce could easily be used by a satirist, their moral import is not satirical. They are in fact the counterparts of such purely saccharine romances as Elinor Glyn's *Three Weeks* and Frances Hodgson Burnett's *Little Lord Fauntleroy*.

Satire can be mistaken for other forms of art and literature, unless its emotional and moral effects are clearly defined and understood. Aesthetic types are not walled off from one another by impenetrable barriers. At their extremes they diverge clearly and unmistakably; but they spring from roots which lie near to one another in the human soul; and, through much of their development, they grow closely together, so that only the boldest and most determined representative of each type appears to define that particular type, while others keep crossing frontiers and mingling powers and competing with one another, just as do people, and languages, and societies. Certain forms of literature are particularly close kinsmen and near neighbors of satire, and often exchange with it both costumes and ideas.

On one side of satire lies its grim gruff old ancestor born in the stone caves, still echoing the martial monotony of the savages' skin drums roaring for the destruction of an enemy tribe, still shrieking with the furious passion of the witch-doctor denouncing a rival. This is Invective, whose parent on one side was anthropoid, and on the other, lupine. Lurking near by is the smaller, weaker, but sometimes more dangerous mutant of Invective: a by-blow born of a snake and a toad, a hideous little creature with a mouth full of poisoned fangs. This is Lampoon, a parasite which has no life of its own and can exist only through destroying its victim.

Usually the lampoon is a poisoned dart, or a shower of filth, discharged with impunity on a helpless victim by his enemy. But sometimes the victim replies with another rain of garbage and venom; and the exchange grows into a regular duel. Each of the duellists endeavors to outshout, outcurse, and silence his opponent, whether by the appalling violence of his abuse, or by its piercing aptness, or by its passionate volubility, or by the unanswerable cleverness with which it is shaped and delivered. Word-duels of this type exist in many cultures, although they seldom emerge into the higher air of fine art and literature. Song-combats (called "drum matches") are recognized methods of settling disputes among the Eskimos of Greenland. Contemporary American Negroes have an institution called "the Dozens," in which rivals sing competing songs of abuse before a crowd: "the one whose fury stultifies his verbal agility loses the contest, and a sure sign of being bested is to hit one's opponent."[1] The hero of the much-loved Argentine poem, José Hernández' *Martín Fierro* (1872-1879), is a roving gaucho who is never without his long knife and his tuneful guitar and loves fighting with either of them. One long section near the end of the poem consists of a duel in song between Martín and a Negro, which very nearly turns into a duel with knives, to the death.[2]

There is no generally accepted word for these exchanges of abuse. However, they are sometimes called "flyting," from the old Scots word for scolding. Normally, they have the following characteristic qualities:

(1) They are, or seem to be, improvised.

(2) They are in strongly rhythmical verse, often married to music.

(3) They are relentlessly personal and outrageously scurrilous.

(4) They are responsive, or amoebaean: that is, when A has uttered his stanza of derision and hate, B must follow him in the same rhythmical pattern. In a close duel, he must use the same sentence-structure and even the same imagery. The challenger therefore has the advantage of taking the initiative, but the responder has always the chance of outdoing him.

(5) They are held in public, before a crowd which derives a complex pleasure from them: admiration of the skill of the contenders, delighted shock at the public use of obscenity and the revelation of secrets, sadistic amusement at the cruel humiliation they inflict upon each other.

Reciprocal exchanges of abuse used to be a popular amusement in Greece and Rome: during the procession from Athens to Eleusis for the rites of Demeter; at weddings in Italy where "Fescennine verses" were sung; at parties and at vintage-festivals. The only real entertainment which Horace and his friends had during their journey to Brindisi was such a duel between two professional comics. (One of them was called Cicirrus, a dialect word for "cock"; and they really put on a verbal cock-fight.)[3] It is likely that the improvised shows called *saturae*, popular in Rome before the importation of genuine comedy from Greece, had such turns in them.

In literature, the slanging-match between Cleon and the Sausage-Seller in Aristophanes' *Knights* is a typical "flyting," and so are most of the contests between opposing half-choruses in Aristophanic comedy. Not all readers of pastoral poetry realize that it has its coarse brutal side, and that the "singing matches" of shepherds in Theocritus and Vergil are sometimes competitions in obscenity and cruelty—although both poets add the charm of elegant expression and subtle imagery: see Theocritus' fifth and Vergil's third bucolic poem.

The fifteenth-century Scottish poet William Dunbar is best known for his "lament in sickness," with its sad refrain *Timor mortis conturbat me*; but when he was well he was full of vigor: he has left fourteen pages of lively abuse exchanged with a fellow-poet, *The Flyting of Dunbar and Kennedy*. It ends with a shout of triumph, calling on Kennedy to "yield and flee the field," and go to hell—

> Pickit, wickit, convickit Lamp Lollardorum,
> Defamyt, blamyt, schamyt Primas Paganorum.
> Out! out! I schout, apon that snowt that snevillis.
> Tale tellare, rebellare, induellar wyth the devillis,
> Spynk, sink with stynk ad Tertara Termagorum.

This flyting is not satire. It is not comedy. Yet it has something in common with both kinds of literature. It springs from some of the same deep roots in primitive society, and in the combative challenging spirit of mankind.

Close to satire on the other side we see, cavorting about and wearing gay masks and putting on funny hats and using unrespectable words and disrupting solemn ceremonies, two other siblings. These are Comedy and Farce. If it wanted to, Comedy could be satire; and in nearly every satire there are some elements of Farce. The main difference is that these two beings are kind. They may be silly; they may tickle the observer, or pinprick him (without drawing more than a drop of blood), or hit him with a blown-up bladder, but they do not hurt. Except to the most solemn or sensitive of mortals, they are inoffensive. Comedy always wishes to evoke laughter, or at least a smile of pure enjoyment. Farce does not care what it does provided that everybody collapses into unreasoning merriment. Most of us ignore this side of art; some of us even ignore this side of life; but the fact remains. The ridiculous is built into human existence. Many of our essential activities, some of our deepest emotions, and several aspects of our physical appearance, are ludicrous. The disrespectful youngster who contrives comedy and the grinning chimpanzee who explores farce both recognize this fact. Out of it they create gaiety which, although temporary, is wholesome; sometimes a joke which lasts; and now and then, almost involuntarily, a work of art.

These, then, are the closest kin of satire: on one side, invective and lampoon; on the other, comedy and farce. Invective and lampoon are full of hatred, and wish only to destroy. Comedy and farce are rich with liking, and want to preserve, to appreciate, to enjoy. The man who writes an invective would be delighted if, after delivering it, he were told that his subject had been overwhelmed by shame and obloquy and had retired into oblivion. The lampoonist would like his victims to die of a hideous disease, or (like the enemies of Hipponax) to hang themselves. The writer of comedy or farce would be saddened by any such news. He likes people, not in spite of their peculiarities, but because of them. He could not endure the notion that all the oddities might disappear, and leave the world to routine and to him. Invective and lampoon look from above and from behind: one is the prosecuting attorney, the other the assassin. Comedy and farce look askance and from below: one is the amused friend who loves his friend's absurdities; the other is the servant who likes his master but cannot keep from befooling and mimicking him. As for satire, the satirist always asserts that he would be happy if he heard his victim had, in tears and self-abasement, permanently reformed; but he would in fact be rather better pleased if the fellow were pelted with garbage and ridden out of town on a rail. Satire is the literary equivalent of a bucket of tar and a sack of feathers.

The purpose of invective and lampoon is to destroy an enemy. The purpose of comedy and farce is to cause pain-less undestructive laughter at human weaknesses and in-congruities. The purpose of satire is, through laughter and invective, to cure folly and to punish evil; but if it does not achieve this purpose, it is content to jeer at folly and to expose evil to bitter contempt.

The purpose of satire is one of its distinguishing marks. Another is the shape which it takes. In narrative fiction and in drama this shape is highly important but is easy to misunderstand. Nowadays it is often misinterpreted not only by readers, but even, to their detriment, by authors.

Have you ever read a novel which started out as a real-istic study of a small community or of a single social prob-lem or of one interesting individual, and then, at intervals, veered backward and forward between straight analysis and grotesque distortion? If so, you have seen the work of a writer who wanted to be two different, and disparate, things at once: a novelist and a satirist. Often we open a new novel and find that the first five or six chapters are devoted to introducing the characters, setting the situation, stating the main conflicts, and establishing the emotional atmosphere. This is done consistently and realistically. A group appears and takes life: you are involved in it. A man and a woman emerge: you feel you know them. And then suddenly, in the sixth or seventh chapter, the whole thing changes. People who have hitherto been normal are transformed into clowns, drunkards, nymphomaniacs, sad-ists, and characters from obsolete motion-pictures. Im-probable conversations are held; meaningless fights break out; regular social relationships are turned upside down. Sometimes the author's pretext for arranging this trans-formation is a party at which everyone gets tipsy, or an unexpected crisis at which hidden desires and follies and hatreds are permitted to emerge. But, unless in the hands of a brilliantly competent novelist, the effect is usually unsatisfactory. In the ensuing chapters, the characters return to their normal selves and resume their established relationships and what had been a realistic novel continues, after an inexplicable interruption, its expected course. For a time, we have enjoyed the peculiar emotions evoked by satire. Before and after, we were carried on by the quite different emotion of participating in a piece of fiction. Now, we cannot wholly believe in the characters of the tale as being real and possibly sympathetic; yet we cannot accept the author's wish that we should see them as utterly laughable and contemptible. We cannot follow the incidents of the story as though it were a transcript of real life; but we feel anxious when asked to enjoy them all, every one, as propaganda distortions. One, or the other: not both.

In the same way, you must often have seen a play in which most of the characters were recognizably real and engaged in normal human relationships, funny, pathetic, or tragic; but which was distorted along one line of stress. Perhaps one character was a professional soldier who did not like fighting, came from a pacific country, and carried as his chief piece of equipment not a revolver but a bar of chocolate; or perhaps an ordinary household was invaded by a fiendish hypocrite who became a monster dominating everyone, and prepared to crush them utterly—until his machinations were destroyed through a quasi-miraculous intervention by God or the King or some other irrational power. In such plays, the dramatist is combining two different types of theatre: normal comedy (or romance, or tragedy) and satiric drama.

It is always tempting for a brilliant writer to mix literary genres. Both Aeschylus and Shakespeare put far more comedy and fantasy into their tragedies than other authors would venture. But it is particularly dangerous to mix realistic fiction (whether narrative or dramatic) with satire. This is because satire—although it pretends to be telling the complete truth about life—in fact presents a propagandist distortion; while dramatic and narrative fiction make a far better balanced selection of material and come much closer to telling the entire truth.

Genuine satiric fiction pretends to be true and real; but it is distorted through and through. Its events are wildly abnormal (as in *Gulliver's Travels*) or linked by preposterous chances and coincidences (as in *Candide*); its hero has superhuman powers of endurance (as in *Don Quixote*), of survival (as in *Baron Munchausen*), of naïveté (as in *Decline and Fall*) or astuteness (as in *Reynard the Fox*); its characters, although often described with every appearance of gravity, are misshapen, exaggerated, and caricatured.

Many famous stories and plays which have been called "satires" are only in part satirical, while far the larger part of their emphasis, far the stronger purpose of their authors, lie outside the field of true satire. Sometimes only a single character or episode is satirical, in a book which is otherwise purely fictional, purely dramatic: for example, Mr. Bumble in *Oliver Twist*, Osric in *Hamlet*. However, when we speak of satires in fiction (whether narrative or dramatic) we shall mean only those books which are predominantly satirical, not those which now and then drop into satire but are mainly designed to present a richer and more balanced picture of life.

The central problem of satire is its relation to reality. Satire wishes to expose and criticize and shame human life, but it pretends to tell the whole truth and nothing but the truth. In narrative and drama it usually does this in one of two ways: either by showing an apparently factual but really ludicrous and debased picture of this world; or by showing a picture of another world, with which our world is contrasted.

2. OUT OF THIS WORLD

There are therefore a large number of satiric tales in the form of visits to strange lands and other worlds. The most famous in English is *Gulliver's Travels*. This terrible book says, by its title and by its scheme, what it means. It is the journey of a gull, or a fool, through various aspects of human life—in four badspells, to parallel the four gospels which Dean Swift expounded in the pulpit. In his travels, the fool, who (like most of us) believed men and women were reasonably honest and wise, finds, stage by stage, that they are ridiculous midgets, disgusting giants, eccentric lunatics, and apelike anthropoids; he ends like Dean Swift himself, isolated in a universe with only one inhabitant and without a God, unable even to take food with his family, unable to look at the rest of mankind without loathing. This spiritual progress into the void is disguised in satiric fiction as a set of traveler's tales. Yet it is quite clear to most readers that Gulliver is not really voyaging to different countries, but looking at his own society through distorting lenses. Lilliput and Brobdingnag are like European countries diminished or magnified (Lilliput resembling the France of Louis XIV and Brobdingnag the Russia of Tsar Peter); Laputa is like the Royal Society translated into Oriental terms; both Balnibarbi and the Yahoos are in different ways like the Irish under English oppression; while the Houyhnhnms are not super-horses but supermen with the virtues of the Age of Reason. In the world opened up to Swift and his contemporaries by exploration, there were many societies far more eccentric and far more instructive than those visited by Gulliver. But satire does not usually compare two real societies: it compares a real and an ideal, or a noble dream with a debased reality. All reality was, for Swift, debased. He could not believe that human beings would ever make use of their capacities for kindness, reason, and nobility; and, although outwardly a member of the Christian church, he believed so strongly in original sin and so little in the supernatural that he saw, neither in his own faith nor in its founder, any possibility of redemption.

In medieval times men and women loved to go on pilgrimages. One of the most important of medieval poems describes a pilgrim's progress in terms which are at least partly satiric. This is *The Man of Many Sorrows (Architrenius)*, written in A.D. 1184 by a virtually unknown author named Jean de Hauteville, in nine books, about four thousand five hundred lines of good, sometimes eloquent, Latin hexameters.[4] It is a tale of moral suffering, search, and redemption. Dissatisfied with his vicious and purposeless life, Architrenius sets out to find Nature, and to learn why she has made him so weak. He passes through regions which are purely allegorical (the abode of Gluttony, the mountain of Ambition), wholly mythical (the palace of Venus), partly mythical (Thule, where he hears instructive speeches by the wise men Archytas, Cato, and Plato), or real and contemporary (the University of Paris); and at last he finds Nature, who delivers an admonitory sermon to him and gives him happiness in the form of a beautiful wife, Moderation. (Curiously, although this is a poem of moral struggle, it almost entirely ignores the Christian church, its teachings, and its promises of redemption.) Since it is usually grave, abstract, and monotonous, *Architrenius* is not really satirical. Stylistically, its chief Latin model is Ovid in his *Metamorphoses*, and, like that poem, it should probably be defined as a blend of epic and didactic poetry. Still, there are some quirks of critical humor in it, several good parodies, and some quotations and adaptations of Juvenal.[5] Like other large medieval poems, then, it is in part but not predominantly or generically a satire.

A famous modern satire in the form of a travel book is Samuel Butler's *Erewhon* (1872). Its very title, *Nowhere* phonetically reversed, and the names of his characters, make us expect to see a looking-glass reflection of his own world. Thus, his host in Erewhon is called by two of the commonest middle-class English names reversed, Senoj Nosnibor; his teacher bears the commonest of all, Thims; and the ruling goddess Ydgrun is the nineteenth-century British juju Mrs. Grundy. Butler's mind was agile, but it was narrow. I personally can never raise up much enthusiasm for a tale in which, after long sufferings and dangerous journeys into an unknown region, the explorer merely finds another Victorian Britain with a few conventions turned upside-down. It is cleverly told and there are some amusing quirks in it. Yet, when we think what wonderful varieties of human society there are on the surface of this globe, and how fantastically and instructively they differ from dear old England, we may wonder whether it was worth Butler's time to cross the untraversed mountain barriers in order to meet with such a commonplace reflection of the men and women whom he knew and did not like. "Sky they change, not heart, who run across the sea," said the Roman satirist;[6] and it is curious to watch Butler spending so much time and energy on constructing an inverted model of his own home, when a few days' ride away from his New Zealand range he would have met a far more interesting and paradoxical people in real life, the Maoris. There is a recent variation on the same idea. In his *Journey to the Land of the Articoles* (1928) André Maurois describes the imaginary island of Maïana in the central Pacific, which is inhabited by two different social groups. The superior group is the Articoles, whose life is wholly given up to artistic experience, painting, and carving, and composing music, and writing. They possess no money, and are supported by the rich Beos (short for Boeotians, i.e. dullards), who carry out all the non-artistic work of the country. The chief problem in the lives of the Articoles is that their existence is too comfortable and too limited to provide them with much material for art. This particularly perplexes the writers. Some of them, however, solve it by introspection. The greatest recent success of Maïanan literature was the confession of an Articole called Routchko, running to sixteen thousand nine hundred pages, and entitled *Why I Cannot Write*.

The only admittedly unrealistic portion of that marvelous little book, *Candide*, is a visit to the imaginary land of Eldorado. The most famous of all such voyages is Thomas More's *Utopia* (1516). Although its tone is calm and restrained, the sharp contrast which its sweetly rational description of Utopian life makes to the irrational condition of contemporary Europe probably entitles it to be styled a mild satire: More himself said it was intended to be both amusing and beneficial.[7] Certainly the funniest travel satire ever written is the fourth and fifth books of Rabelais' *Pantagruel*, the long voyage parodying the quest of the Holy Grail, in which the gigantic prince and his courtiers sail to find the Oracle of the Holy Bottle, and touch, en route, at all sorts of satirical islands which emblematize the weaknesses and follies of this world. One of them is called Medamothy, which means, just as Utopia does, Nowhere.[8]

OTHER WORLDS

Sometimes, again, the traveler makes his way quite outside this earthly realm to a region inhabited by beings who are inhuman, or superhuman, or else peopled by human creatures on a different plane of existence. It is one of the oldest of our dreams, the flight through space and the visit to another world. Manifestly the description of such a journey need not be satiric in purpose. It may be

heroic, as in Odysseus' interview with the ghosts of his
dead comrades. It may be mystical, as in Dante's ascent of
Mount Purgatory and flight through the spheres. It may
be fanciful, like Wells's *First Men in the Moon* and the
innumerable "space fictions" which are now pouring out
of a newly tapped reservoir of the subconscious.[9] It may be
comic, like Dionysus' descent to hell in Aristophanes' *Frogs*
and the flight of Trygaeus to heaven on a dung-beetle in
Aristophanes' *Peace*. But when it involves criticism of life
in this world, with exposures of human vices and weaknesses and bitter or teasing humor, then it is satire. The
brilliant Menippus of Gadara (following Aristophanes)
wrote of his visit to the world of the dead, where he con-
sulted the wise soothsayer Tiresias about the best way to
live, and got the same advice which, two thousand years
later, was given to Candide: to shun public affairs, and
τὸ παρὸν εὖ θέσθαι, "make the best of his lot."[10] There, too,
he saw how easily death strips the rich and powerful of their
wealth and their dignity, how frail and trivial are the
externals of this life, which we struggle so hard to get and
keep. The same Menippus flew up to the sky in order to
test the philosophers' theories about astronomy; and thence
he looked down on the earth, seeing the pettiness and
confusion of human life, the folly of the human prayers
which ascend constantly like smoke to heaven.[11] These
two themes recur often in the work of satirists, and even,
as episodes, in more august types of literature. In Ariosto's
Madness of Roland there is a delightful flight to the moon,
where the chevalier Astolfo finds the wits lost by hapless
lunatics of this world, together with a vast deal of deceits
and magics and trumperies. On this model Milton inserted
into *Paradise Lost* a short satiric description of the dump-
heap of vanities, on the outer rim of our universe, whither
they are blown by the wind.

Then might ye see
Cowls, hoods, and habits, with their wearers, tossed
And fluttered into rags; then reliques, beads,
Indulgences, dispenses, pardons, bulls,
The sport of winds: all these, upwhirled aloft,
Fly o'er the backside of the World far off
Into a Limbo large and broad, since called
The Paradise of Fools.[12]

Some of the more successful satiric pieces by Menippus's admirer Lucian describe, in dialogue form, visits to and conversations in the underworld and the home of the Olympian deities: Menippus himself and other Cynics appear as characters in them, laughing philosophers who are the very incarnations of satire.[13]

An imaginative writer may describe a visit to an extra-terrestrial region either as a journey or as a vision. The difference between the two is often a matter of emphasis. Dante, who is so careful to remind us that he retained his own physical body (suffering pain and pleasure, and even, to the astonishment of the souls of the dead, casting a shadow), and who describes with vivid detail the modes of movement which take him from one stage to another of his journey, is not a visionary but a voyager. Rabelais, however, sends one of his characters to the world of death and brings him back with miraculous ease and rapidity. Perhaps he had at the back of his mind the magnificent revelation of the world of eternity which (according to Plato in his *Republic*) was vouchsafed to the Armenian warrior Er while he lay apparently a corpse and yet not wholly dead. If so, as he did with nearly all his models, he parodied it and made it satirical. Prince Pantagruel's squire Epistemon (whose name means Knowledgeable) was killed in the battle with the giants: his head was smitten off; his soul left his body and moved among the dead. But Panurge stitched his head back on again, dusting it with powder of diamerdis, and restored him to life. Epistemon then reported what he had seen. It was a complete inversion of the fates and fortunes of this world—and thereby betrayed its ancestry in the satires of the Cynic Menippus. Diogenes was a monarch with a robe and a scepter, while Alexander the Great was a mender of old clothes; Epictetus the poor beggarly Stoic was now a rich gentleman with wine and women, while Cyrus the conqueror cadged farthings from him; a famous Pope had become a pie-peddler, and the Knights of the Round Table were bumboat-men, rowing the devils back and forward on the river of Styx.[14]

Between a mystical journey and a mystical vision the most important difference is that, in a journey, the stages are described in some detail, and the author tries to make them seem real, while the visionary either is transported by a miracle to and from the scene of his vision, or else, in a spiritual rapture, sees it all with the inward eye. Epistemon's visit to Hades was therefore a vision, seen by his spirit while his body lay cataleptic. Satirical visions of the hereafter are not common in Christian literature, for obvious reasons, but the Greek and Roman pagans were less squeamish about making fun of eschatology. One of the most brilliant and scandalous, but effective, visionary satires in Latin is the *Apocolocyntosis* of Seneca.

The eccentric Emperor Claudius, partly crippled by cerebral palsy and even more emotionally disturbed than the majority of his disastrous family, after reigning for fourteen years, was poisoned by his wife Agrippina in a doctored dish of mushrooms. Quickly, before any scandal could spread or any disorder arise, Agrippina's young son Nero was proclaimed Emperor. Claudius was given a magnificent state funeral, at which Nero read a solemn eulogy of his adoptive father's virtues and achievements written for him by Seneca: it was listened to at first in respectful silence and then with roars of irresistible laughter. Next, Claudius was declared to be a god and given a place in heaven beside Augustus and Romulus, with temples, and altars, and priests, and sacrifices, and holy festivals, on earth below. Claudius, who had been made Emperor half in jest by the bodyguard of his murdered predecessor, who had governed through a collection of his ex-slaves (Greeks, and Orientals, and what not), whose wife Messalina had publicly married another man, and who, after signing the order for her execution, had forgotten all about it by dinner-time, Claudius who could scarcely walk without tottering and speak without slobbering—a god! It was an important moment when he was deified. Julius Caesar with his baleful brilliance had something supernatural in him, like Alexander. Augustus was the Savior who had brought peace to the war-maddened world. These men could well be accepted as deities, and revered, and worshipped. But when Claudius was deified, everyone felt it was a ridiculous and almost blasphemous convention, and the court knew it was a diabolical stratagem.

The philosopher Seneca, Nero's tutor, wrote a satire on the deification of Claudius. It begins as a parody of history (because the truth about Claudius was too ridiculous to write down as fact), and then becomes a vision of heaven and hell inspired ultimately by Menippus. It tells how Claudius, after being only half alive for many years, finally expired. He went to heaven and demanded admittance. The gods discussed his claim to divinity, and some of the old-fashioned eccentric ones moved to accept him; but his own ancestor Augustus, speaking for the first time in that august assembly, denounced him as a bad man and an evil ruler. Claudius was rejected, and taken down to hell, where he was finally handed as a slave to his crazy predecessor Caligula. Such is Seneca's satire, the *Apocolocyntosis*.[15]

It is so cruel and mean and personal, the *Apocolocyntosis*, that it would be a lampoon, if it did not contain a serious moral judgment. It is basically a farcical description of Claudius trying to reach heaven and being sent to hell; nearly all of it is funny; it is full of jokes, puns, parodies, paradoxes, and epigrams; but it contains a serious warning to Claudius's successor Nero himself, in the form of a speech by Augustus, the founder of the Empire. (Nero did not take the warning, and ended more miserably, even more ludicrously, than Claudius.) Because Seneca was a clever man and a skillful teacher, it is a brilliant and instructive satire. Because he was a moral weakling, it is a disgusting piece of brutality and flattery. But it is an important historical document. It is the first extant book to say openly that the Roman emperors were human, and less than human, and far from godlike—and thereby to impugn the entire system of monarchy founded by Julius Caesar. Seneca's vision of the shambling stammering Emperor trying vainly to get into heaven prepares for the stern refusal of the Christians to sacrifice to the false god on the imperial throne.

Long afterward, in A.D. 361, when the Christians were already conquering the Empire, another satire on the same theme was composed. In a vision of heaven called *The Drinking-Party*—also inspired by Menippus and also written for the Saturnalia—the last pagan Emperor, Julian the Apostate, described his imperial predecessors as being invited to attend a banquet of the gods in heaven, and one by one gaining acceptance or suffering contumelious rejection. It is amusing in Seneca to watch the efforts of Claudius to win his divine citizenship; it is still more amusing in Julian to see the long procession of Augusti presenting themselves and waiting for the verdict of the Olympians upon their godability. Julian's portraits are sharp, unconventional, often cruel. He knows well that a principal purpose of satire is destructive criticism. Therefore at the end he introduces not only his uncle Constantine, the first Christian Emperor, but his own Galilean enemy, Jesus of Nazareth. He makes Constantine adopt soft Luxury as his own patron divinity, because Julian himself was a severe Stoic who (like Nietzsche in a later age) despised Christianity as a meek mild milksop creed. And he even twists the summons of Jesus, "Come unto me, all ye that labor and are heavy laden, and I will give you rest" (Matthew 11.28), and the rite of baptism, into "Whoever is a seducer, whoever is a murderer, whoever is polluted and loathsome, let him be of good cheer and come. For I shall immediately make him clean by washing him with this water; and if again he falls into the same sins, I shall give him the power to become clean again by beating his breast and banging his head." With its bitterness, its ruthless energy of attack, and its pungent salty wit, Julian's *Drinking-Party* is in the true tradition of Greek and Roman satire.[16]

The most illustrious of Spanish satirists, excluding Cervantes, is Francisco Gómez de Quevedo y Villegas (1580-1645). He has left a group of prose *Visions* which are all of the same type: revelations of the proud shams and disguised vices of this world, laid bare as at the last judgment, scorched with fiery humor and cauterized with acid wit. The style is hard, brisk, often brutal, often too coarse to suit the tender sensibilities of Quevedo's contemporaries. The most peculiar feature of his *Visions* is one which recurs in Rabelais' underworld chapter and in other such fantasies of this kind. It is that, although he is dealing with an essentially Christian theme—the judgment of God between good and evil, the revelation of all that in this world was hidden, and the penalties of the condemned—he does not mention the Christian deity. The divinity who presides over the last judgment is called Jupiter and shown as naked, "clothed in himself."[17] Quevedo does mention angels and fiends, the Ten Commandments, the apostles and the saints, and certain institutions of the church (for instance, the monastic orders); and he makes great play with the Accuser, the devil himself. But, as God is not introduced, so Jesus is not mentioned as the Saviour and Redeemer of mankind.

In the same way as it is difficult for a devout Christian to write a tragedy, so it is almost impossible for a devout Christian to compose a Christian satire dealing with death and the judgment and the next world. Therefore both Quevedo and Rabelais transfer the theme of judgment and punishment back beyond Christianity to the milieu in which it first entered Western thought: the ancient Greek mystical beliefs called Orphism, which are best known to us from the eschatological visions of Plato; and they both paint those visions with the vivid satirical colors of the Cynic Menippus. Quevedo's book of *Visions* begins with an explicit allusion to Dante's *Comedy*, and the largest of them is a sort of parody of Dante's *Hell*; but even there we meet something which only a very unorthodox Christian would have even dreamed of writing. In the place of punishment, Quevedo sees Judas Iscariot. Dante, seeing Judas, did not speak to him and could not.[18] But Quevedo speaks to him. He reproaches him. Judas does not accept the reproach. He replies, "No, no, there have been many since the death of my Master, and there are today, ten thousand times more wicked and ungrateful than I. They buy the Lord of Life, as well as selling him."[19] This is caustic and piercing satire; but it will not fit into Christian thought, and we see why the satirist was forced to hark back to the old pagan philosophical jester for his chief model.

EXTRA-TERRESTRIAL VISITS

There are interesting variants on the satirical voyage to an unknown world. One is the visit of extra-terrestrial beings to this planet. In 1959 the cartoonist Alan Dunn produced a book of deft pictorial satire on this theme. It shows a team of Martians endeavoring to solve the question *Is There Intelligent Life on Earth?* (Soon after landing, they visit the new Guggenheim Museum of Modern Art in New York, which interests and alarms them. Its structure reminds them of the planet Kokeye, and they speculate, "It might even be the Kokeyed Legation, and indicate that they had gotten here before us.") On the same topic Voltaire, perhaps inspired by Gulliver in Lilliput, wrote a charming little satiric tale called *Micromegas* (1752). In this, an enormous inhabitant of a planet attached to Sirius, after being exiled for heresy, visited Saturn, and then dropped off on our world, where he discussed the same question with a Saturnian (modeled on the intelligent Fontenelle). The Saturnian reached a conclusion in the negative: "This globe is so badly constructed, it is so irregular, and so absurdly shaped. Everything is chaotic. Look at these little streams, not one going straight; these pools, neither round nor square nor oval, nor symmetrical in any way; all these little pointed dots [he meant what we call mountains]. And see how flat this sphere is at the poles, and how awkwardly it turns round the sun, so that the polar areas must be deserts. I think there is no life on earth, because I don't believe any intelligent people would ever consent to make their home here."[20] However, Micromegas happened to drop the diamond necklace he was wearing. The Saturnian picked up one of the diamonds and found that it magnified like a lens. With its help the two visitors saw a living organism in the water—which proved to be a whale—and then something a little bigger, a ship full of scientists just back from exploring the Arctic Circle. What amused Micromegas most was to see these miserable microscopic animalculae talking and moving and engaging in corporate enterprises, just as though they were real.

Another variant of the satiric narrative is the voyage into the future. Most such visions are naively optimistic, such as Edward Bellamy's *Looking Backward 2000-1887* (1888), or grimly pessimistic, such as H. G. Wells's *Time Machine* (1895) and *When the Sleeper Wakes* (1899, revised and reissued in 1906 as *The Sleeper Awakes*). These it is difficult to describe as satires, since they usually arouse neither laughter nor contempt nor disgust, but merely wonder or horror. Yet there are some episodes of satire in a few of these fantasies. For instance, the awakened Sleeper finds that newspapers have been replaced by loud-speakers which scream out sensational news like this:

> "Yahaha, Yahah, Yap! Hear a live paper yelp! Live paper. Yaha! Shocking outrage in Paris. Yahahah! The Parisians exasperated by the black police to the pitch of assassination. Dreadful reprisals. Savage times come again. Blood! Blood! Yaha!"

In our generation, the most famous vision of the future (at least in English) is George Orwell's *Nineteen Eighty-Four*. Published in 1949, it sounded grim enough then. Now, only twelve years later, it sounds even grimmer. It is a story of the spiritual birth and death of an Englishman called Winston Smith. (Born in 1945, he was naturally christened after Churchill.) By 1984, the world has been divided into three superstates, Oceania, Eurasia, and Eastasia. Britain has become a province of Oceania called Airstrip One. The three powers are permanently at war, although sometimes, to gain an advantage, one will make a temporary "alliance" or even "peace" with another. Oceania is governed by a single totalitarian party. Partly through the injuries of war, and partly because of the enormous waste of energy and material which the party encourages in order to keep its power, Britain has become an impoverished, grim, and hopeless land, ruled by an

oligarchy more exclusive, more ruthless, and only tech-
nologically more efficient than medieval feudalism. Winston Smith attempts, although he is a member of the "Outer
Party," to assert his intellectual and emotional independence. He is watched, and arrested, and tortured until (like
the victim of Koestler's *Darkness at Noon*) he abandons
all the convictions which had made him a little more hope-
fully human than the others.

In all this the reader can feel little or nothing of the
bitter amusement and free-moving contempt which true
satire should inspire. It is a tragic story. Yet many of the
incidental antitheses and paradoxes are magnificently satirical. For instance, the terrible windowless fort, heavily
guarded and filled with scientific instruments of torture,
where Winston Smith is converted into a self-confessed
traitor and a screaming imbecile, is officially called the
Ministry of Love. The building where (before his arrest)
he works, altering the records of the past—even yesterday's
newspaper—to suit party policy and intrusive facts, is the
Ministry of Truth. After sufficient Minilove persuasion
has been applied to him, he admits that

Two and Two Make Five.

(Galileo, after being brainwashed by the Holy Inquisition,
is said to have retracted his suggestion that the earth goes
round the sun; but, as he rose from his knees, to have
murmured "E pur si muove." "Yet it does move," he said;
but Winston Smith dare not even think so; cannot even
think so.) The personification of totalitarian personal
power, whose face stares out from every wall, and whose
subordinate eyes watch everyone in public and in private
through telescreens, is called Big Brother. The intellectuals
of 1984 are developing a fresh language, designed to
diminish the range of human thought. It is called New-
speak. The logic of the single totalitarian party, by which

a fact can simultaneously be true and be untrue, is Double-think.

For everyone, except perhaps the student of satire, it is daunting to think that even Orwell's terrible vision of the future is obsolete. He wrote of Airstrips and Floating Fort-resses and the occasional rocket bomb. Since his time air-strips have become—because of technological advances—almost outmoded; and most of the surface of the globe may be rendered uninhabitable, if scientific progress continues at its present rate.

This prospect too has been described in a satirical vision of the future. Aldous Huxley's *Ape and Essence* (1948) takes us forward five generations, to the year 2108. An expedition from New Zealand, which was not radio-acti-vated, is visiting the North American continent, which was. The descendants of the survivors, they find, have re-verted to savagery—or rather to a savage parody of what were once civilized mores. Two of the most powerful human instincts, religious awe and the sexual urge, have of course survived, and (like the human beings who carry them) produced new and hideous mutations. Degraded as their manifestations are, however, they are scarcely worse than the social life of several nations which have existed in the not-so-distant past: so that *Ape and Essence* is an effective satire, not so much on the future of war-befuddled humanity, as upon what Mr. Huxley considers an unholy duality, religion and sex. It is always difficult for a visionary satirist to know how to present his vision. Cervantes, un-happily, bungled it by saying that Don Quixote lived several centuries earlier, and that he was translating his biography from an ancient Arabic manuscript. Mr. Huxley does not make his satire more convincing by couching it in the form of a motion-picture script. The format, the very atmosphere of such a thing inhibit the sensitive reader from believing, even for a moment, what he reads. Even a satirical fantasy should be, while it is being read, convincing.

Peace has its horrors, no less debased than war. One modern voyage into a peaceful future world is a satire so brilliant and so bitter that it is almost the *Gulliver* of our time. In Aldous Huxley's *Brave New World* (1932), a young man who combines some of the strengths of our past and our present (being spiritually part Amerindian and part Shakespearean) is transported from a time capsule (in the form of a savage reservation) into the "progressive" future which has all the advantages toward which we are striving: stability, peace, machines to do all the hard work and conditioned human and subhuman beings to do most of the easy work, an emancipated sex life, perfect birth-control, handy but harmless drugs, frequent orgies of togetherness, wise control from above, and nothing disquieting such as education or creation or experiment in literature, art, philosophy, or pure science. It sounds almost perfect, although at present six hundred years ahead, in the Year of Our Ford 632. Many an idealistic "social engineer" of the type of Bernard Shaw and Sidney Webb, after imbibing his glass of warm milk and ingesting his energy tablets, used to go to bed and dream about it; and the beauty of Huxley's satire is to show that, for a human being, it would be absolutely unendurable.

Vladimir Mayakovsky, an idealist who began by hymning the Russian revolution, ended by satirizing it (and incidentally the Russian character) in a pungent extravaganza called *The Bedbug* (1929). A rough tough workman is by an accident preserved in ice (like Wells's cataleptic Sleeper) until 1979. Revived then, he finds himself a stranger, a fossil, a coelacanth. All voting is done by gigantic machines, and all discussion carried on by huge loudspeakers. Artificial trees bear real fruit, changed daily. Everything is hygienic and orderly. The survivor from the

old world carries microbes with him, and infects the new
world with ancient maladies long forgotten: the men with
a liking for beer, the girls with a fancy for dancing and
lovemaking. But at the end, he is safely caged, alone with
his sympathetic fellow-survivor, an old Russian bedbug
from the warm untidy disorganized past.

FANTASTIC VOYAGES

Of course not all fantastic books of travel can be called
satires. Many dreamers have journeyed far and high in
their dreams—across the earth into unknown regions,
twenty thousand leagues under the sea, out into the in-
conceivable distances of inter-galactic space. Pascal was in
a minority when he said "The eternal silence of these
infinite spaces terrifies me." Some dreamers simply want to
display human courage and explore human imagination,
and to have marvelous adventures without any critical
reference to the world which, in real life, they inhabit.
Such adventures are not satirical. When Sindbad the Sailor
told of his explorations and his shipwrecks, he enjoyed
recalling them and his guests enjoyed hearing them, for
the sake of mere wonder. The adventures of Baron Munchausen seem to us to be rhapsodies, conjuring tricks, pure
fantasies, flights into the manifestly incredible, like the
"tall stories" told by the first explorers of the American
West. Their chief author, Rudolph Raspe, was a liar and
a crook; but the soldier of fortune whose name he attached
to his imaginings was a real man, Hieronymus Karl
Friederich, Freiherr von Munchausen, who had long enjoyed the harmless pastime of telling whoppers with a
straight face.[21] Conceivably, therefore, the Singular Adventures of the Baron were meant both to satirize that
perennial type, the Boastful Soldier, and to ridicule the
inexhaustible credulity of mankind. In the Advertisement
to the second edition, Raspe added a "certificate, sworn

at the Mansion House" of London, with affidavits by Gulliver, Sin[d]bad, and Aladdin, to witness of his truth. It is a fair division. Two-thirds of Munchausen's adventures are mere fantasy; the other third, perhaps, are satirical. But we, reading them nowadays, think of them purely as dreams. The same applies to Lewis Carroll's books about Alice. From a child's point of view they are often satires, criticizing the absurd conventions by which grown-up people run their world; there are some touches of adult satire in them too, ridiculing law and authority and mechanical system and eccentric power-holders (such as the King and the Duchess). Most of us read them, however, in the same spirit as we listen to cheerful young music, such as Debussy's *Children's Corner.*

And what of the most influential of all travel fantasies, Lucian's *True History?* It has long been the most popular of all Lucian's works, and has spawned a lively brood of impossible voyages—for instance, Rabelais' personal trip down Pantagruel's throat, visiting Gulletville and the cities of Larynx and Pharynx.[22] Like *Munchausen*, it is a string of arrant impossibilities, which its author scarcely even tries to make credible. Nearly all the *True History* is pure fun. It leaves scarcely any aftertaste of bitterness; it makes us feel no contempt; it is a Disney dream. If so, is there anything in it that can be called satiric? The title itself implies some criticism. This book, obviously a pack of lies, is "true"; all other tales of travel and exploration are therefore false. And there is in it an amusing touch of satire aimed at another target: the reading public. Lucian is kidding his readers, by writing rubbish and then bamboozling them into reading it. This particular trick is a favorite of Rabelais: he will go on and on, listing hundreds of games or hundreds of absurd book-titles, column after column, just to see how long the suckers will go on reading them.[23] If this is satire, it is a unique kind of satire: for the reader is himself its victim.

3. ANIMAL TALES

Satiric voyages and visions produce their effect by contrasting this world of ours with another, distant in time or space and different in quality. The other main type of satiric narrative and drama depends on showing a ludicrous or debased picture of this world.

One way to do this is to depict men and women as animals, or rather as non-human animals. Beast stories in themselves are not necessarily satiric. Some tales about animals, although they show animals talking and exchanging ideas and doing other human things, are not about people but about animals: they are attempts to explain the behavior of beasts, using human standards of judgment. (Unhappy attempt. One of the main efforts of modern zoologists is to explain why animals do not behave like people, but like machines with built-in biochemical controls.) Other animal stories are only externally about animals. Their characters are human beings disguised in animal skins. In them, animals do things which are just a little like normal animal behavior, but are really lessons for human beings. They are proverbs made visible and memorable in what was (as we can see from the cave-paintings) for many millennia the most vivid and familiar form known to mankind. Such tales are not often funny, seldom critical, usually gently smiling and wisely warning. Although, like the proverb which they embody, they may become part of a satire, they are not usually satiric themselves. "Go to the ant, thou sluggard," says the Book of Proverbs in its minatory tone, "consider her ways, and be wise." Robert Benchley once did this. He said he watched an ant all through a long summer afternoon, considering her ways; and all that he learned was that, if he carried too large a crumb on his head, he would walk sideways.

However, a few of the huge collection of animal fables are sharp enough and sour enough to be defined as satires; and from the Middle Ages we have one of the great satires of the world, in the form of a biography of one of the cleverest of all animals, Reynard the Fox.²⁴ This is very nearly a satiric epic. If the eighteenth-century critics had not been so short-sightedly devoted to the Greek and Roman classics, they should have cited this, in discussions of the connection between epic and satire, epic and comedy, rather than the virtually non-existent *Margites*. It mirrors the world of the Middle Ages, taut, narrow, pyramidal, authoritarian, and unintelligent. On top sits His Majesty King Noble the Lion. Next come his barons, Bruin the Bear, Isengrim the Wolf, Tybert the Cat; and then one of his most energetic and productive subjects, Chanticleer the Cock. Over against them all stands Reynard the Fox. They are society; he is anti-social. They are rich and powerful; he is clever. They are orthodox and gullible and polite; he is unorthodox and inventive and rude. In any society (except during short revolutionary periods) it has always been difficult for a poor or isolated man to find what Napoleon called "a career open to the talents." In the Middle Ages it was exceptionally difficult, unless through the church, which entailed many sacrifices, or through the profession of war, which entailed other abnegations and greater risks. Reynard the Fox thinks the entire system is absurd, and so he lives the life of an active satirist, exposing it and showing its folly. Once, after twenty glasses of wine, he sings out what he really believes:

> Ever since I was born,
> I've felt bitter scorn
> For worthy respectable people;

Reynard the Fox honored by King Lion

So with merry heart sing
Here's a fig for the King;
Nought care I for law, crown, or steeple.

'Tis my honest belief
An industrious thief
Is a blessing to all good society;
To the humdrumming round,
Wherein most men are bound,
He furnishes pleasant variety.[25]

Plato made Socrates say that the greatest tragic poet should also be the greatest comic poet. Certainly if you want to understand any age, you ought to read not only its heroic and philosophical books but its comic and satirical books; and so, after reading such a noble chivalrous medieval work as Malory's *Morte Darthur*, I try always to spend an hour or two with its satiric counterpart *Reynard the Fox*.

Not a clever fox, but a stupid donkey, is the hero of another animal tale which was popular enough in its time: *The Fools' Mirror*, in Latin verse, written shortly before A.D. 1180 by Nigel, a monk of Canterbury. Chaucer knew it as the book of "Daun Burnel the Asse."[26] It is an expansion of a simple little animal fable into a long, rambling, ill-proportioned story with more talk than action and more serious homilies than satiric adventures. In some four thousand lines of Ovidian elegiac couplets (useful for epigrammatic wit but inappropriate for serious or satiric narrative poetry) it tells how the donkey Burnellus or Brownie tried to get a tail long enough to match his ears, but instead lost half his tail and both his ears and was recaptured by the master from whom he had escaped. This (Nigel tells us in his preface) symbolizes the overthrow of ill-judged ambition among churchmen. Crude as this is, it would have been more effective if Nigel had kept it short and clear. But he confused it. He made the donkey behave sometimes like an animal, thinking about his ears and tail, and sometimes like a man, enrolling in the university of Paris and aspiring to become a bishop or a cardinal. Burnellus is so asinine that, after seven years in Paris, he can only say Hee-haw, and cannot remember the name of the city because a traveling companion confused him by saying a PAternoster; but he utters long and superficially intelligent monologues, criticizing wicked greedy monarchs and lewd hireling bishops, comparing the merits of the various religious orders and inventing a new one of his own. Nigel wrecks the continuity of the story, already distorted to admit these improbable homilies, by squeezing in other animal fables and allegorical tales; and he finishes with a dispute between the donkey's owner and a rich man of Cremona, neither of whom has entered the story before. It would, perhaps, be too flattering to suggest that Nigel wished to make his story resemble its hero, and end with an amputated tail; but perhaps he did divine the original meaning of satire, a hotch-potch, and tried to write a story full of the heterogeneous and the unpredictable.

The Fools' Mirror is only one of a group of medieval Latin poems about animals which are mainly satiric in intention. The earliest is *The Prisoner's Exit* (*Ecbasis Captivi*, a rather affected title half Greek and half Latin), written by a monk of Lorraine about A.D. 940. It tells how a calf escaped from its stall and was almost eaten by the wolf: the moral for young monks is "Fret not at your cloister's narrow room." Its author was a good Latinist, widely read. He must have known Horace pretty well by heart, for he took over one-fifth of his lines from Horace. (See how satirical material is handed on. The fable of the sick lion who could not persuade the fox to visit him inside his cave, told by Aesop, retold by Lucilius, and summarized by Horace, is here expanded and told once more, this time by the wolf.) One of the best and most popular of all is *Ysengrim*, a satire against monasticism in seven books of elegiac couplets telling how the wolf (i.e. the monk) was deceived by the fox. Its author, Nivard of Ghent, who wrote about A.D. 1150, was a competent and sophisticated satirist.[27]

Surely the strangest of all the satirical books about animals is the *Metamorphoses* of the North African sophist Apuleius, written, in eleven books of astoundingly complex and versatile Latin prose, about A.D. 180.[28] The hero, who begins as a naïvely intelligent and romantically sensual young Greek and ends as Apuleius himself, visits Thessaly, traditionally a great center of magical practices, as adventurous modern investigators visit Haiti to study voodoo. He tries to change himself into a bird, but uses the wrong formula and becomes a donkey. His mistress and accomplice knows the cure: if he eats fresh roses, he will become a man again. Before she can bring him the roses, he is stolen by robbers, who load him with plunder and drive him to their cave. Thenceforward, fully human in mind and emotions, but in voice and appearance an ugly ass, he passes through increasingly dangerous and degrading adventures, painful even for an animal, almost unendurable for a man—until, the night before being compelled to make a public exhibition of his sexual prowess with a woman criminal who, after this degradation, is to join him in death, he escapes from prison, runs to the sea-shore, plunges into the purifying waves, and sees a vision of the goddess, the mother of all nature. She alone pities him. In a speech filled with intense beauty and transcendental nobility, she expounds her love and her power, welcomes him as a devotee, and tells him that next morning, instead of being humiliated and slain, he will find fresh roses in the hand of one of her priests. So he becomes human again: but not the silly youth he was. He becomes a tranquil, humble, self-denying, self-forgetting, serious, happy man.

This extraordinary story is, first and foremost, a tale of growth and education through suffering—what the Germans call, in an untranslatable word, a *Bildungsroman.* Lucius moves from sensuality through bestiality to purity; from silliness through asininity to wisdom; from irresponsible vagabondage through slavery and floggings to the life of a pious pilgrim; from black magic through crimes and orgies to a higher religion. (Apuleius himself was seriously accused during his lifetime of practicing magic, and generations later was still believed by some of his fellow-Africans to have been a wizard.)[29] Since it describes this process through a narrative which is grotesque and impossible, often grossly comical and often disgusting, it is a satire. Some, though by no means all, of the adventures experienced by the hero or told in his hearing, are satiric in purpose and in tone. The chief difficulties in appraising the book are, first, its superlatively elegant style (we do not expect a violent and ridiculous story to be told in prose more recherché than that of Marcel Proust, and yet Apuleius is not parodying any particular school of writing), and, second, the genuine charm and sweetness of its conclusion, and of a few famous episodes, notably the tale of Cupid and Psyche. The explanation of the first is that plain prose, blunt and factual, would be both gross and unconvincing. Apuleius is following the most eminent of all conjurors, Ovid, who makes incredible transformations credible by describing them with eloquent imaginative detail and suave grace. His prose is as scented and as sinuous as a magical spell. Secondly, the loveliness of the Cupid and Psyche story and other scenes is intended to enhance the cruel satiric contrast of ideal and real, soul and body, virtue and vice, nobility and crime, aspiration and debasement, which is the basic theme of the book. That is why, a tale of ideally happy marriage attained through hideous ordeals, it is told to a terrified maiden by a drunken hag in a bandits' cave.

There have been many satires which, like *Reynard*, pretended to be about animals, while they were really about people. The Houyhnhnms of the final book of *Gulliver* are certainly not horses. Horses are delightful creatures, and from the pictorial point of view highly decorative, but their power of reasoning is even smaller than that of human beings, and their emotions are wildly disorderly. One of the sad things about the development of humanity is the fact which Dean Swift was trying to avoid: that the ape, although it looks hideously like us, is the most intelligent of the lower mammals.[30] Once there was a world like that described in Gulliver's fourth Voyage. It was the Old Stone Age, the Palaeolithic. The Yahoos were the Old Stone Men. They had not thought of capturing and taming the horse (they had only just invented the dog), but they did hunt the horse. They drove the poor Houyhnhnms over cliffs in enormous stampedes, because they were cleverer and crueller, and then they ate the bodies. Outside the cave of Solutré in Burgundy a Stone Age deposit of tens of thousands of horse-skeletons was found: the bones had been split to extract the marrow. We may—as Dean Swift caricatured us and as scientists have assured us—be nearly apes; but we are intelligent, and it is a grievous satiric distortion to show us as inferior to other animals in that one talent. It is other qualities that we lack. But in fact neither the equine Houyhnhnms nor the simian Yahoos are animals. Both are types of human beings: the reasoning minority and the ignorant multitude; or else two aspects of the human soul itself, with its cool tranquil idealism and its low bestial impulses. *Houyhnhnm* itself sounds like an esoteric human language, the parlance of philosophers; while every human being can say *Yahoo*, and some modern poets and statesmen are even shouting it to the accompaniment of drums.

Penguin Island, published by Anatole France in 1908, is an occasionally witty but usually sour and labored attempt to satirize the history of France from an extreme left-wing point of view. The French are caricatured as a special race of penguins, discovered by an early Christian missionary on an Arctic island, baptized into the Church through a regrettable error, converted by a special act of divine grace into human beings, and by another miracle transported, island and all, to the neighborhood of Brittany. Most of us are unconvinced by this parallel between the sober, uniformly dressed, and austere penguins and the tasteful, elegant, epicurean French—especially when we recall that most penguins are monogamous, and that in their society sexual deviations are virtually unknown. However, Anatole France chose penguins because he shared the conviction of many French intellectuals that their fellow-citizens are (although of course superior to other Europeans) fundamentally *bêtes.* In any case, he virtually dropped the idea one-quarter through his satire, apart from a few comic names like Greatauk and Porpoisia.[31] Then he transformed the book into a distorted burlesque of French history, passing over the Renaissance and the age of Louis XIV in a few rapid pages, but devoting an entire book to a satirical version of the Dreyfus case, and ending with a hideous picture of the future world. His picture is a black variant of the apocalypse of Karl Marx: a monstrous megalopolis inhabited by hordes of debased workers, dominated by a few decadent multimillionaires,[32] but—instead of being taken over by the victorious proletariat under the guidance of the Communist party— eventually destroyed by anarchists using an explosive based on radio-activity. The implication of the latter half of *Penguin Island* is that the history of France—indeed, of all the West—began in superstition and barbarism and will culminate in greed and butchery; and that the destruction of Western civilization by atomic bombs is the only possible solution to the problem of human obduracy, selfishness, and stupidity.[33] This satire is, like *Gulliver's Travels*, wholly negative, utterly pessimistic: it belongs to the powerful tradition of the Cynics. As a work of art, however, it is far inferior to *Gulliver*, because the biases and rancors of its author distorted its structure, making it not one single book but three incompatible fantasies.

Less than two generations later, George Orwell, who had watched, first with enthusiasm, then with disappointment, and finally with horror, the building of a new socialist society, wrote a satire upon it. *Animal Farm* (1945) is a bitter attack, worthy of Swift, on the Communist revolution in Russia and on its betrayal by Stalin and the Communist bureaucracy. Although it is ostensibly a story about animals, we know that it is about types of people. When we see pigs training dogs to guard them instead of biting them, when we hear the talking raven telling the farmyard congregation about Sugarcandy Mountain in the sky, and still more at the end, when we observe the pigs drinking beer and playing cards with the human farmers of the neighborhood, we know that we are seeing an animated cartoon in which the spiritual distortion of human beings is imaged by their physical disguise as lower animals. This too is a wholly negative satire. There is no hope, it says, for the poor beasts. The sheep will always bleat and run in crowds, the hens will always cackle and lay eggs and have them stolen, the cattle will always do what they are told, and the horses will work until they drop. Pigs and dogs will dominate. Although *Animal Farm* was immediately inspired by the rise of Communist state monopoly and "the cult of individualism associated with J. V. Stalin" (as the Communist propagandists now describe a genera-

*"All animals
are equal,
but some are more equal than others."*

From *The Animal Farm*, by George
Orwell. Harcourt, Brace & World, Inc.,
1946. Illustrations by Joy Batchelor
and John Halas

tion of odious tyranny), it is broad enough and cruelly
realistic enough to apply to any revolution which has ever
been betrayed.

It is more difficult to put human beings disguised as
animals onto the stage than to describe them in a narrative: therefore satiric dramas in which animals behave like
human beings, and vice versa, are rather uncommon. The
graceful and melodious non-human characters in Aristophanes' *Birds* are not satirically drawn. They are idealized
creatures, who live afar from the sphere of our sorrow, in
Cloudcuckooland. The satirical impact of the comedy falls
on the poor human beings and inefficient divinities who
have so far mismanaged their world as to make it necessary
for the birds, eldest of warm-blooded terrene species, to
found a new world-order, and create the universal happiness which neither men or gods have been able to achieve.
This satiric play therefore belongs to another category:
the visit of human beings to a visionary world, better than
their own.

However, in another of Aristophanes' wonderful satiric comedies (which has evoked delightfully apt music from the imagination of Vaughan Williams), we find a group of wasps who talk human language. They are the poor elderly unemployed tax-supported citizens of Athens who fill the law-courts, serve on all the juries, and sink their stings deeply into those public enemies, the rich. Not bees, who live to gather honey and help their community, but wasps, who are purely selfish and sting without remorse, they harbor a special poison that prevents them and their victims from living a wholesome happy life.

Karel Čapek, the Czech genius who wrote that famous vision of the mechanized future, *R.U.R.*, created in collaboration with his brother Josef a satirical *Insect Comedy* (1920), with only one principal human character, a drunken tramp. In a forest glade he watches, first the courtship dances and intrigues of the butterflies who image the life of rich, frivolous, hypersensitive men and women; then the struggles and squabbles of the dung-collecting beetles and the home-loving crickets and the murderous ichneumon flies who resemble the ruthless acquisitive bourgeois; and at last those perfectly social insects, the ants, working like machines and fighting like mass armies of human beings. In their notes on the play, the brothers Čapek call it a "travesty" and refer to *The Battle of Frogs and Mice*. It is indeed a satire, but far more bitter and pessimistic than the little Homeric parody. One of the most touchingly absurd figures in it is a Chrysalis, who throughout two acts proclaims the future, when it will at last become fully alive and reveal the secret of life to the world. Immediately after its metamorphosis, still exultant and pulsating, it drops down, a little dead moth.

An important component of all drama, as Aristotle said, is the probable impossible.[34] As the quotient of probability falls, the satirist's work becomes more difficult. Therefore when Eugene Ionesco produced *The Rhinoceros,* whose theme was that the human population of an entire town— with one solitary exception—was transformed into roaring, rampaging, thick-skinned, happily brutal rhinoceroses, he was challenging one of the central problems of dramatic satire. In spite of a weak and farcical first act and a disappointing conclusion, he solved it in one big scene. To see the quiet undemonstrative hero on the stage, confronting one of his friends who visibly swells out and alters his shape and changes his nature until he is one of the herd whose bellows and tramplings can be heard off-stage, himself every moment less human than pachydermatous, this is to appreciate not only the experience of satire, but the amused and tormented emotions of the satirist. Ionesco himself has variously described his play as being a critique of Nazification (which he conceives as a perversion of intellectualism), of totalitarian government, and of collective hysteria. It is all that, and more. As he puts it, "Once ideologies become idolatries, . . they dehumanize men."[35]

The Rhinoceros showed men becoming animals. One of the bitterest satirical plays ever written shows men who retain their human shape, but in spirit are so close to being beasts that they bear the names and follow the behavior-patterns of cruel and treacherous animals. The hero of Ben Jonson's *Volpone* (1607) is well named Fox. His parasitic attendant is Mosca, a fly; while his legacy-hunting false friends are greedy raptors:

> Vulture, kite,
> Raven and gorcrow, all [the] birds of prey
> That think [him] turning carcase.

In a satiric story, not all the human beings need be disguised as animals. A deft satirist can produce the right effect by introducing only one animal, and showing it as equal, or in some ways superior, to its human associates. Thus, in Peacock's *Melincourt*, there is an admirable ape which has been brought from Angola to England, taught the usages of polite society, and christened Sir Oran Haut-ton. (Peacock evidently did not distinguish between the East Indian orang-outang and the African chimpanzee.) Its patron has bought it a baronetcy, and intends to have it sent by a pocket borough into Parliament. Sir Oran cannot speak, but after all many of the English gentry pride themselves on their impenetrable reticence, and say very little except "Ha—hm." Otherwise he is eminently acceptable. True, he is rather hairy, but whiskers were fashionable then. He has a tendency to leave the room by jumping through the window, but the English admire both athletes and eccentrics. Sir Oran Haut-ton drinks as heartily as any landed gentleman, and has the unexpected social talent of playing the flute.

In a trenchant modern satire, *His Monkey Wife, or, Married to a Chimp* (1930), John Collier introduces the female of the simian family. She is called—like the heroine of the first great love-story in the English language— Emily. Dutiful, taciturn, devoted as Griselda, she loves her dear master Mr. Fatigay, and endures many humiliations so as to be near him. She cannot talk, but she can type. *My gracious silence*, he sometimes calls her, laughingly. When he is deceived and mistreated by a cheap selfish human girl, she weeps for him. When she herself becomes a star dancer (her dark Spanish beauty setting men's hearts on fire), she uses all her wealth to redeem him from the degradation into which his amorous disappointment has thrown him. At last, in a melodramatic (and monstrously improbable but satirically acceptable) substitution at the very altar, she marries him. An ape she may be; but she is far better than the ordinary woman, whose skin may be smooth and white, but whose soul is cankered, whose muscles, like her heart, are stunted, and who has the congenital defects of frivolity, infidelity, and garrulity. Written with bitter elegance, this novel is a satire not only on modern womanhood, but on the modern ideal of romantic love: its very title contains a cynical allusion to the cheapest amorous fiction, and its chapters are punctuated by quotations from Tennyson's *Locksley Hall*.[36]

4. DISTORTED VISIONS OF THIS WORLD

A satirical picture of our world, which shows only human beings as its inhabitants, must pretend to be a photograph, and in fact be a caricature. It must display their more ridiculous and repellent qualities in full flower, minimize their ability for healthy normal living, mock their virtues and exaggerate their vices, disparage their greatest human gifts, the gift for co-operation and the gift for inventive adaptation, treat their religions as hypocrisy, their art as trash, their literature as opium, their love as lust, their virtue as hypocrisy, and their happiness as an absurd illusion. And it must do all this while protesting that it is a truthful, unbiased, as nearly as possible dispassionate witness. This is difficult. It is most successfully achieved by authors who are, or pretend to be, themselves part of the ludicrous and despicable pattern of human life; or by authors who, while standing outside their stories, still relate them either with wide-eyed and apparently honest naïveté or with what looks like mild indulgent humor. Satiric novels which are predominantly harsh and bitter, like Céline's *Journey to the End of the Night*, are difficult to write; and often their authors spoil them by veering away from the true purpose of satire into true realism or somber tragedy. A tone of indulgent comedy is best; and the satirist's flag bears the device half-true and half-false, *ridentem dicere uerum,* "to tell the truth with a laugh."[37]

Because he neglected this principle, Gustave Flaubert failed in his grand design of writing an effective satirical novel about stupidity. *Bouvard and Pécuchet* (left unfinished at his death in 1880) told the story of two middle-aged men, office hacks like Charles Lamb, who retired to the country on a lucky legacy and started to study all the intellectual disciplines for which they had never previously had leisure. Without experience, they try farming; they attempt to learn chemistry, geology, medicine, etc., from books; and they fail in everything because of the contrariness of human beings and the idiotic inconsistencies of authors. In an improbable scene which may be an unfunny parody of Goethe's *Faust I,* they decide to commit suicide, but are dissuaded by seeing the celebration of the Christmas midnight mass in a little country church. "They feel something like dawn rising in their souls"; but in the very next chapter they become sharp and deeply-read critics of Christianity, citing Tertullian and Origen like trained scholars. And so they go on, through phrenology, to education, to politics. Like Sir Hudibras,

> Their notions fitted things so well,
> That which was which they could not tell;
> But oftentimes mistook the one
> For th' other, as great clerks have done.[38]

At the end of the book Flaubert planned to make them withdraw from the world and take up their old trade of copying. Copying what? A dictionary of human stupidities. Flaubert had already compiled its basis, a *Dictionary of Accepted Ideas*—which reminds us of Swift's *Complete Collection of Genteel and Ingenious Conversation.* But there is an important difference. Both Swift and Flaubert were convinced that the mass of men were "as well qualified for flying as [for] thinking";[39] both were moved to nausea by the spectacle of human folly; but Swift retained, even in his grimmest moods, a sense of humor, while Flaubert bored both himself by his search through third-class books for examples of third-class thinking, and his readers by the banality of his examples. There is something comic in even the silliest exchanges in Swift's *Conversation*.

> *Miss.* Well, comparisons are odious; but she's as like her husband as if she were spit out of his mouth; as like as one egg is to another. Pray, how was she dressed?
> *Lady Smart.* Why, she was as fine as fi'pence; but truly I thought there was more cost than worship.
> *Lady Answerall.* I don't know her husband. Pray, what is he?
> *Lady Smart.* Why, he's a concealer of the law; you must know, he came to us as drunk as David's sow.[40]

But most of Flaubert's *Dictionary* is merely flat.

> CROCODILE. Attracts people by imitating the cry of a child.
> DIAMOND. One of these days they'll make synthetic ones! And just think, it's only carbon!
> GULF-STREAM. Celebrated town in Norway, recently discovered.
> YAWNING. Always say, "Excuse me, it isn't boredom, it's my stomach."
> WALTZ. Denounce it.

Page after page of the novel is an arid waste of sentences such as this: "The *Catechism of Perseverance*, by Gaume, had disgusted Bouvard so intensely that he took up the volume of Louis Hervieu." The total effect resembles those collections of cigarette-stubs, torn bus-tickets, hair-combings, fragments of dirty newspaper, and broken bottles, which the Dadaists used to frame and exhibit as *collages*; and sometimes the patient reader, as he watches the novelist laboriously sieving out a huge intellectual rubbish-dump, wonders whether Flaubert himself in this project was not unconsciously providing a prime example of human stupidity. The satirist should enjoy his subject, however gruesome it may be; however stupid, it should give him a snarling laugh.

One of the leading contemporary satirists in English began his career when he was still young enough to laugh at folly and to cock a snook at sin. This was Evelyn Waugh, whose first book, published in 1928 when he was only twenty-five, bore the mock-portentous title *Decline and Fall*, with the subtitle "An Illustrated Novelette." ("Novelette" in England is a non-U word, meaning "cheap romance." The illustrations, some of them very amusing, were by Waugh himself.) The book is a novel of modern life, with a plot almost as outrageous as that of *Candide*. Its hero, Paul Pennyfeather, is a quiet little undergraduate at Oxford who intends to become a clergyman. A group of drunken noblemen, reeling out of a party, meet him in the quadrangle, and, because he is apparently wearing the tie of a club to which he does not belong, "de-bag" him, or take his trousers off. He is then expelled "for indecent behavior," with his career ruined. He gets a job as a schoolmaster in an inferior private school in Wales, with an aristocratic English clientele and a staff composed of eccentrics and criminals. At the school sports, a chic and beautiful lady called Mrs. Margot Beste-Chetwynde (doubtless pronounced Beast-Cheating) comes down to see her son. She falls in love with Paul, finds a place for him in her business, the Latin-American Entertainment Company Ltd., and is about to marry him, when he is arrested: the Latin-American Entertainment Company Ltd. has been exposed as an organization which ships girls to Latin America for one specific and generally disapproved type of entertaining. Paul spends some time in prison, is smuggled

"The social balance was delicately poised."

From *Decline and Fall*, by Evelyn Waugh. Little, Brown, 1949.
Evelyn Waugh's own drawing of the Llanabba school sports.

out under a fake death certificate, and returns to Oxford to continue studying for the church.

The main point of this is the double-edged satire that the good are dull and stupid, and that the beautiful and rich are corrupt and ruthless: the world is not governed by moral principles, or even by orderly reason, but by chance and the power of the absurd. But along its blades there are many diamond-sharp facets: jokes against movements and personalities, some of which are still alive and prominent, while others have receded, since 1928, into history. There is, for instance, a progressive German architect who hates people and loves machines: his name is Otto Friedrich Silenus, and he will remind some people of Walter Gropius. There is an intensely cultivated Negro named Sebastian Cholmondeley ("Chokey" for short) who has a fine singing voice and declares "My race is a very spiritual one": Mr. Waugh may have been thinking of Paul Robeson. Almost every detail in the book could no doubt be paralleled from some real person or incident; but when put together they form a pattern which is a delightful and painful distortion of life. It is an entirely successful satire.

In 1931, after some years of preparation, Wyndham Lewis published an outstandingly savage satirical novel about British aesthetes and millionaire Bohemians. It was called *The Apes of God,* and contained ferocious caricatures of the leading lights of Bloomsbury and of a group closely resembling the Sitwell family. In the same year, Roy Campbell (who appeared in *The Apes of God* as "Zulu Blades") turned the same subject into a poetic satire, *The Georgiad.* Kindred areas of intellectual and social snobbery were explored in a series of brilliant tales by Aldous Huxley. This type of satire was probably initiated in English by Thomas Love Peacock. Although there are occasional patches of luminescence in Peacock's novels, their plot structure and their narrative style now seem painfully artificial; and we read them chiefly for their amusing portrayals of the mannerisms and conversation of Coleridge, Shelley, Southey, and others: for this kind of satire specializes in personal caricature.

However, to enjoy the satire, it is not necessary to recognize the characters. When I first, in my teens, read Huxley's novels, it never occurred to me that the fantastic figures in them might portray living people. (Being bred in Scotland, I thought they were merely imaginary eccentrics from southern England.) Now I understand that the majority of them were easily identifiable. The absurd Burlap in *Point Counter Point* (1928), to me incredible, was in fact the critic Middleton Murry, drawn so harshly that his enemies rejoiced and he himself was deeply wounded. (Like Byron on reading Southey's gibe at his hot temper, he thought of challenging Huxley to a duel. We must regret that he abandoned the idea, for it would have produced one of the funniest scenes in all literary history.) Recently the American satirist Mary McCarthy wrote a novel called *The Groves of Academe*. Her subject was a girls' college headed by a "liberal" president, and she played with it as affectionately as a cat with a newly caught mouse. Not long afterwards the poet Randall Jarrell produced a novel called *Pictures from an Institution*. This also portrayed a girls' college with an eccentric staff and a boyish president, but one of its chief comic characters was a woman novelist with a feline smile and a cool uncharitable eye: a figure apparently strong, but harboring humiliating weaknesses of its own.

Most dramatic satires are of this type: caricatures of contemporary life. Yet the frontier between comedy and satire on the stage is a thin and wavering line. It is easy enough to recognize a true satire like *Patience*, but many plays are blends of satire and comedy, or even satire and tragedy. Sometimes, as in Shakespeare, the plot and most of the characters are gay, harmless, close to reality on the humorous side; one man—Parolles in *All's Well* and Malvolio in *Twelfth Night*—is drawn in harsher lines, befooled, and exposed to bitter scorn. So in Shaw's *Doctor's Dilemma* the main characters and the plot are lively and credible, but the consulting doctors are gross travesties. In Molière's *Tartuffe* the villain is bigger than life-size, viler than any normal reality; and yet, because such hypocrites are often more intense and convincing than ordinary men, he is real enough. Still, we do not laugh at the end of *Tartuffe*, as we do when a comedy closes. We shudder; we want to spit. It is a satire both on the hypocrite and upon the fools who believe him.

To produce the full effect of satire on the stage, exaggeration is usually needed. Is it possible to imagine the First Lord of the Admiralty explaining to the crew of one of Her Majesty's ships that he reached his position by sticking to his desk and never going to sea? or to conceive a naval captain placed under arrest for saying "Damme" to one of his men? No; but Disraeli gave the Admiralty post to a publisher who knew more of politics than of seafaring, and the reforms of British naval custom had mollified much of the old harsh discipline. The satire in these cases, as in others, consists in a *reductio ad absurdum*: "if that," the satirist says with a ruthless smile, "why not this?"

Serious-minded students of the classics often complain that Aristophanes' picture of Socrates in *The Clouds* is not lifelike. True, the actor wore a mask bearing the well-known features—so comical that they scarcely needed exaggeration. But Socrates appeared in a space-vehicle, in which he said he could "move through air and contemplate the sun"; and one of his pupils described an ingenious experiment in which Socrates measured the length of a flea's jump. Critics of Aristophanes say that the real Socrates paid little attention to astronomy and biology but concentrated on ethical teaching. How true! They might add that he did not live in an isolated Phrontisterion, or Thinkstitute: he walked about the streets conversing with anyone and everyone. But Aristophanes is writing satire. Satire, which pretends to be true, is usually a distortion. Long after the gay dramatic satires of Aristophanes had left the stage, they were succeeded by the melancholy romantic comedies of Menander. An admiring critic exclaimed, "Menander! Life! Which of you copied the other?" This is not what anyone—except perhaps a modern philologist—would cry after seeing a play by Aristophanes. Satire is often funny, but a comedy is not a satire.

TALES OF TRAVEL AND ADVENTURE

Another group of satires on contemporary life contains those stories which involve travel and adventure. The extravagant pictures of society such as Peacock's novels, although they contain alarums and excursions, are essentially static. These satires move, and their heroes see a great deal of the world. Sometimes the hero is a passive observer, enduring and, in silence, criticizing; sometimes he is a sort of knight-errant, who irrupts into various groups and upsets both them and himself.

Not every fictional tale of travel is a satire. Some are perfectly serious; some are purely humorous; some are boldly romantic. And, because many authors are not clear in their minds about the distinction between satire and other types of writing, it is common to find a novel which passes from straight narrative to broad comedy, thence into satire, and thence again into romance. For instance, much of the plot of *The Pickwick Papers* covers the travels of the Perpetual Chairman, with his friends and his servant. The Club itself is a mildly satirical sketch of the new intellectual societies, such as the Athenaeum, which were being founded in Dickens's young days: hence the title of Mr. Pickwick's paper, "Speculations on the Source of the Hampstead Ponds, with some Observations on the Theory of Tittlebats." Some of the voyages of the Chairman are truly satiric. We can see which, by observing those in which the names are cruelly distorted, the characters rather ridiculous and repulsive, and the adventures unduly rough—for example, the visit to a town called Eatanswill, where the election is fiercely contested by Buff and Blue, and where the lion-hunting hostess (who reads a parodic ode "To an Expiring Frog," in the costume of Minerva) is called Mrs. Leo Hunter. But other episodes of the novel are purely comical or harmlessly romantic; at last, when we reach the Fleet prison, the story leaves satire behind altogether, and even the picaresque Mr. Jingle becomes a figure of true pathos.

In these varied episodes, Mr. Pickwick is sometimes a passive spectator, occasionally an unconscious object, sometimes an active catalyst. In the intensity of their activity, the heroes of satiric travel-books differ widely. Thus, in *Scott-King's Modern Europe* by Evelyn Waugh (1949), a quiet middle-aged English schoolmaster, who has translated an otherwise unknown baroque Latin poet, is invited to attend a celebration of the poet's tercentenary in Neutralia, the country of his birth. He is plunged into the absurd intrigues of modern totalitarian politics, swept away into the underground like a piece of paper in a sewer, and finally delivered—without taking any action whatever—as a displaced person in an illicit immigrants' camp in Palestine.

On the other hand, in *Don Quixote*, the hero and his squire spend their entire lives careering through an otherwise fairly stable society and disordering it. The satirical amusement comes partly from our pleasure in watching their invincible craziness, and partly from the surprises which are provided by its conflict with other people's illusions. Such also is the result produced by the stolid but shrewd stupidity of the Good Soldier Schweik, who lived through the First World War and threw the entire Austro-Hungarian army into confusion by simply doing exactly as he was told by his superior officers.

But here once again we meet the difficulty that many authors put on and take off the mask of satire, without thinking that this spoils their effect. One of the few good books written in Germany during the disastrous seventeenth century is *The Adventurous Simplicissimus*, by Hans Jakob von Grimmelshausen. This is a remarkable book, almost as rambling and versatile as Goethe's *Faust*. The name *Simplicissimus* (later adopted for an important satirical weekly) means Utter Simpleton: the hero is an innocent, like Voltaire's Candide and L'Ingénu, and Margites. The first idea that its author had was a fine one. His hero was kidnapped as a boy of ten, when his entire family was killed or outraged in a guerrilla action of the terrible Thirty Years' War; he was brought up in the woods, by a hermit; then he went into a world disordered by war and corruption, to see it with the eyes of an infant, or a saint. This concept, if the author had worked it out, might have been wonderfully successful: a series of candid-camera pictures of an atrocious age, to match the simple but terrible etchings of Callot. But Grimmelshausen lost hold of it somewhere. He made his young hero become a court fool, and then—quite irrationally—the boldest marauder in all the armies, ambushing and looting, dueling and plundering. With the change in the hero, the change in the book ruins it: it has turned from satire to picaresque, and soon it changes again from picaresque to romantic comedy. A good idea was wasted, because in a chaotic time it is hard to be consistent.

The Image of Satire
Frontispiece from 1669 edition of Grimmelshausen's
Simplicissimus Teutsch

The same applies to Byron's *Don Juan*. By nature, Byron was a satirist: many of his letters and much of his private conversation were witty, distorted, obscene, and basically moral. But he was also a romancer, with a soft and ardent heart; and something of a hero, with a taste for bold adventure. The result was that, averse as always to planning, he wrote a poem as disorderly as his life, a poem which was intended to be a satire, but which for long periods veered off into other tones and other emotions, and must therefore be pronounced an artistic failure. Satire must be various, but it ought not to lose its special astringent tone.

Here it is worth discussing one peculiar little travel satire, because its author is so illustrious and its point so obscure. In the fifth poem of his first book of satires, Horace describes a slow, uncomfortable, and laborious journey which he and some friends made from Rome to Brundisium. Nothing very much happened. Although there were some brilliant and charming men in the party (Vergil, for instance, and Maecenas) not a word of their conversation is recorded: apparently the high point of the trip was a vulgar slanging-match between two professional buffoons at a party. On the surface the poem is a tissue of trivialities.

To understand its satiric point, we must recall the political tensions of the time when it was composed. The year was 37 B.C. Three years before, the rivals for supreme power in Rome, Mark Antony and Octavian (later Augustus) had agreed to partition the Roman world into eastern and western "spheres of influence." Now Octavian, fighting a difficult war in the west against the heir of Pompey, asked Antony for help. Antony replied by appearing off Brundisium with a fleet of three hundred ships. This was a great deal more than Octavian expected. It looked as though Antony proposed to take over the war, finish it, and become supreme. On their own initiative, the authorities of Brundisium kept him out of the harbor. He sailed off to Tarentum. Near there, a few weeks later, the rivals met, and renewed their uneasy alliance. (It was to end six years afterwards, in the battle of Actium, followed by Antony's suicide.)

One of Octavian's principal advisers was the adroit Maecenas. It was in his suite that Horace and Vergil went to Brundisium. His journey—which would normally have taken nine days and which he prolonged for fifteen days, apparently in order to study Antony's intentions—was an early move in a complex and important diplomatic chess-match. In Horace's poem, however, the political problems are scarcely mentioned. We hear only that Maecenas and another man were "sent as delegates on great issues," that they were "accustomed to reconcile estranged friends," and that a third member of the party was "first among the friends of Antony." Octavian is never mentioned; nor, apart from that one phrase, is Antony. The struggle with Sextus Pompey is not hinted at, nor is the imminence of Antony's war fleet. Everything seems peaceful, even sleepy. There is no trace of excitement. After the earlier treaty, in 40 B.C., Vergil wrote a poem full of rapturous happiness and hope: his fourth Bucolic, foretelling the advent of a new Age of Gold, with peace on earth at last. But now Horace feels no comparable excitement. His entire poem is a catalogue of the unimportant. Here the fire smoked because the fuel was wet. There the water was bad. Horace got a touch of ophthalmia. Vergil had indigestion. Their host at Beneventum nearly set fire to the kitchen. A girl said she would join Horace in bed, but didn't. The bread is exceptionally good in Equus Tuticus. And so on, to a suitably flat conclusion:

> The end of this long road, and screed, is Brindisi.

Now, why is it all trivialized? Did Horace think the entire trip was a waste of time? Did he despise both Octavian and Mark Antony, and contemn their shrewd advisers? This is out of the question. He was no fool: he admired Maecenas and Octavian greatly; he had already written deeply serious political poems about the crisis of the Roman world, and he knew how much was at stake.

Scholars generally adduce only two reasons for his publishing such a poem. Horace, they say, wanted to write "a masterly description of ordinary experiences," "a lively picture of a journey." And he wished to rival his predecessor Lucilius, who had composed a travel-poem about a trip to Sicily.[41] These explanations might be sufficient if Horace had taken an ordinary journey as his subject—a casual jaunt with a few friends chosen at random. But this particular journey was so important that he must have had further purposes in treating it satirically.

In part, he is satirizing himself. He is the little man who moves on the fringe of great events without having the power, or even the wish, to influence them. He knows very well that, since his father was a slave, he will be bitterly criticized if he grasps at power and dignity. (This is indeed the theme of the next satire in this same book.) His talent is for poetry, not politics.[42]

But he is also satirizing the outsiders, those who misconceive his true relation to Maecenas. (He elaborates this topic in the ninth poem of this book.) Thousands of people would have liked to know what went on during the days preceding this important conference, and at the conference itself. Elsewhere Horace complains that he is constantly cross-questioned by acquaintances who think he knows, and will betray, important secrets of state.[43] Therefore, to mock the curiosity of such busybodies and their misapprehension of his friendship with Maecenas, he writes a poem which describes with photographic clarity everything except what they really want to know. Such delicate mockery can sometimes be almost too mild for satire; and some readers have concluded that not only the journey but the poem itself was pointless. This is a mistake. The satire is a subtle study in contrast.

In satires disposed as tales of travel through regions of the real world, the target is sometimes the places themselves with their inhabitants as observed by a quizzical visitor, and sometimes the visitor himself, who is shown as simple, easily puzzled, easily bamboozled, and easily shocked. In the satiric episodes of Byron's *Don Juan* the hero is both amused and bewildered by the coarse corruptions of Catherine's Russia and by the more civil sensualities of Regency England. In one of its most successful imitations, Linklater's *Juan in America* (1931), a naïve but energetic and amorous young Britisher savors both the dangers and the delights of America during those wild days when the consumption of liquor was enormously encouraged by the Prohibition Amendment, and sexual activity more than kept pace with the intake of fermented liquors. Among the bitterest of modern satiric travels is Evelyn Waugh's *Black Mischief* (1932), the tale of an unscrupulous young Englishman in the African kingdom of Azania (which is not wholly unlike Abyssinia). Told not with the usual romantic fervor but with cool acerbity, it has a climax which makes a fine satirical comment on the current idealistic doctrine that all races are brothers under the skin. The hero, Basil Seal, attends the funeral feast of the dead Emperor Seth, and even pronounces a funeral eulogy upon him before the eating and drinking begin. The main dish at the feast is stew, and its main ingredient is Basil's mistress, Prudence Courteney, daughter of the British minister. He does not discover this until, engaged in the passive process of digestion, he sees her red beret decorating the head of one of his hosts.

Waugh plays a variation on the same theme in *The*

Loved One (1948), which is basically a satire on the famous idealistic cemetery of Southern California, Forest Lawn. Most of the book describes, with gruesome charm, the process of embalming and cosmeticizing the corpses (dead through surgery, "strangulated," or drowned and sea-changed, it makes no difference) and makes fun of the elegant language of a funeral home where the dead are Loved Ones, their relatives the Waiting Ones, and the mortuary the Slumber Room. But the hero is an English amateur crook (one of Waugh's favorite types, a smaller version of Basil Seal): he regards Southern California as a crazy and inconceivably remote foreign country, from which—like a Conrad hero—he must by any means escape before it absorbs and engulfs him; and the book ends with his imminent departure from a land which even native-born Americans sometimes feel belongs to another far-distant world.

A few satires may be called inverted travel books. In these, the writer disguises himself as a foreigner from far away, visits his own country, and then describes its customs with humorous amazement tempered by disgust. The most important of these is the series of *Persian Letters* published anonymously at Amsterdam in 1721, and written by the young Charles de Montesquieu (later famous as the author of *The Spirit of Laws*).[44] The book purports to be a collection of correspondence to and from two educated Persian gentlemen visiting Europe, which they find interesting but often incomprehensible. The best satirical letters are those which turn upside down the ethnocentrism of Europeans and Christians: for instance, the thirty-ninth, in which a Hajji, writing to a Jewish proselyte of Islam, explains the tremendous miracles which attended the birth of Mohammed, and concludes, "After so many striking testimonies only a heart of iron could refuse to believe his holy law." Montesquieu contrived to satirize the church by making his Persians refer to all Catholic priests as "dervishes" and the Pope as "the Mufti." Unfortunately, being French, he felt he must bring in Amour; and so he gave a sort of narrative continuity to the correspondence by inserting a series of highly improbable letters from the wives of one of his Persians, passionate ladies left at home in the seraglio, unhappy, ill-disciplined, and reduced to despair, corruption, suicide. This romantic fiction may have interested his eighteenth-century readers, but spoils the effect of the satire for us, since we conclude that a man who could not govern his own household could scarcely criticize a foreign kingdom with any cogency. Once again we see how dangerous it is to intersperse satire with other types of literature, unless they are very close to it in spirit.

5. THE STRUCTURE OF SATIRIC STORIES AND PLAYS

Apart from their general satiric intention, we can trace certain distinguishing marks in all these stories and plays.

If they are long, they are usually episodic. Although the satirist pretends to be telling a continuous story and gives his fiction a single unifying title, he is less interested in developing a plot, with preparation, suspense, and climax, than in displaying many different aspects of an idea; and, as a satirist, he does not believe that the world is orderly and rational. Therefore gaps and interruptions, even inconsistencies, in the story scarcely concern him. His characters flit from one amusing humiliation to another with scarcely any intervals of time and reflection. Seldom do they develop by degrees, as people in real novels do. They may display more of their character as the story drops them into new situations, but they do not grow.

At the very end, they sometimes undergo a radical change—which corresponds to the change which the satirist

himself wishes to induce in his readers. Candide believes
in the optimistic theory of Leibniz through twenty-nine
chapters of hideous and comical misadventures, and is only
converted to realism in the thirtieth and final chapter, by
a total stranger. Lucius is an ass for ten books, until the
day fixed for his death: only then, by a divine miracle,
is he made a man. After a hundred and twenty-six chapters
Don Quixote is still as mad as ever: if he is prevented from
being a knight-errant, he is determined to become a figure
from the unreal world of pastoral, "the shepherd Quixotis";
it is only in the next, the final chapter, that he regains his
senses and dies. Lemuel Gulliver was naive and coarse
when he visited Lilliput; he indeed does grow and change
during his two succeeding voyages; but only in the island of
the Houyhnhnms does he realize that he is a Yahoo. Thereafter he will make no further voyages, but can scarcely
endure to live in what he once believed was his happy home.

The comedies of Aristophanes are so disorderly, with so
many apparently improvised scenes and so many characters
irrupting apparently at haphazard, that the plan underlying their structure was discovered only three generations
ago.[45] Even then, it is rather a sequence of episodes than
a single development. (Such also was the original Latin
satura, on which see chapter 5 of this book.) We can easily
see one of the main differences between satire and comedy
if we read one of Aristophanes' rambling fantasies and then
one of Menander's suave and symmetrical studies of reality.
Menander takes a thin slice of life, extracts the impure
and the extraneous from it, and folds it into a neat omelette.
Aristophanes pours Bacchus into a huge mixing-bowl, jollies
us into a dozen toasts, paints our face with wine, plays
kottabos with it, splashes it on the walls, and carries us off
with him into a world of intoxicated inconsequential
imagination where happiness is not found through logic.

Certain non-dramatic works of satire also are merely

Candide, Encolpius, Schweik, Simplicissimus—they have a preternatural gift of survival.

Their situations are equally improbable. Apuleius asks us to believe that a young man interested in magic went to a country where it was commonly practised, and was changed into a donkey. Aristophanes tells us that his hero wanted to bring Peace back to earth; since Peace lives in heaven, he had to fly up to bring her down: so he trained a large flying beetle (*Geotrupes stercorarius*, which eats dung as fuel) to carry him, and it teleported him into the Peace Belt. The pygmies of Lilliput and the giants of Brobdingnag are impossible, even physically, and the wise benevolent horses who are served by mindless anthropoid villains are so absurd that, in reading the fourth of Gulliver's travels, we attend only to the satiric message without even trying to believe its fictional structure.

Satiric tales of trickery—are they reality or fantasy? They sound highly improbable, most of them, and still. . . . The Inspector-General of Gogol was a fraud so transparent that he virtually exposed himself, and anyone, we think, should have seen through him; but more outrageous frauds have been perpetrated and have succeeded. In Romains' admirable satiric comedy *Knock, or The Triumph of Medicine* (1923) we are asked to believe that a quack physician with meager training and rude experience takes over a large community of healthy thrifty suspicious French peasants, and converts it into a gigantic sanatorium full of obedient hypochondriacs. In real life, the regional medical association would have checked his qualifications and wrecked his enterprise long before it matured—or so we say to ourselves, and then we remember the fake specialists who proliferate like cancer cells both in country communities and in large cities; and we feel the impact of satire. Of all the improbabilities with which satire deals, the most plausible and the closest to real life is the fraud, the hoax, the swindle.

It is easy for scientists to test the limitations of human endurance under conditions of acute strain; but the height and depth and breadth and absorbent power of human stupidity cannot be described by the most eloquent of satirists, or exhausted by the most inventive of satiric swindlers. (Just before writing this paragraph I read the biography of a man who really sold the Eiffel Tower to *two* different scrap-metal merchants. He posed as an agent of the French government, which as usual needed money; and he told them it must be kept confidential.)

To mock and expose the gullibility of mankind is one of the chief functions of Panurge, the clever unprincipled rascal who is the associate and friend of Prince Pantagruel. They make a strange couple, the good prince and the bad courtier: they do not closely correspond with the other master-and-servant pairs who are notable in satire and comedy: Dionysus and Xanthias, Don Quixote and Sancho, Don Juan and Leporello. They are closer to Prince Hal and Falstaff, but the difference between the two pairs is still great. Pantagruel, who is a wise, benevolent, and cultured monarch, does not treat Panurge (whose name means Clever Scoundrel) as an amusing companion met for an hour and then forgotten. He takes him into his service, and spends much time talking with him. Panurge can in no sense be called an adviser or a minister of his prince: he is much more like a court fool, having, instead of a humpback or a dwarfish body, an incorrigibly naughty mind. Yet it is impossible to excise Panurge from Rabelais' wonderful story. He represents one of the essential elements in satire, as Pantagruel represents another.[46] The princely giant who swallows an entire group of pilgrims by accident, and rearranges long-standing disputes by superhuman gestures of strength and wisdom (and occasionally of ridicule), personifies satirical scorn for the small, and the mean, and the prejudiced, and the conventional. The crook who plays cruel jokes on pretty girls and well-dressed men, and can out-gesture a symbolist, out-jargon a psychologist, out-language a semanticist—he personifies the mischievous, destructive force of satire, evil in itself, and only potentially good when attached to a good prince or a good principle. When a Roman general of the republic won a great victory, he was privileged to go, in a procession called a triumph, to make a sacrifice of thanks to the supreme god. He wore a costume of unique grandeur. His family and friends all followed his chariot as it moved through the shouting streets. The victories he had won were shown in pageants followed by his captives and his rejoicing army. For a time, he was raised high above ordinary humanity. But behind him marched his troops, often singing songs of edged derision and cheerful satire: his physical weaknesses, his bad habits, his equivocal reputation, all resounded among and sometimes above the shouts of applause. And (according to some authorities) a slave stood behind the triumphator in his chariot, holding above his head a golden crown, but saying in his ear, "Remember, you are human." Within the court of Pantagruel, so free and gay and powerful and irresponsible, Panurge plays the part of that slave and sings that mocking song. Three hundred years later he appears in Goethe's *Faust*, where he is one of the two principal characters: Mephistopheles, the spirit who says always "No." Satire is not positive, but negative.

And yet, like Mephistopheles, a higher power may determine that it always aims at evil and always does good.

The exploits of Panurge typify another feature of satiric narratives. This is that they are usually shocking. Their heroes are beaten, soused in filth, threatened with instant execution. Their heroines are raped, enslaved, eaten by cannibals. In ways equally outrageous, the satiric hero sometimes abuses and humiliates the rest of mankind. He steals the bells of Notre Dame cathedral, urinates over the royal palace (of course, on the side containing the queen's apartments), befools priests, nobles, and monarchs, enjoys the absurd sufferings of others. Stones and dirty words whistle through the air of satire. In its world no one can preserve decorum, maintain virtue, or expect happiness. The pulchritudinous princess ends as a monopygous hag; the courageous explorer is condemned to read the works of Dickens aloud to a sentimental jungle tyrant, or is made to straddle the nipple of a female giant, or is carried off by a monkey and stuffed with the half-chewed food from its cheek; the husband has to watch his wife vomiting at the dinner-table; the lover penetrates his darling's bedroom, to find it full of unwashed clothes and stale excrement.[47] This, says the satirist, is the world we all inhabit; but while the cataract of sentiment doth grossly blind our eyes, we cannot see it. He sets out to cut away our blindness without any anaesthetic except a whiff of laughing gas, and to cure our delusions by shock therapy.

Yet satires are not horror stories. They nearly all appeal, closely or distantly, to our sense of humor; and the great satirists are those who have been best able to convey a disgusting or ghastly message, and make it palatable by making it ridiculous. Would it be possible to jest about eternal hell? Scarcely, we think, and then we remember Quevedo and Rabelais and even a few scenes in Dante. About being hanged? Surely not; yet there is the indestructible Dr. Pangloss in *Candide*. About cannibalism? Impossible. Yet in modern times there is the hero of *Black Mischief*, consuming the heroine. And in antiquity there is a magnificent scene in the *Satyrica* of Petronius, just at the end, where some satirical fate mutilated our poor surviving manuscripts. An elderly poet has represented himself as a dying millionaire, and thus (like Jonson's Volpone) wheedled gifts and courtesies from legacy-hunters.

At last, his will is read aloud—a will intended to discourage even the greediest. "All my heirs shall receive their legacies on condition that they cut up my body and eat it in public. Let them gulp down my flesh as eagerly as they damned my soul." And, as the manuscripts dwindle to their tantalizing end, someone is saying very persuasively, "It is easy. Just close your eyes and think it is not human flesh, but half a million dollars. There are sauces, relishes. People have done worse things in time of siege. . . ."

6. HISTORY AND BIOGRAPHY

Historians do not tell the truth. They tell parts of the truth, selected and arranged by their own emotions, ignorance, or moral and political bias. Historical narratives, being usually solemn, can be classified with sermons, fiction, and propaganda. But occasionally there emerges a historian who, using a scornfully humorous sense of incongruity and employing certain satirical devices, writes history that can be called satire. The fifteenth and sixteenth chapters of Gibbon's *Decline and Fall of the Roman Empire*, in which he examines the causes of the rise of Christianity within the pagan world, are in their use of keen unsmiling irony one of the finest examples of historical satire. The orthodox explanation is of course that Christianity is the only true faith, founded by Almighty God incarnate in Jesus of Nazareth, and that it was therefore inevitably bound to prevail. No doubt, says Gibbon, but "as truth and wisdom seldom find so favorable a reception in the world, and as the wisdom of Providence frequently condescends to use the passions of the human heart, and the general circumstances of mankind, as instruments to execute its purpose, we may still be permitted, though with becoming submission, to ask, not indeed what was the first, but what were the secondary causes of the rapid growth of the Christian church."

And he goes on, in terms of the profoundest outward respect for Christianity, to explain that it rose to the domination of the western world partly because it was a tightly organized and fanatical cult, growing out of Jewry, which demanded toleration from other creeds and then, once entrenched, refused it to its competitors; partly because the early Christians claimed to perform miracles, and guaranteed immortality to their adherents; partly because the tolerant Romans did not persecute them with continuous energy and a true annihilation policy. These and the other causes which Gibbon sets out may well be true; many devout Christians would accept them; yet Gibbon thought, and wished his enlightened readers to believe, that the first reason was deplorable, the second rubbishy, and the third unfortunate. He could not say so. Therefore he said the opposite, in irony, or put the dangerous comments in the mouths of others.

On the Old Testament. "There are some objections against the authority of Moses and the prophets which too readily present themselves to the sceptical mind; though they can only be derived from our ignorance of remote antiquity, and our incapacity to form an adequate judgment of the Divine economy. These objections were eagerly embraced and as petulantly urged by the vain science of the Gnostics. . . . The God of Israel was impiously represented by the Gnostics as a being liable to passion and to error, capricious in his favour, implacable in his resentment, meanly jealous of his superstitious worship, and confining his partial providence to a single people, and to this transitory life. In such a character they could discover none of the features of the wise and omnipotent Father of the universe."

On the Second Coming. "In the primitive church the influence of truth was very powerfully strengthened by an opinion which, however it may deserve respect for its usefulness and antiquity, has not been found agreeable to experience. It was universally believed that the end of the world, and the kingdom of heaven, were at hand. The near approach of this wonderful event had been predicted by the apostles; the tradition of it was preserved by their earliest disciples, and those who understood in their literal sense the discourses of Christ himself were obliged to expect the second and glorious coming of the Son of Man in the clouds, before that generation was totally extinguished which had beheld his humble condition upon earth. . . . The revolution of seventeen centuries has instructed us not to press too closely the mysterious language of prophecy and revelation; but as long as, for wise purposes, this error was permitted to subsist in the church, it was productive of the most salutary effects on the faith and practice of Christians."

On the exclusion of the pagans. "The condemnation of the wisest and most virtuous of the Pagans, on account of their ignorance or disbelief of the divine truth, seems to offend the reason and the humanity of the present age. But the primitive church, whose faith was of a much firmer consistence, delivered over, without hesitation, to eternal torture the far greater part of the human species."

On the miracles. "But how shall we excuse the supine inattention of the Pagan and philosophic world to those evidences which were presented by the hand of Omnipotence, not to their reason, but to their senses? During the age of Christ, of his apostles, and of their first disciples, the doctrine which they preached was confirmed by innumerable prodigies. The lame walked, the blind saw, the sick were healed, the dead were raised, demons were expelled, and the laws of Nature were frequently suspended for the benefit of the church. But the sages of Greece and Rome turned aside from the awful spectacle, and, pursuing the ordinary occupations of life and study, appeared unconscious of any alteration in the moral or physical government of the world. Under the reign of Tiberius, the whole earth, or at least a celebrated province of the Roman empire, was involved in a preternatural darkness of three hours. Even this miraculous event, which ought to have excited the wonder, the curiosity, and the devotion of mankind, passed without notice in an age of science and history."

With these passages should be ranked the grim chapters in which Tacitus, as coldly as a psychiatrist watching a hopeless schizophrenic, traces the delusions and vices of the early Roman emperors. They behaved as gods, and even called themselves divine before their deaths; but (he seems to say through tightly closed lips) they were worms feeding on the half-dead body of what had once been a strong and noble republic.

There are some biographies which qualify as satires: for instance, biographies of petty scoundrels treated as though they were great men, and biographies of important men treated as though they were petty scoundrels or shallow fools. Here, as always, the emotional response of the reader is the test. If a life-history, real or fictitious, arouses simple amusement or the excitement of adventure or—like a recent biography of Paul Joseph Goebbels—unmixed revulsion, it should not be styled satirical. But if it produces that unmistakable blend of amusement and contempt, then surely we must classify it as satire. Thus, in Lytton Strachey's *Eminent Victorians* (1918), the study of Florence Nightingale opens sympathetically, does justice to that remarkable lady's achievements, and closes with a quaint but generous picture. Very old, and (although Strachey does not say so) imbecile, Miss Nightingale was given the highest British award of its kind, the Order of Merit. " 'Too kind, too kind,' she said, and she was not ironical." This has the charm of age and modesty; if, here and there in his sketch of her career, Strachey does satirize Miss Nightingale's subordinates and antagonists, that does not alter the central effect of his biographical essay. But on the first page of his study of Gordon, we meet the general tripping about Palestine with a Bible and a solar topee, trying to identify the places mentioned in the Hebrew scriptures—a practice which Strachey implies is a ludicrous eccentricity. And although Gordon's courageous death, surrounded by savages and defending a distant outpost of which all others despaired, is seriously described, his biography ends not there, but with a mocking account of Her Majesty Queen Victoria's *very* emotional tributes to his *dear* memory, and the subsequent moves of British diplomacy, "and a step in the peerage for Sir Evelyn Baring." A ludicrous figure, the brave and crazy Gordon; contemptible, the suave sanctimonious imperialists who used him as a tool. So we are meant to think. We are not supposed to remember that Strachey's father was himself a general in the British army, and a builder of the British Empire; nor are we meant to feel the full force of that passionate Voltairian indignation which Strachey's friend Clive Bell says was his main motive.[48] We are intended simply to smile a scornful smile, and to turn away from the Victorians with disgust.

Several of Strachey's biographical studies are subtle satire. There are far less delicately written biographies which are nevertheless satirical in their effect. These are lives of eminent rogues, composed sometimes (fictionally) by themselves and sometimes by their pretended admirers. They are called picaresque stories, from the Spanish word for a rogue, *picaro*. There must be thousands of them. Not all, by any means, can be classed as satire. In many of the best of them, we are meant simply to enjoy the high spirits of the trickster, to be astonished at the ingenuity of his stratagems, and to be excited by the trials and dangers through which he chooses to pass. For instance, there is a delightful collection of stories by O. Henry called *The Gentle Grafter* (1908) which plays on all these emotions, but contains no sneers, arouses no contempt, and blends the sweetness of its laughter with not a drop of acid.[49] A number of tales of crime and outlawry are meant to be read with perfect seriousness, and carry no overtones that could be called satirical. Into this field satire enters only when the author has a special purpose beyond telling a story. When Le Sage writes of the adventures of Gil Blas of Santillana (parts 1-2, 1715; 3, 1724; 4, 1735), he is ostensibly narrating the exploits of a brilliant rogue for the sake of our amusement and excitement; but in fact he is commenting on the corrupt state of society. He implies that his era produces, even encourages, rascals; and that in his corrupt world open rascality is really more admirable than villainy masquerading as virtue. So *The Adventures of Hajjî Baba of Ispahan* by the British diplomat J. J. Morier (1828), which was actually modeled on *Gil Blas,* might have been considered a straightforward autobiography if it had been composed by a native Persian; but the fact that it was set down by a foreign observer made it appear to be a satiric comment on the devious character and maladjusted social system of a nation which has usually considered itself far above criticism.[50]

Satire is a blade with two edges. Only a few years after *Gil Blas* appeared, the other edge was used by Henry Fielding in his biography of a contemporary crook, *Jonathan Wild the Great* (1743). Jonathan Wild was one of the first men to organize metropolitan crime on the same big scale as business and political jobbery. He was hanged in 1725;

but after his death he became even more famous than during his life. For various reasons he was admired as something like a hero. To attack this cult, Fielding wrote his biography in a tone of ironic seriousness, treating him like a figure of vast historical significance. He traced his ancestry back to the Saxon invaders of Britain, paralleled him to Caesar and Alexander, and compared the portents announcing his birth to those which heralded the advent of Cyrus the Great. Then he recounted all Wild's base and mean acts, with the same wide-eyed interest and solemnity as Plutarch in telling the exploits of his Greek and Roman heroes; finally he conducted him to his "glorious" death and reported the maxims for achieving greatness which he bequeathed to posterity. This was a well-conceived satire. Its execution, unfortunately, was imperfect. Fielding always found it difficult to stick to one single tone in his books; here he branched off from mock-heroism into sentimentality, and brought in, as a contrast to the Great Jonathan Wild, a flawlessly good and innocent man called Heartfree—thus breaking the satiric illusion and rendering his feigned admiration for Wild ridiculous. *Jonathan Wild the Great* satirized not only the prosperous criminal admired by the foolish, but—without mentioning his name—an eminently successful politician: Sir Robert Walpole, who had just retired after a long career distinguished by what his enemies called the subtlest forms of corruption and a bold hypocrisy comparable to that of Wild himself.

7. DESCRIPTIVE SATIRE

Have you ever been to a party where everything went wrong? From the instant you rang the bell, and heard the angry voices inside and the baby crying and the dog barking, through the moment when you stepped inside and smelled the burnt cooking and met the flushed faces set in glacial politeness and heard the viperine whispers with which the host and hostess interspersed their greetings, to the introductions when you met the grotesque anthropoids who were to be your fellow-guests, you knew that everything, from that time onward until the hour of leavetaking, would be simply agonizing. Lucky, in such a case, the man who is happily married: he and his wife exchange a glance of sympathy and strength. The single man, if he has the mind of a satirist, may survive. He will not expect to enjoy himself in the usual way. He will know that the meal (if it ever arrives) will be interrupted, graceless, and inedible; that the conversation will be spasmodic; and that the gaiety will at best be a few forced jokes, which, if the host keeps the drinks circulating, will change into hysterical laughter and end in angry shouts or whooping sobs. The entire evening will be punctuated by deliciously unpredictable accidents. Small children will appear, dirty and crying. Inexplicable strangers will lurch through the room and vanish. Loud arguments will take place just out of the range of intelligibility. At intervals there will be crashes of glass and crockery, smothered screams, and door-slams. For the unmarried guest it will be difficult not to excuse himself and escape. If he does stay, he may develop a piercing migraine headache; but if he can live through this and observe everything that happens, he will have had a superb satiric experience.

Such an experience is the basis of a special literary form allied to satiric narrative: satiric description. Instead of saying, "Listen, here is the story of an event," the satirist says, "This is a complete picture of a bizarre adventure, a lifelike portrait of an absurd and revolting person." The distinction between a narrative of an event which took several hours or days to complete, and a description of a grotesque scene which could scarcely be grasped all at once, is unimportant. In both cases, the satirist says, "This is as though some foreign observer of American mores were to describe Diamond Jim Brady—who began dinner with a quart of orange juice and three dozen oysters and gave his mistress Lillian Russell a gold-plated bicycle with jeweled hubcaps—as a typical American gentleman. It is hard to see how any scholar could make this mistake, since even the disreputable heroes of Petronius constantly find themselves amused but revolted, and finally run away from Trimalchio's mansion in disgust.[52] But some philologists, although skilled in the subtleties of language, have little opportunity, and even aptitude, for observing the nuances of social behavior; and this is the penalty of the satirist— he exaggerates and selects, but he pretends to be telling the truth, and simple-minded readers take him literally.

In modern times I believe it was the clever Italian satirist Francesco Berni (1497/8-1535) who, with ironic descriptions of the lovely peaceful time of the plague and the beauties of the chamberpot, introduced the technique of satiric photography. He had many Italian followers, notably Cesare Caporali (1531-1601), who was admired and imitated by the first French satirist in this style, Mathurin Régnier (1573-1613). I cannot trace the theme of the excruciatingly disagreeable dinner-party back, in the Renaissance, beyond Régnier. His tenth satire, *The Absurd Supper*, starts with an adaptation of Horace, goes on to close borrowings from Caporali, and ends realistically with an argument developing into a fight. The narrator then escapes into a Bad Lodging, described in the eleventh satire with some masterly detail and some rascally reminiscences of Petronius.[53] These are diffuse but amusingly realistic poems. Disgust is more neatly and wittily expressed, although with far more restraint, in Boileau's third satire, *The Ridiculous Meal*. The tradition of the dismal dinner later passed into the semi-satirical or satirical novel: for example, the Veneerings' banquet in chapter 2 of Dickens's

Our Mutual Friend, which is stamped as satirical by the very names of the guests—Lady Tippins, the Podsnaps, Boots, Brewer, and two stuffed Buffers, all attended by a butler described as the Analytical Chemist. With modern changes in manners and styles of entertainment, it has now been succeeded, as in Evelyn Waugh, by the Painful Party.

"Oh, Nina, *what a lot of parties.*"

(. . . Masked parties, Savage parties, Victorian parties, Greek parties, Wild West parties, Russian parties, Circus parties, parties where one had to dress as somebody else, almost naked parties in St. John's Wood, parties in flats and studios and houses and ships and hotels and night clubs, in windmills and swimming baths, . . . dull dances in London and comic dances in Scotland and disgusting dances in Paris—all that succession and repetition of massed humanity . . . Those vile bodies . . .)[54]

Even one episode in a party can be made into satire: even one moment, one aspect so apparently trivial as the design of the guests' monocles, when seen by Marcel Proust.

The Marquis de Forestelle's monocle was tiny and rimless, and since it constrained his eye—in which it was encrusted like a superfluous cartilage bizarre of substance and inexplicable of presence—to clench itself incessantly and agonizingly, it gave his face a melancholy refinement, and made women think him capable of suffering deep pangs of love. But that of M. de Saint-Candé, surrounded by an enormous, a Saturnian ring, was the centre of gravity of those features which kept rearranging themselves around it, a quivering red nose and protrusive sarcastic lips which strove to distort themselves into grimaces as striking as the brilliant firework shower of wit which sparkled from his crystal disc, a face more attractive than the handsomest eyes in the world to snobbish and degenerate young women who saw in it a promise of artificial delights and voluptuous refinements; while behind his monocle M. de Palancy, round-eyed and huge-headed like a carp, slowly passed through all this gaiety, from moment to moment unclenching his jaws as though attempting to orient himself, and looking as if he carried with him an accidentally detached, perhaps wholly symbolic, fragment of the glass of his own aquarium.[55]

CARICATURES

It is also possible to write satiric description in the form of more or less loosely connected character-sketches. One of the most famous Renaissance satires is little more than a series of portraits of contemporary types, all identified and described as fools, although all (in their own eyes and the eyes of most contemporaries) quite normal. This is *The Ship of Fools* (1494) by Sebastian Brant. Although his central idea was to describe the world as a ship manned by fools and steered toward the fools' paradise of Narragonia (*Narr* is the German for "fool"), his book has no plot and no continuous story: it amounts simply to a group of mildly amusing but disconnected literary caricatures.

The long parade of evil and hateful wives which forms Juvenal's pageant of bad women (Satire 6) is a series of portraits done in this manner. It has had many descendants. One, particularly remarkable, is a prose satire by Boccaccio, called *Il Corbaccio* (which probably means *The Courbash, The Heavy Whip*) or *The Labyrinth of Love.* He wrote it in 1355, when he was over forty and beginning to feel his age. It is so intensely personal that we cannot strictly classify it as belonging to any one type of satire. However, its core is a satirical monologue, based on Juvenal's sixth satire, and combining many of its portraits of bad women into one sinister and monstrous caricature. Boccaccio, unhappy and humiliated by a capricious widow whom he loves, is visited by her dead husband, who has been released from

THE SHIP OF FOOLS

From Brant's *Ship of Fools*, 1494 edition. (Truliner's facsimile, 1913).
New York Public Library Prints Division

purgatory to save Boccaccio from the error he himself committed. The ghost delivers a long homily on the folly of loving any woman (dirty, unchaste, quarrelsome, and cruel as they are) and the particular folly of loving this particular woman—whose habits he describes in nauseating detail, with many direct quotations from Juvenal.[56] (It makes an odd parallel to Boccaccio's early love-story, *Fiammetta*, in which he sublimated his own agonies over the cruelty of his beloved Maria d'Aquino by writing a story in which a young girl suffered from her lover's cruelty.) This is one of a long series of satires on women, written by embittered men who wished to show that, although women are outwardly attractive, they are really, when known intimately, monsters of filth and horror. Such is the sow-woman of Semonides. Such is the enchantress of Lucretius against whom the true Epicurean must harden his heart.

> After all, there are others; we lived without her before;
> after all, she does (and we know it) the same as the uglies:
> she makes her own scents, poor thing, revolting smells
> which put her maids to flight, giggling behind their hands.
> Meanwhile the wretched lover, locked outside, and weeping,
> covers her haughty door with flowery wreaths, and smears
> its posts with perfume, and plants kisses on its planks.
> Yet if he were let in, and met, as he advanced,
> one single breeze, he would excuse himself and leave,
> dropping his long complaints of cruelty and wrong,
> damning his own stupidity because he thought
> his lady more than mortal, superhuman, a goddess.[57]

The same theme was taken up and made more concrete and more grotesquely comic by Juvenal:

> Meanwhile, a foul and funny spectacle, her face
> bulges plastered with bread or sweats with fat Poppaean
> cream-lotion, viscid on the lips of her poor husband.
> She only cleans her face to visit her lover. . . .
> Listen, that thing, so overlaid, so richly poulticed

with patent medications and with heaps of soaking
dough fresh from the oven, is that a face, or an ulcer?[58]

The Christians took it over from the pagan satirists, and
used it in a thousand years of denouncing women after
the manner of Hamlet: "God hath given you one face, and
you make yourselves another."[59] Adapting the topic to the
civilities of the baroque era, Boileau introduced into it
some truly charming effects of oxymoron.

> Dans sa chambre, crois-moi, n'entre point tout le jour.
> Si tu veux posséder ta Lucrèce à ton tour,
> Attends, discret mari, que la belle en cornette
> Le soir ait étalé son teint sur la toilette
> Et dans quatre mouchoirs, de sa beauté salis,
> Envoie au blanchisseur ses roses et ses lys.[60]

Dean Swift's pathological horror of the human body and
in particular of its excretory functions would have made it
difficult for him to love even a healthy, well-exercised, well-
bathed, scentless Greek beauty; but, surrounded by the
lazy, unwashed, flea-bitten women of the eighteenth century, who covered their smells with perfumes and their
pimples with "beauty patches," he was driven nearly insane
with disgust at the thought of exploring a lady's dressing-
room.

> But oh! it turned poor Strephon's bowels,
> When he beheld and smelt the towels:
> Begummed, bemattered, and beslimed,
> With dirt, and sweat, and ear-wax grimed.
> No object Strephon's eye escapes;
> Here petticoats in frowsy heaps.
> Nor be the handkerchiefs forgot,
> All varnished o'er with snuff and snot.[61]

The eighteenth century. That was the era when a lady of
the French court would have an enema administered to
her while she was chatting with her guests. That was the
era. when Lady Mary Wortley Montagu, on being told

that her hands were rather dirty, replied, "You should see my feet!"

This kind of literary satire is very close to satire in the visual arts, which—although it is a heavy inadequate word—is generally called caricature. In the Middle Ages, not only preachers in the pulpit and Goliards in the tavern, but sculptors in the cathedral produced satirical representations of vice and folly personified in human (and even in animal) form. Lustful ladies and greedy merchants and proud prelates, seen by critical eyes and carved with loving hatred, still look down on us from the walls and columns of many a Gothic cathedral. During the Renaissance the greatest artists enjoyed creating satire through pictures. Leonardo drew grotesque and comically hideous faces with the same loving care as a saint or a madonna, and Dürer's illustrations for Brant's *Ship of Fools* are actually more effective than Brant's little poems. In the eighteenth and nineteenth centuries several fine artists put all or most of their energy into caricature. For eighteen years, Louis-Philippe, the heavy-jowled "citizen king" of France, was caricatured as a gross bulbous pear. With a coarsely vigorous sense of humor, a strong moral sense, and a hearty contempt for the follies of mankind, Hogarth, Rowlandson, Gillray, Cruikshank, Gavarni, Grandville, and the marvelous Daumier drew scenes of contemporary life which fulfilled every possible requirement of the genus satire, and indeed surpassed in energy most of the poets of their own era.

One of Hogarth's masterpieces is a pair of pictures, "Gin Lane" and "Beer Street" (1751), showing the contrasting evil and good social effects of cheap spirits and sound English beer. Although every detail in "Gin Lane" is realistic and could no doubt be documented from contemporary records, the accumulation of horrors produces the exaggeration and distortion typical of satire; and besides, there

Two monks, satirically portrayed on the tombs of the
Dukes of Bordeaux:
one personifying pride, the other, with his purse, avarice
Gothic sculpture, Cathedral of Bourges
Photograph by Giraudon, Paris

are, here and there throughout the picture, touches of sordid but undeniably comical humor.

"Gin Lane," Hogarth called it. It was a real place, a London slum known as the Ruins of St. Giles. Most of the buildings we see in the picture are ramshackle. One is actually collapsing as we look. Only four places of business are visible: an undertaker's, a distiller's, a pawnbroker's, and in the cellar a dram-shop, bearing the advertising slogan which has become famous in histories of England:

> Drunk for a Penny
> Dead drunk for two pence
> Clean Straw for Nothing.

The scene is full of activity, perverse, painful, and absurd. The central figure is a young slatternly woman who may once (judging by the bone-structure of her face) have been handsome. She is now a hopeless wreck, wearing nothing but a loose gown indecently open and a rag on her head. Her legs and face are scarred, perhaps with syphilitic chancres. With a smirking affectation of aristocratic nonchalance, she is taking snuff, while her baby boy, who has been stretching and fidgeting in her arms, falls unnoticed over the banister into the area. Nevertheless, she is comical, with a satirical incongruity. The figure beside her is ghastly: a living skeleton kept alive only by drink, and at this moment unconscious. He seems to be an itinerant singer and seller of ballads (one of which is hanging from his basket), but he is so besotted that he has pawned shirt, stockings, and waistcoat, and wears nothing but shoes, breeches, an open coat, and a shapeless hat. He is moribund. The first cold night will kill him, unregretted by all except his dog, which stares gloomily at his nipperkin. The third main foreground figure is Mr. Gripe the pawnbroker, who is trying to think how little he can offer for a carpenter's saw and his Sunday coat, while a ragged woman (the carpenter's wife?) waits in turn to offer her cooking-pot and tea-kettle. These two are giving up the effort of living decently, and will soon be destitute. In front of them is a man so truly destitute that he is sharing a bone with a cur, and a woman so stupefied that a snail is exploring her arm.

In the middle distance, great jollification. A woman is dosing her baby with a slug of gin to keep it quiet; an old woman, so drunk she must be wheeled home in a barrow, is being given one for the road by her daughter or daughter-in-law.

In the background, two young creatures, chantry-girls from St. Giles's church, are pledging each other in gin. A pair of cripples are fighting savagely, watched by a crowd gathered round the distillery door. Further back, three corpses: a barber, hanged in his own ruinous garret; a child (apparently fallen out of window) impaled on a spit carried by a roistering cook; a beautiful young woman, sadly wasted, being coffined beside a weeping child. In the remoter distance, ruinous houses and a tall, pompous, baroque monument.

It would be possible to translate the sordid details and grotesque overall effect of "Gin Lane" into a satire of a hundred couplets; but unless the couplets were by Swift or Byron, the poem would be inferior to the picture. Swift himself described the Irish Parliament as a mob of lunatics in Bedlam, and then, with unexpected but not unjustified modesty, called on Hogarth for his collaboration.

> How I want thee, humorous Hogart!
> Thou, I hear, a pleasant rogue art;
> Were but you and I acquainted,
> Every monster should be painted;
> You should try your graving tools
> On this odious group of fools;
> Draw the beasts as I describe 'em;
> Form their features, while I gibe 'em,
> Draw them like, for I assure you,
> You will need no Car'catura.[62]

Hogarth's *Gin Lane*

V   CONCLUSION

LAST of all, a few fundamental definitions and descriptions.

1. NAME   The name "satire" comes from the Latin word *satura*, which means primarily "full," and then comes to mean "a mixture full of different things." It seems to have been part of the vocabulary of food. We have the recipe of a sort of salad called *satura*; a dish full of mixed first-fruits offered to the gods was called *lanx satura*; and Juvenal, no doubt in allusion to this strain of meaning, calls his satires by the name of another mixed food, *farrago*, a mishmash of grain given to cattle. Other types of literature have been given food-names: "farce" means "stuffing," "macaronic" poetry was a crude mixture of Latin and Italian, and so forth.[1] The essence of the original name therefore was variety—plus a certain down-to-earth naturalness, or coarseness, or unsophisticated heartiness. Let the rich and refined have their *truite au bleu* and breast of guinea-hen. The ordinary man likes stew, or fish chowder, or *minestrone*, or *paella*, or *pot-au-feu*, or *garbure*, or a platter of mixed cold cuts with pickles and potato-salad and a couple of slices of cheese, in fact a *satura*. To be true, therefore, to its original derivation and first conception, a satire must be varied, it must be large enough to fill the bowl, and it must be coarse and hearty. Highly stylized, polite, and sophisticated satires have been written, of course, particularly in the field of parody—*The Rape of the Lock* is a little masterpiece of aristocratic satire; but they are untypical, almost paradoxical.

The name has nothing to do with the Greek beings

called satyrs, shaggy creatures partly human and partly bestial, often rudely goatish in their behavior. They are never mentioned in connection with satire by Romans or by Greeks (except by one late critic, and in some versions of the title of Petronius's book). The spelling *satira* or *satyra* only came in long after the classical period, largely so that scholars could explain the shocking coarseness of satire by saying that it was inspired by the funny obscene satyr-folk.[2]

We know who first wrote poems and called them *saturae*, "medleys": it was Ennius, the Chaucer of Roman poetry. But long before him, the Romans were enjoying something they called *saturae*. These were variety shows on the stage. They were not real plays, because they had no continuity and no sustained plots: the higher art of dramaturgy had still to be brought in from the Greek world. They were apparently groups of "turns" or "skits" with dialogue (doubtless mainly comical and often spicy) and dancing and imitation of real-life situations: the same sort of low-grade entertainment that always hits the taste of the ordinary public, whether it is called vaudeville, or revue, or the latest Saturday-evening television show. At first these shows were improvised by amateurs; later the professionals took them over. At their highest, they may have been rather like the Italian *commedia dell' arte*, which also relied heavily on improvisation—although the *commedia* had a single basic plot or range of plots, and owed something to the sophisticated Greek and Latin comedy. There is only one really good ancient authority who says anything about these "dramatic *saturae*," and some scholars think his source invented the whole thing, in order to give the poor uncultivated Romans a sort of original primitive drama corresponding to the early stages of Greek drama.[3] But the Italians had a native talent and liking for exactly this kind of show, improvised verse dialogue, competitions in comic abuse and scurrility, mimicry: and it sounds extremely likely that shows of this kind did exist. Perhaps they contained little scenes of cheating and thieving, comparable in a small way to those which appeared later in regular comedy with Plautus. Almost certainly there were character-sketches of real persons or of types, and jokes about local peculiarities—for these things appear, highly developed, in Naevius, the first original Roman comic dramatist.[4]

Therefore, when Ennius called his poems *saturae*, he meant not only that they were a mixed dish of simple coarse ingredients, but that they grew out of an improvised jollification which was (although devoid of plot) dramatic, since it mimicked and made fun of people and their ways, and contained dialogue sung or spoken. All or most of these elements have remained constant in most satire: variety, down-to-earth unsophistication, coarseness, an improvisatory tone, humor, mimicry, echoes of the speaking voice, abusive gibing, and a general feeling, real or assumed, of devil-may-care nonchalance. When Lucilius (as we saw in the second chapter) added to this salty mélange the vinegar and pepper of personal and social criticism, satire assumed its true and final nature.

2. FUNCTION

The function of satire has been variously, and never quite satisfactorily, defined. Since it did not exist in Greek as a clearly marked separate genus of literature, there is no Greek discussion of its nature comparable to Aristotle's analysis of tragedy. Menippus, the Cynic who satirized other philosophers, was called σπουδογέλοιος, "the man who jokes about serious things."[5] This combination of jest and earnest is a permanent mark of satiric writing, but it cannot be called its function. It is the central *method* of satire.

Horace is apparently translating σπουδογέλοιος when he says he wants "to tell the truth, laughing": after saying so he continues with a serious, though lightly phrased, discussion of a social and ethical problem.[6] He has therefore moved from the method of satire to its purpose, or one of its purposes, combined with one of its methods. The satirist, though he laughs, tells the truth.

Many satirists repeat this. But often they declare that their truth is what people do not want to hear. Persius, after saying that Lucilius spoke out boldly and Horace tactfully, goes on:

> I mustn't whisper? in private? into a hole? nowhere?
> Yet here I'll bury it. Book, I myself have seen it:
> everyone has a pair of ass's ears! This secret,
> this laugh of mine, this nothing, I will sell for no
> *Iliad!*[7]

Juvenal asserts that the truth which is his subject-matter is so easy to see that he need only walk through the streets of Rome, or stand at a busy crossing with a notebook.[8] But for him truth is limited to the triumph of wickedness. Immediately after stating that all human life from the days of the Flood is "the farrago of his book," he cries

> And when was there a richer crop of vices?[9]

Soon afterward he adds that to tell these truths, naming names or even saying "That's the man," is dangerous, and will bring the satirist to a fearful death. He determines therefore to describe vice and crime, which are permanent, endemic, in Rome, but to use the names of scoundrels long dead when describing them.[10]

Therefore when the satirist claims to be telling the truth, he may mean that he is trying to help his friends and the public by giving them valuable advice and warnings which they need, or that he is bringing out, into the open, scandals which would horrify the world if they were seen in the light of cruel day. If the first, he expects the truth to do good; if the second, he expects it to hurt many people and to endanger himself.

There are, then, two main conceptions of the purpose of satire, and two different types of satirist. One likes most people, but thinks they are rather blind and foolish. He tells the truth with a smile, so that he will not repel them but cure them of that ignorance which is their worst fault. Such is Horace. The other type hates most people, or despises them. He believes rascality is triumphant in his world; or he says, with Swift, that though he loves individuals he detests mankind. His aim therefore is not to cure, but to wound, to punish, to destroy. Such is Juvenal.

The two types have different beliefs about evil. The misanthropic satirist believes it is rooted in man's nature and in the structure of society. Nothing can eliminate or cure it. Man, or the particular gang of miserable manikins who are under his scrutiny, deserves only scorn and hatred. If he laughs at them, it is not the laughter of fellowship, there is no joy in it, no healing warmth. He laughs with contempt at their pretensions and incongruities and base hypocrisies. This satirist is close to the tragedian.

Many a reader has turned away in revulsion from his work, asking, "Why should he concentrate on such disgusting subjects? What pleasure is there for him, or for us, in gazing on these foul scenes?" Women in particular, with their kind hearts, are prone to make this criticism: very few of them have ever written, or even enjoyed, satire, although they have often been its victims.[11] But this is like asking why the tragic poet must show us only the horrors of extreme suffering: the son kills his mother, the loving husband strangles his faithful wife, the savior of his people is blinded or crucified. For Sophocles or Racine the fundamental fact of human life, so far as it can be put into words, is the hopeless defeat of the best and noblest among us:

martyrdom its own crown. The misanthropic satirist looks at life and finds it, not tragic, nor comic, but ridiculously contemptible and nauseatingly hateful. His vision makes his mission.

This view of life, rather than the tragedian's, is close to that of orthodox Christianity, which holds that all pagans and all heretics together with many professing though sinful Christians, the illimitably greater portion of the human race, are doomed to eternal torment, and that they deserve it. As he thinks this, the Christian sighs. The pessimistic satirist smiles a grim smile, or curls a contemptuous lip.

The other type of satirist is an optimist. He believes that folly and evil are not innate in humanity, or, if they are, they are eradicable. They are diseases which can be cured. They are mistakes which can be corrected. To be sure, there are many cruel and foolish people in every time and every country. Some of them are incurable. Let us make warning examples of them, therefore, in order to help all the others. If we show our fellow-men the painful and absurd consequences of certain types of conduct, personified in Lady Slop and Lord Belial, no doubt these two specimens will suffer when they are pinned down and dissected, but others will be cured; and most people can be cured. This view can be traced back to Socrates. He constantly preached the simple strange doctrine, "No one errs willingly." Stated otherwise, "Virtue is knowledge." Merely understand what good really is, and you needs must love and follow it. Sinners are not devils, fallen forever. They are men self-blinded, and they can open their eyes. The chief Greek philosophical schools followed Socrates in emphasizing the power of reason. If you understand, they said, you will do right. Indeed, you must do right, if you understand. Only strive to see the truth.

Satirists such as Horace believe this. They are kinder,

gentler. They persuade more than they denounce. They laugh with wholesome laughter, oftener than they sneer, far oftener than they shout and shake the fist and point the finger. At the utmost, they will say that the world is topsy-turvy, and what a comical spectacle it makes! (But the pessimistic satirist says the world is hell, why, this is hell, nor are we out of it.) Usually they cut up a few ridiculous or despicable people, in order to warn the rest, the majority, of their readers. If their satire does prick us a little more deeply than is comfortable, it is merely a hypodermic: the pain and the swelling will generate healthful antibodies.

Since there are two divergent types of satirist, there are two different views of the purpose of satire. The optimist writes in order to heal, the pessimist in order to punish. One is a physician, the other an executioner. One sees a world in which the natural condition of man is health—although far too many of us spoil our metabolism by stupidity and catch diseases by carelessness; also, there are certain typhoid-carriers and even reservoir-poisoners and drug-peddlers wandering among us, who must be found and convicted and then put away. The other sees a world populated by recidivist criminals, incurable drug-addicts, gibbering lunatics, ineducable morons, simian savages; full of goats, monkeys, wolves, cobras, leeches, and lice, in human form. For such a world there is no remedy. Some have gone mad even from looking at it. The pessimistic satirist, so that he may not go mad, howls with savage derision, hisses with hate.

But the satirists refuse to be marshaled into two armies, the white and the black. They are willful and independent fellows. The flag of satire is not particolored, white on one side and black on the other. It is polychromatic. *Satura* is variety. A single author will write one satire as an optimist, and follow it by another of the bitterest pessimism. A beginning satirist will erupt like a Paricutin with a thundering fountain of boiling lava, searing all it touches and petrifying black over the ruins and the corpses; but then, some years later, the fire-shotten clouds have rolled away, and the mountainside (although still grimly wrinkled) begins to smile with new lush growth. In a single book, even in a single page, we can see the multiple emotions of a satirist struggling against one another for mastery; and ultimately it is this ferment of repulsion and attraction, disgust and delight, love and loathing, which is the secret of his misery and his power.

3. MOTIVES

The motives of the satirist? They are as complex as the emotions he wishes to evoke, as various as the forms with which he works.

First, he is always moved by personal hatred, scorn, or condescending amusement. Frequently he disclaims this, and asserts that he has banished all personal feelings, that he is writing only for the public good. But he always has a rankling grudge, however well he tries to conceal it, or a twitch of contempt, however gracefully he turns it into a smile. He differs from the writer of acknowledged hate-poetry (such as Hipponax) in that he contrives to generalize and justify his hostility, and usually to make his readers share it.[12] A whole book could be written to unravel the curious links between a satirist's subjects and his private life. For instance—

Thousands of readers have been delighted by the rough but ingenious practical jokes which a little group of friends, in Jules Romains' novel *The Pals,* play upon two small French towns. The towns, it seems, are chosen at random. The pals are in a Montmartre restaurant, drinking and making jokes. Bénin, the gayest of them, goes a little too far. The others throw him out, regret it, and welcome him when, dusty and dishevelled, he returns. He says he has been in the attic. On the wall he saw a large map of France, divided into its eighty-six regional "departments," each with its own shape, like a conglomeration of strange living beings. The towns in each department gaze out like eyes. And two of these eyes, says Bénin, have a nasty expression: disrespectful, even hostile. He takes his friends to the attic, and shows them these malevolent urban eyes. It is true: they seem to squint, to leer at the onlooker. Are the friends to endure this insult passively? No! Retribution must be sought. Revenge must be wreaked. The towns are Issoire and Ambert. They must suffer for it. And, in the rest of this gay satire, suffer they do.

Issoire and Ambert are real places: remote little towns in the center of France. Apparently the friends have chosen them through a humorous whim, to be the subject of a "gratuitous act" of satire. Any other little provincial towns would have been equally appropriate victims. *Les Copains* are Parisians, making fun of the provinces.

So it seems. So the book reads. Nothing, surely, could be more Parisian and sophisticated than its author, Jules Romains, of whose genial imagination the friends are projections.

Yet if we look up his biography, we find that he is not a native Parisian. He was born at Saint-Julien-Chapteuil, which is a tiny place in the Auvergne, about fifty miles from Ambert and Issoire. His real name is not the classically noble Jules Romains, but Louis Farigoule, which sounds countrified and even funny ("Farigoule fait rigoler," he must have been told when he went to Paris). Therefore his novel is not only a Parisian's satire on the backwardness of the provinces, but a provincial's mocking revenge on his own origins.

Or consider Rabelais. Much of the First Book describes a terrible war between Gargantua's father Grandgousier

(Bigthroat) and the neighboring King Picrochole (Bitterbile), ending in a glorious victory for Gargantua command-
ing his father's army. It reads like a parody of all grand
heroic warfare: even Gargantua's address to the defeated
enemy is modeled on a speech by the Roman emperor
Trajan, and contains allusions to recent historical events
such as Charles VIII's subjugation of Brittany. But in fact
the war is a comical exaggeration of a dispute between
Rabelais' own father and a neighboring landowner over
certain fishing and water rights in the river Loire; even
the minor characters bear the names of men who were involved in the lawsuit; and the cities and fortresses of the
war are all tiny places near Rabelais' own home.[13] Therefore Grandgousier is Rabelais' father, Picrochole is the
rancorous neighbor, and Gargantua—

A noticeably large number of satirists have been im-
pelled by a rankling sense of personal inferiority, of social
injustice, of exclusion from a privileged group. Menippus
was a slave. Bion's father was a slave and he himself was
sold into slavery. Horace's father was a slave, although
Horace was born free. Pope was a Catholic in a Protestant
England which penalized all Papists. Lucian was a Greek-
speaking Syrian. Swift and Joyce were Anglo-Irishmen;
Byron, Orwell, and Waugh, Anglo-Scots. (Byron, though
he called himself an "English bard," was brought up in
Scotland speaking broad Scots. George Orwell's real name
was Eric Blair: his family background was Scottish and he
spent his last years in Scotland. Evelyn Waugh's father was
an Edinburgh publisher, and his elder brother is called
Alec; he also suffered from going to a not-very-good public
school and a not-very-good Oxford college, and he is a
Roman Catholic convert.) Pope was tiny and painfully
deformed; Boileau was nervous and sickly; Cervantes had
a maimed hand; Byron had a crippled foot. Juvenal, Cer-

vantes, Gogol, and Parini were all men of talent forced into careers which they felt to be useless or degrading.

In fact, most satirists seem to belong to one of two main classes. Either they were bitterly disappointed early in life, and see the world as a permanent structure of injustice; or they are happy men of overflowing energy and vitality, who see the rest of mankind as poor ridiculous puppets only half-alive, flimsy fakes and meager scoundrels. Such are Aristophanes and Rabelais and Lucilius and Tassoni and Petronius and Dryden and Quevedo and Browning and Campbell and Abraham a Sancta Clara.

But there is always one person, or one type, or one group, or one social class, or one national structure, on which the satirist focuses most of his amusement and his loathing, and from whom he derives the strength to generalize and vivify his work.

The second impulse is openly avowed by many satirists. They wish to stigmatize crime or ridicule folly, and thus to aid in diminishing or removing it. "The true end of satire," says Dryden, "is the amendment of vices by correction." He goes on to say that the frank satirist is no more an enemy to the offender than the physician is an enemy to his patient, when he prescribes a harsh remedy to make surgery unnecessary.[14] That may not be universally, or even commonly, true; but at least the first, the general statement, is correct. If the satirist is ironical, he avows it in reverse. ("Young my lord," says Parini deferentially, "let me explain the full beauty and importance of Your Grace's daily routine.") If not, he makes it explicit, either in prologues and epilogues, or at important points of the text. Thus at the very end of Cervantes' masterpiece, Don Quixote dictates his will, and leaves all his property to his niece, on condition that, if she marries a man who knows anything whatsoever about romances of chivalry, the entire legacy will go to charity.

Aesthetic, in a strange way, is the third motive. It is the pleasure which all artists and writers feel in making their own special pattern, manipulating their chosen material. The patterns of satire, as we have seen, are interesting because they are so complicated. Any writer who sets out to use them must be attracted by their difficulties. He needs a huge vocabulary, a lively flow of humor combined with a strong serious point of view, an imagination so brisk that it will always be several jumps ahead of his readers, and taste good enough to allow him to say shocking things without making the reader turn away in disdain, as one does from an obscene graffito on a wall. Unless he is writing a parody (in which case his pattern is already given) he must appear to be improvising, and yet afford us the satisfaction, when we reflect on his work, of seeing an underlying structure. There is a paradox in this aspect of the satirist's work. Most artists like to paint handsome men, beautiful women, rich landscapes, positive energetic forms and textures. Few can look at and immortalize on canvas the contents of a garbage can, the colors of an open sore, the lingering currents of a stream of sewage. Yet the satirist must do this. He enjoys it. For him, a rotten fish shining and stinking in a dark pantry is more fascinating than an opening rose; a rabble of rats fighting over a corpse is more compelling than a swarm of butterflies dancing over a meadow; the senseless boasting of a dandiprat and the serpentine evasions of a politician enthrall him more than a wise man teaching or a lovely girl singing. Such is his material. Out of that, with a curious mixture of love and hate, he makes the pattern which is satire.

Fourth is a motive which is not operative for all satirists: the pessimists will not admit it, the jokers seldom think about it. Still, certain satires gain greatly from it. They are protreptic. Not only do they denounce in such a way as to warn and to deter. They give positive advice. They set up an exemplar to copy. They state an ideal. Thus, in his fifth satire, Juvenal describes a dependent's dinner in a great nobleman's house: a hideous evening, bad food, worse wine, deliberate humiliations. No moral is drawn, except that it would be better to beg in the streets. But in his eleventh poem, after a short introduction on the absurdities of Roman gourmandise, he invites a friend to a quiet dinner in his own home, and describes the modest but tasteful menu. Although the satire contains some keen points of criticism, its strongest part is its positive statement of the ideal of moderation, that healthy tranquil retiring pleasure which is truly Epicurean. So also Rabelais first describes, with much ludicrous and sordid detail, a thoroughly ill-bred youth, Prince Gargantua, talented and energetic but allowed to grow vulgar and stupid; then he puts him under a new teacher and describes his ideally good education.[15] So later, after the war against King Bitterbile has been described, with much blood and many wounds, Rabelais explains the constitution of the victorious Gargantua's new foundation, the Abbey of Thelema, which is an ideal society for handsome and cultivated young ladies and gentlemen. Although some are too embittered, others too convulsed with laughter, to give voice to their positive beliefs, all satirists are at heart idealists.

Hail, Satire! Hail, clear-eyed, sharp-tongued, hot-tempered, outwardly disillusioned and secretly idealistic Muse!

ABBREVIATIONS

THE names of periodicals and standard works of reference are abbreviated according to the system set out by the *American Journal of Archaeology* in 1958: *CP* = *Classical Philology, PL* = Migne, *Patrologia Latina,* and so on.

Other abbreviations are the well-known survivors of Latin: cf. = compare, init. = beginning, med. = middle, fin. = end, ibid. = in the same book or in the same passage; c. means both chapter and circa (about).

NOTES ◈

I. INTRODUCTION

1. Juvenal 1.51-57 and 6.634-661.

2. Juvenal 3.232-248 and 254-261. Although apparently informal, this fine passage covers an entire twenty-four-hour day in the city, from the sleepless night (232-238) through early morning (239-248) and the lunch hour (249-253) to the afternoon rush (254-267) and so into the horrors of a metropolitan evening (268-301) and night (302-314).

3. Hobbes, *Leviathan*, Part 1, c. 13.

4. Pope, *Dunciad* 3.101-117.

5. Gibbon, *Decline and Fall of the Roman Empire*, c. 71.

6. Pope, *Dunciad* 3.36.

7. *Candide*, c. 23. The victim was John Byng, Admiral of the Blue, who was court-martialed and shot for failing to relieve Minorca.

8. The speech by Johnson's ghost is in the Smith brothers' *Rejected Addresses* (1812): see p. 142 of this book.

9. Swift's letter to Pope dated November 27, 1726.

10. On Plato's *Menexenus* see p. 137 of this book.

11. Juvenal 1.30.

12. This is in the introductory letter addressed by Erasmus to Thomas More.

13. Pope, *Dunciad* 3.165-170.

14. J. C. Squire, another beery poet, was satirized by Roy Campbell in couplets directly inspired by Pope:

> A speedy death to all his verse he fears
> Who so attempts to pickle it in tears,
> Taking as raw material for his lays
> The good old English beer he loves to praise,
> To which all other exit he denies
> Save through the whizzing hosepipe of his eyes.

(*The Georgiad*, London, 1931, p. 23.)

15. Ruskin, *Aratra Pentelici*, Lecture III, "Imagination," paragraph 85.

16. Voltaire, *Candide*, c. 10 fin.

17. Juvenal 3.261-267.

18. *Troilus and Cressida* 5.10.33-57.

19. Swift, *Proposal for Correcting the English Language*, eds. Davis and Landa (Oxford, 1957), 243.

II. DIATRIBE

1. Horace, *Sermones* 1.10.48-49. On *rudis et Graecis intacti carminis auctor* (1.10.66), often supposed to refer to Ennius as chronologically the first Latin verse-satirist, see E. Fraenkel, *Horace* (Oxford, 1957) 131 n. 3, who quotes and accepts Nipperdey's interpretation, that *auctor* means, not Ennius (who after all was a Hellenist) but any crude writer.

2. Lucilius (ed. F. Marx, 2 vols., Leipzig, 1904 and 1905), in the second satire of Book 9.

3. In an apt image characteristically exaggerated, Persius (1.115) says Lucilius "broke his jaw-tooth" on his victims.

4. *Serm.* 1.4.1-7.

5. *Ep.* 2.2.60.

6. Marx in his edition of Lucilius (cited in n. 2) compares fragment 836 with Aristophanes, *Wasps* 184; but there Lucilius is really parodying *Odyssey* 9.366-367, while Aristophanes is apparently mocking a recent play by his rival Cratinus.

7. It is strange that Horace should say there was no difference between Aristophanes and Lucilius except their meters, and totally neglect the dramatic character of the Greek comedies (*Serm.* 1.4.6-7). Did he fail to see that the Old Comedies were plays (because they were so disorderly, and were never staged in his time), or did he imply that Lucilius's satires could be put on the stage? Heinze, in his note on this passage of Horace, says that Greek and Roman literary critics believed meter was extremely important in defining and distinguishing literary genres; but surely a sensitive poet such as Horace cannot have used such a superficial standard?

8. Such is Satire 2, which was apparently built around a scene in a law-court: compare the trial in Aristophanes' *Wasps* and the contest of Aeschylus and Euripides in *The Frogs*.

9. The link between comedy and satire in both Lucilius and Horace is strongly emphasized by M. Puelma Piwonka in *Lucilius und Kallimachos* (Frankfurt a/M, 1949) 60-63, who cites, among other passages, Horace's comparison of the realistic quasi-prosaic styles of satire and comedy in *Serm.* 1.4.39-56. However, there are not nearly so many direct quotations and imitations of Old and New Comedy in either author as Mr. Piwonka implies. I believe also that some of his parallels and reconstructions go too far, as when he finds a dramatic *Paraklausithyronszene* in a mention of Tantalus (Lucil. frg. 140) and in the crudely comic episode of Horace's sexual disappointment (*Serm.* 1.5.82-85). That little adventure is almost the exact reverse of "love locked out": Horace is not standing in the cold street but waiting in his bedroom, and he does not stay awake all night weeping and singing serenades. Again, it is far-fetched to

say that one remark in Lucilius ("God preserve us from dirty language," frg. 899) means that Lucilius himself will avoid obscenity in his satires: for he certainly does not do so, and the tone of the remark sounds much more like one of his comic characters—perhaps, as Marx suggests, a shocked lady.

10. Hor. *Serm.* 2.3.11-12.

11. Hor. *Ep.* 2.2.59-60.

12. The metaphor by which wit is called salt is too common in Greek and Latin to make it necessary for us to interpret the phrase as an allusion to the fact that Bion's father sold salt fish.

13. For a description of some of these gypsy priests see Apuleius, *Metamorphoses* 8.24-30.

14. For an elaboration of this point see P. Wendland's *Hellenistisch-römische Kultur* (Tübingen, 1912) 245-246. On St. Paul's use of some of the methods of the diatribe and on the connection between the diatribe and Christian preaching generally, see E. Norden, *Antike Kunstprosa* (Leipzig, 1898) 2.506 n. 1, and 2.556-558. There is a good analysis of the style of the diatribe in the same work, 1.129-131. The whole subject is clearly and penetratingly treated in an old but still useful book, S. Dill's *Roman Society from Nero to Marcus Aurelius* (London, 1905²), Book III, c. 2, "The Philosophic Missionary."

15. We know Bion chiefly through his life in Diogenes Laertius 4.46-57; see also von Arnim in *PW/RE* 3.483-485 and C. Wachsmuth, *Sillographi graeci* (Leipzig, 1885²) 73-77. His discourses have disappeared, but they can be reconstructed from quotations, and descriptions, and imitations by his follower Teles, whose work has been well edited by O. Hense (*Teletis reliquiae*, Tübingen, 1909²). On Teles see also A. Modrze in *PW/RE* 2.5.375-381, and U. von Wilamowitz-Moellendorff, *Antigonos von Karystos* (*Philologische Untersuchungen* 4, 1881) Excurs 3, pp. 292-319.

16. Eratosthenes in Diogenes Laertius 4.52, and Theophrastus in Strabo 1.15: both possibly referring to the fact (which Bion himself bluntly admitted) that his mother had been a whore.

17. Wilamowitz, on p. 307 of his study quoted in n. 15 above, suggests that the diatribe as Bion practiced it was a cross between the Socratic dialogue and the display speech of the sophists; but this rather overlooks the studied informality of the diatribe, which is far removed from the elegantly symmetrical sentences and gracefully turned platitudes or paradoxes of the *epideixis*.

18. There is a useful list of the principal themes of the diatribe in A. Oltramare, *Les Origines de la diatribe romaine* (Geneva, 1926), Introduction, section 4. On their survival see P. Wendland, "Philo und die kynisch-stoische Diatribe," in P. Wendland and O. Kern,

Beiträge zur Geschichte der griechischen Philosophie und Religion (Berlin, 1895).

19. In c. 1, sections 4 and 5, of his book cited in n. 9 M. Puelma Piwonka draws a sharp distinction between the *sermones* of Lucilius and Horace on one hand and diatribe on the other. First, he says, diatribe is aimed at the general public, while Lucilius and Horace speak to a relatively small audience of friends (Lucilius 26.592-596; Hor. *Serm.* 1.10.74-91). Second, the diatribe is a monologue, while the *sermo* is more like a conversation. Third, Lucilius dislikes philosophy, and Horace, though more inclined to philosophizing, is still rather a dilettante. And, fourth, the philosophical teachers who make most use of the diatribe, the Cynics and Stoics, are odious to both satirists, as extremists, *immoderati, inepti.* The argument is valuable, but a little exaggerated. Lucilius (as far as we can tell from his remains) did not care for philosophy; but Horace knew quite a lot about it, and enjoyed discussing it. He thought the Stoics were absurd doctrinaires and he despised the Cynics, but he did not refrain from using some of their arguments. Although his *sermones* are often addressed to individuals and pretend to be conversations, still, such important satires as the first of Book 1 (to Maecenas on discontent) and the third of Book 2 (a discussion of the Stoical theme that all non-Stoics are insane) are but diatribes arranged as conversations: meant to be, as it were, overheard by the public. In a useful article, "Satire as Popular Philosophy," *CP* 15 (1920) 138-157, C. W. Mendell points out that the Roman satirists were more concerned with ethical themes than with invective (which is why Juvenal and Horace are called *ethici* in the Middle Ages). Horace's satirical works are full of important moral terms such as *sapiens* and *stultus, uirtus* and *uitium.* See also c. 7 of Oltramare's book, cited in n. 18.

20. Diels, *Fragmente der Vorsokratiker* (6th edn. by W. Kranz, Berlin, 1951) B15, pp. 132-133.

21. Fragments of Homeric parody in Wachsmuth, *Sillographi* 191-200.

22. Σπουδογέλοιος, Strabo 16.2.29 and Diogenes Laertius 9.17; the alternative form σπουδαιογέλοιος appears (according to Liddell-Scott-Jones) only in an inscription. The thought, if not the actual word, comes up in a jolly chorus of Aristophanes, *Frogs* 389-390: πολλὰ μὲν γέλοια εἰπεῖν, πολλὰ δὲ σπουδαῖα. Menippus wrote a Descent to the World of the Dead, in which he saw and (like a true Cynic) relished the humiliation of those who in this life had been great men. From Lucian's imitations of it, it appears to have been a burlesque of the visit of Odysseus to the dead in *Odyssey* 11; but it may also have been inspired by the comic *katabasis* of Dionysus in Aristophanes' *Frogs.* We hear also of a Flight to Heaven, modeled (as

Helm in *PW/RE* 15.1.889 infers) on the flight of Trygaeus in Aristophanes' *Peace*. We may say therefore that Menippus was the first philosophical satirist to make his entire work funny, and that he modeled it on Aristophanic comedy.

23. Menippus was a Syrian, from Gadara. *The Arabian Nights* constantly slip into rhyming prose and thence into verse: see Burton's "Terminal Essay," c. 5, in his translation. Professor Moses Hadas, to whom I owe the suggestion that the shape of Menippean satire was Semitic in origin, explains that there is an Arabic form of humorous philosophical discussion in prose mingled with verse, called the *maqama* or "session." See his *Ancilla to Classical Reading* (New York, 1954) 58; but also O. Immisch, *NJbb* 47 (1921) 409-421.

24. Lucian says he "dug up" Menippus: see his *Twice Accused* 23. The *Symposium* of Menippus was an ancestor of Julian's remarkable satire on his predecessors, Συμπόσιον ἢ Κρόνια, on which see p. 167.

25. On Lucilius and Callimachus see M. Puelma Piwonka's book (cited in n. 9), especially c. 4, section 7. Lucilius 698 quotes and criticizes Archilochus, and Marx in his edition suggests that all his twenty-seventh book was devoted to a critical discussion of Archilochus. On Archilochus and Hipponax in Horace's epodes see *Epod.* 6.13-14; on Archilochus as an inspiration for Horace's *sermones, Serm.* 2.3.12. C. M. Dawson has a good study of Callimachus's iambics in *YCS* 11 (1950) 1-168.

26. Margites is an extension of μάργος, "mad," as Thersites of the Aeolic θέρσος, "boldness."

27. Few if any scholars now believe *Margites* was composed by the author or authors of the *Iliad* and *Odyssey*. It looks like folk-material put into a sophisticated meter about the time of Archilochus. The fragments and testimonia are on pp. 152-159 of the fifth volume of T. W. Allen's edition of Homer (Oxford, 1912). Aristotle's mention of the poem has misled some people into assuming that it must have been a mock epic; but it was not called a παρῳδία, rather a παίγνιον. See F. J. Lelièvre, "The Basis of Ancient Parody," *Greece and Rome* 1 (1954) 80 n. 22. A papyrus with 21 fragmentary lines (hexameters irregularly mingled with iambics) which may be part of *Margites* was edited by E. Lobel in *Oxyrhynchus Papyri Part XXII* (London, 1954) no. 2309. They are interpreted and the poem is reconstructed in an extremely ingenious essay by H. Langebeck in *HSCP* 63 (1958) 33-63. He appears to me to make it probable that the hero was not a dull clod, but a bogus intellectual who thought he knew everything and was easily hoodwinked. I might suggest that the emperor Claudius in the *Apocolocyntosis* is stamped from the same mold.

28. Ennius's *Hedyphagetica* was a translation of *Hedypathia* by the fourth-century Sicilian author Archestratus. This poem goes

into great detail on the best varieties of fish and other delicacies. Since it is in hexameters, and uses the diction of Homer and other lofty writers for a trivial subject, it looks like a satiric parody; and yet the author seems to take the subject quite seriously, with no trace of contempt or amusement. Perhaps it should be classified (like Ovid's *Art of Love*) not as a satire but as a frivolous didactic poem. On the *Attic Dinner* by Matro of Pitana see note 15 on chapter III. (These authors are both edited and explained by P. Brandt in Volume 1 of the *Corpusculum Poesis Epicae Graecae Ludibundae*, Leipzig, 1888.) As for Ennius, Horace does not speak of him as a satirist. Yet Ennius did publish four books of poetry called *Saturae*, which contained some of the characteristic features and some at least of the critical function of fully developed satire. Their remains are on pp. 382-395 of E. H. Warmington's *Fragments of Old Latin* I (Cambridge, Mass., 1935). In 14-19 we have part of a monologue by a parasite exposing his own impudence; in 21 we hear Ennius's own voice; on p. 394 there is a reference to a dialogue between two hypostatized figures, Life and Death; and on p. 389 to a charming fable translated by Ennius from Aesop in the popular meter of trochaic tetrameters. All these might well occur in satiric poetry, and indeed the monologue of the parasite reminds us of Juvenal's ninth satire. But there is no evidence that Ennius in his satires ever attacked any individual personally, as Lucilius did; and it is because of these personal attacks that Horace praises Lucilius and calls him the successor of the Attic comedians, the founder of Roman satire (*Serm.* 1.4.1-8, 1.10.46-51). M. Puelma Piwonka, in c. 3, section 2 of his book cited in n. 9, attempts to dissociate Ennius still further from Lucilius and Horace.

29. Hor. *Serm.* 2.5, the interview between Ulysses and Tiresias, may well have been inspired by Menippus's *Nekuia*, although not directly modeled on it; see R. Helm, *Lucian und Menipp* (Leipzig, 1906) 19.

30. *Apologia* 37c8-d1.

31. The extant monologue satires in Latin (excluding the satires of Lucilius and Varro, which are so fragmentary that we can never be quite sure of their original shape) are: Horace 1.1, 1.2, 1.3, 1.4, 1.6, 1.10, 2.2, and 2.6; Persius 1, 2, 3, and 5; all Juvenal's poems except 4 and 9. Some of these satires open by addressing a real person—who, however, does not reply (e.g. Horace 1.1 and Juvenal 6); and many have short passages of dialogue with an imaginary interlocutor or interlocutors; but they are basically monologues. Then there are monologues disguised as dialogues: Horace 2.1, 2.3, 2.4, 2.5, 2.7, 2.8, and Juvenal 9. In six of these the chief speaker is not the poet himself but another character: Horace 2.3, 2.4, 2.5, 2.7, 2.8,

and Juvenal 9; and in Horace 2.5, the poet does not appear at all. Horace 2.8 is an oddity, for it is really a narrative in the form of a monologue with Horace acting as interlocutor. Juvenal 15 contains a detailed and vivid narrative, but most of the poem is an indignant monologue commenting on the story. Satires in the monologue-form of a letter are uncommon in Latin, but Horace's poetic *Letters* are quite close to satire (e.g. 1.18), and Persius 6 looks like a letter. Of the other Latin satires, Horace 1.5, 1.7, 1.9, and 2.8 (mentioned above as a hybrid) are narratives, as is Petronius's *Satyrica*; some of Varro's best satires—*Endymiones, Eumenides, Sexagessis*—are narratives too. To complete the classification, Horace 1.8, Juvenal 4, Seneca's *Apocolocyntosis*, and probably Varro's *Sesculixes*, although narrative in form, are basically parodies: Horace parodying a dedicatory epigram with an aetiological addition, Juvenal an epic poem by Statius, Seneca a historical monograph, Varro the *Odyssey*. On Petronius see p. 114.

32. Satire and epic, Juvenal 1.51-57; satire and tragedy, 6.634-661. Juvenal's satires also received much of the power of the monologues on ethical and political subjects, called "declamations," which were fashionable in the first century A.D.

33. Weinreich remarks on p. xc of the Introduction to his *Römische Satiren* (Zürich, 1949) that the very titles *Against Eutropius* and *Against Rufinus* are not right for satire, which is true. They stand half way between satire and invectives such as Cicero's attacks on Antony and Catiline. In satire their closest relative is Juvenal 4, which opens (1-27) with a fragment of Juvenal's *In Crispinum*.

34. The *Graeculus esuriens* of Juvenal 3.58-125 is someone quite like Lucian, even in his volubility and versatility. Not even the ridiculous flatteries of the Greeks in Juvenal 3.86-108 are as bad as Lucian's toadying panegyric of the beauties of Panthea, the mistress of Verus Caesar, in his *Pictures*; and, as Juvenal observed, he was not Greek by blood:

Syrus in Tiberim defluxit Orontes (3.62).

However, there is no good evidence that the two men knew each other: see G. Highet, *Juvenal the Satirist* (Oxford, 1954) 252 and 296.

35. In an interesting essay, "La satire dans les *Lettres* de Saint Jérome," *REL* 43 (1945) 209-226, C. Favez explains how the satiric spirit in St. Jerome overflowed in his violently imaginative and drastically colloquial denunciations of heretical Christians and other backsliders, but, by implication, shows that the saint did not think he was writing satire. A much richer study by D. S. Wiesen, *St. Jerome as a Satirist* (Ithaca, N.Y., 1964), explains that Jerome had all the bitter critical temper and the caustic tongue of the satirist (even sometimes to his own embarrassment as a Christian) and that

he and others occasionally thought of himself as doing a satirist's work; but that, except in one or two books such as *Against Rufinus*, he seldom showed the variety and wit which are essentials of satire.

36. What happened in the Middle Ages was that satire of the monologue type was displaced by invective or "complaint." This process is well described by Mr. John Peter in c. 2 of his *Complaint and Satire in Early English Literature* (Oxford, 1956). Section 3 of that chapter discusses, clearly and illuminatingly, the question whether Bernard's poem is a real satire.

37. This is from "Against the Pride of the Ladies," on pp. 153-155 of *The Political Songs of England from the Reign of John to that of Edward II*, ed. T. Wright (London, 1839). I have slightly adapted the text: in particular, "jewels" (which goes so well with "jowls") is in the original "clogs." There is also a good satire "On the Consistory Courts" which were trying to punish the peasants for having love affairs: see pp. 155-159.

38. The satirical passage from St. Bernard is *Sermo 33, Super Canticum (PL* 133, col. 959), cited by Owst, pp. 271-272. The selection from Bromyard is in Owst, pp. 316-317; the idea, as Dr. Owst explains, also occurs in *Piers Plowman* and in an early satiric poem attributed to Walter Map.

39. For Golias *De conjuge non ducenda* and the poems of Walter Map see *The Latin Poems Commonly Attributed to Walter Mapes*, ed. T. Wright (London, 1841).

40. Owst, on p. 386 n. 3 of his book cited on p. 45 says that the entire *Wife of Bath's Prologue* is no more than a series of variations on the theme of the gadabout woman, taken by preachers from the short description in Proverbs 7.10-12. This seems a little like over-simplification.

41. *As You Like It* 2.7.50-51.

42. Abraham a Sancta Clara differs from Bion in the fact that Bion was almost wholly negative and sceptical, while Abraham was a devout Christian; but there are many marked coincidences in their styles. Bion said about wives that an ugly one was a ποινή and a pretty one a κοινή (Diog. Laert. 4.48). So Abraham warns his readers of the dangers of love and marriage, saying that Venus is We-nuss: "We, was manche harte Nuss muss der Verliebte aufbeissen!" (*Judas der Erzschelm*, Book 3, p. 69); in marriage one must choose carefully, "damit man nit anstatt einer Gertraut ein Beeren-Haut, anstatt eines Paulen einen Faulen, anstatt einer Dorothee ein Ach und Wehe, anstatt einer Sibill eine Pfefferl-Mühl heyrathe" (*Judas*, Book 1, p. 15). In the address to the reader before Book 3, he says that he does not want "der Heil. Lehr einen Fassnacht-Mantel anlegen," which is like τὴν φιλοσοφίαν ἄνθινα ἐνέδυσεν of Bion (Diog.Laert.

4.52). There is a sound, though rather unsympathetic, portrait of Abraham in c. 2 of R. A. Kann's *Study in Austrian Intellectual History* (New York, 1960).

43. Roy Campbell, *The Georgiad* (London, 1931) 16-17.

44. For identifications of most of the characters in these novels and an account of Miller's life while he was writing and living them, see Alfred Perlès, *My Friend Henry Miller* (New York, 1956).

45. Mort Sahl is famous enough to have been the subject of a full-length character-sketch in *Time* (August 15, 1960). It contains some good specimens of his butterfly-plus-wasp diatribes.

46. Commenting on Terence's *Phormio*, Donatus explicitly says that the parasite Phormio's speech in 339f. is not taken from the Greek original of the comedy, but from Ennius's satires: he then quotes six lines. They can be found in Warmington's *Remains of Old Latin* I (Loeb series, Cambridge, Mass., 1935) 388-389. A contemporary monologist, Bob Newhart, who has probably never heard of Ennius, delivers a diatribe on the same plan. Speaking in the character of a disgruntled common soldier in George Washington's army, he piles up Army gripes about all the great figures of the War of Independence. "You hear what Nutty George pulled last night? The dollar across the Potomac, you didn't hear about that? You know he had us out till three in the morning looking for the damn thing? . . . There was some nut flashing a light on and off in the church tower all night. The minute he quits, this drunk goes riding through town screaming. . . . Here comes one of the real weirdos of them all—Benny: the one with the square glasses. Next time we have a thunderstorm, watch him!" (*New York Times*, April 17, 1961.)

47. In his charming introductory letter dedicating *The Praise of Folly* to his friend Thomas More (partly because "folly" in Greek is *moria*, with a long o) Erasmus defines it as a satire, by saying it is both funny and biting, by pointing out that, although ostensibly a piece of foolery, it has a serious meaning, and by listing among its predecessors Athenian Old Comedy, *The Battle of Frogs and Mice,* Seneca's *Apocolocyntosis*, and a work by Lucian.

48. Browning called these serious monologues *Dramatic Idyls* and *Dramatic Romances*. They bear about the same relation to regular poetic drama as his satiric monologues to satiric comedy.

49. Aristotle, *Nicomachean Ethics* 1108a22 and 1124b30.

50. *Hamlet* 3.2.97-99 and 312-314. See a detailed analysis by N. Knox: *The word irony and its context, 1500-1755* (Durham, N.C., 1961).

51. A. R. Thompson, in a good little book called *The Dry Mock* (Berkeley, Cal., 1948), says that dramatic irony was first so named and described by Connop Thirlwall, the British scholar, in 1833

(pp. 143-148). On p. 34 he gives a fine epigram by Max Eastman summing up the effect: the playwright exchanges with the audience "a gruesome wink." He distinguishes three types of dramatic irony, all based on contrast: irony of speech, in which the words of a statement contrast with the facts behind them; irony of character, in which a man's outward appearance and behavior are at variance with his real nature; and irony of events, in which we see the contrast of expectation and fulfillment.

52. *Personal Recollections of the Life and Times . . . of Valentine Lord Cloncurry* (Dublin, 1849) 46.

53. "You call your satires, libels: I would rather call my satires, epistles," wrote Pope to Swift: see his *Correspondence*, ed. G. Sherburn, vol. 3 (Oxford, 1956) 366. I owe the quotation originally to Mr. Ian Jack, *Augustan Satire* (Oxford, 1952) 100. Incidentally, I believe he is a little off the mark in describing the Latin *satura* as "in essence an informal ethical epistle, without a plot." An ethical epistle would not naturally have a "plot"; and apart from that, letters for the Romans were rather more formal than speech. The obscenities and absurdities of much Latin satire would have been impermissible in a letter, but are excused by the fact that they are supposed to be ebullitions of lively talk. Still, the connection of *sermo* and *epistula* is close: see M. Puelma Piwonka (cited in n. 9) 91-93.

54. On the *épîtres du coq-à-l'âne* see O. Rossettini, *Les Influences anciennes et italiennes sur la satire en France au XVIᵉ siècle* (Florence, 1958) 46-48.

55. On St. Jerome's letters see n. 35.

56. Byron, *Vision of Judgment*, stanzas 75 and 78.

57. Pope, *Epilogue to the Satires, Dialogue II*, 20-25. Mr. Ian Jack, in note 2 on p. 112 of his book cited in n. 53 above, points out that the distinction between a poetic letter [or monologue] and a dialogue was, for the Augustan poets, purely one of rhetorical structure and convenience, and that Pope actually converted his third *Moral Essay* from an "epistle" into a dialogue.

III. PARODY

1. See R. Lebel, *Marcel Duchamp* (tr. G. H. Hamilton, New York, 1959) 44-45. The title was L.H.O.O.Q., which appears to be a distortion of LOOK, but if spelled out letter by letter in French becomes the vulgar phrase "Elle a chaud au cul." This masterpiece is reproduced on plate 90 in Mr. Lebel's book: it is now in a private collection in the United States.

2. See K. Clark, *The Nude* (New York, 1956) 122 and 356.

3. There is a useful article called "The Basis of Ancient Parody" by F. J. Lelièvre in *Greece and Rome* 1 (1954) 66-81, which shows

that parody meant two things, principally, in Greece and Rome: one, reproducing a passage from an author and applying it to a comic, humble, or otherwise inappropriate subject; the other, reproducing the general style and thought of an author while exaggerating his salient characteristics, and not necessarily quoting any passage verbatim.

4. Cf. Sophocles, *Antigone* 1.

5. So says Clytemnestra to Cassandra, in Aeschylus, *Agamemnon* 1060-1061.

6. Scarcely exaggerated at all: e.g. Sophocles, *Philoctetes* 1230-1234.

7. This parody, attributed to "an anonymous delegate from a country of the Eastern Hemisphere," was published in the *New York World-Telegram and Sun* for April 20, 1960.

8. *Judas der Erzschelm*, Book 2, p. 84. In the same work, Book 3, p. 103, Abraham produces a sort of rhyming parody of the 110th Psalm. He says that many men when they sing vespers are thinking of worldly things, like this:

DIXIT DOMINVS DOMINO MEO
heut gehen wir zum Herrn Leo
SEDE A DEXTRIS MEIS
heunt werde ich gewinnen, das ist gewiss
DONEC PONAM INIMICOS TVOS
gestern hab ich verspilt drey Mass
SCABELLVM PEDVM TVORVM
heunt wird sich das Glück kehren um
VIRGAM VIRTVTIS TVAE
was gilts ich werd haben *figuri tre*
IN SPLENDORIBVS SANCTORVM EX VTERO ANTE
              LVCIFERVM GENVI TE
so dann bezahlen mich alle
IVRAVIT DOMINVS ET NON POENITEBIT EVM
ich will sehen, dass ich bei Zeiten komm
TV ES SACERDOS IN AETERNVM SECVNDVM ORDINEM
              MELCHISEDECH
sauff ich zum meisten, und sie bezahlen die Zech
DOMINVS A DEXTRIS TVIS
schau dass wir eine Ganss jagen an die Spiess
CONFREGIT IN DIE IRAE SVAE REGES
eine gute Jausen ist nit böss. . . . [*etc.*]

So, from Byzantium, we hear of attacks on a drunken monk and on a man who refused to wear a beard, in formulae arranged on the lines of the Mass (Baynes and Moss, *Byzantium*, Oxford, 1949, p. 250).

9. Hesketh Pearson, *Labby* (New York, 1936) 256. Labouchère also commented on Queen Victoria's polyphiloprogenitive nature in

a slightly blasphemous parody of Jesus' aphorism in Matthew 6.34: "Sufficient for the reign are the grandchildren thereof." (*Ibid.* p. 252.)

10. S. N. Behrman, *Portrait of Max* (New York, 1960) 89-97.

11. *Goody Blake and Harry Gill.*

12. *Simon Lee, the Old Huntsman.*

13. *Miscellaneous Sonnets*, Part III, xiii. I cannot resist quoting a delicious piece of self-parody by the Parnassian Catulle Mendès: the first line of his poem *Le Disciple*:

Le Bouddha rêve, ayant dans ses mains ses orteils.

14. J.K.S. (i.e., James Kenneth Stephen), *Lapsus Calami, new edition*, Cambridge, 1891.

15. The name of Pigres of Halicarnassus, who was the brother of Queen Artemisia (allied with Xerxes in his invasion of Greece), is traditionally connected with this poem; but it looks more like a product of the age of Aristophanes, some fifty years later. There are a good article, with bibliography, s.v. *Pigres*, by W. Aly, in *PW/RE* 20.2.1313-1316, and a little treatise full of interesting side information by G. W. Waltemath, *De Batrachomyomachiae origine, natura, historia, versionibus, imitationibus* (Stuttgart, 1880). There are two different accounts of the origin of parody in Greece. Aristotle (*Poetics* 1448a12) says it was first written by Hegemon of Thasos, a man who lived during the Peloponnesian War. Polemo, quoted by Athenaeus (15, 698b), asserts that the inventor of parody was the bitter lampoonist, Hipponax, who lived much earlier, about 540 B.C. But there is nothing to support this, except four lines of denunciation by Hipponax which are certainly epic in tone although applied to a disreputable subject: it would be more correct to describe them as merely abusive, like the angry speech of Achilles in *Iliad* 1 and the invectives of Hesiod in *Works and Days*. Parody as an individual type of poetry was therefore introduced by Hegemon, who had originally been a rhapsode, a serious reciter of epic poetry. His most famous work was a *Battle of Giants*, which amused the Athenians even in the grim days of their Sicilian expedition. For the surviving fragments of Hipponax and Hegemon, and discussions, see Brandt, *Corpusculum* 1.31-36 and 37-49.

On the other hand, since so much Greek literature grew out of folk-poetry, it is tempting to think that Hegemon did not "invent" parody, but rather stylized an existing form. F. W. Householder, ΠΑΡΩΙΔΙΑ, *CP* 39 (1944) 8, suggests that after serious recitations of epic poetry by the professional rhapsodists, there appeared amateur parodists who made fun of their matter and style. So a tragic trilogy was followed by a satyr-play; and tragedies by comedies. It would be a shame not to mention a magnificent parody by Matro of Pitana, the *Attic Dinner* (c. 315 B.C.), a hungry man's description of a banquet in Homeric terms. It shows an almost incredible verbal facility and a knowledge of Homer which must have been virtually complete from the beginning of the *Iliad* to the end of the *Odyssey*; it plays with words in many different fashions—puns, unexpected line-endings, farcical assimilation of great lines to small subjects. It is one of the wittiest parodies ever written; and yet it has a reverse effect and satirizes Matro himself. It is always disgusting to read the Greeks boasting about the free delicacies they gobbled down at another man's table (this is one of the things that makes Athenaeus unreadable), and it is worse when one of the guests is Stratocles, the vile flatterer who persuaded the Athenians to grant quasi-divine honors to their Macedonian conquerors and to house the Macedonian governor in the Parthenon.

16. *Batrachomyomachia* 114 Brandt.

17. *Batrachomyomachia* 253-257 Brandt.

18. Because of the peculiar character of the fight, between land-animals and water-animals, who are not usually natural enemies, and because of the tradition that the poem was written by a contemporary of Xerxes, it has been believed that the *Batrachomyomachia* is a parody of a real epic about the war between the water forces of Greece and the land forces of Persia. Yet it is hard to think of it as being written before the *Gigantomachia* of Hegemon, which is dated fairly accurately to 415 B.C. (see note 15). More probably the mice are the Peloponnesians and the frogs, whom Athena tries to help, the navy-minded Athenians.

19. Quoted by Jack Simmons in his *Southey* (London, 1945) 168-169.

20. Professor L. A. Marchand, in his thorough biography of Byron (New York, 1957), suggests that Byron was thinking of Quevedo's first satiric vision, *The Vision of the Skulls*, which deals with the Last Judgment. (See vol. 2, note on p. 932, 1. 27.)

21. K. Clark, *The Nude* (New York, 1956) 244-246, 260-261.

22. K. Clark, *The Nude* 260 and 405-406.

23. The British musical critic Ernest Newman once reviewed a song recital and briskly disposed of a song by a Russian composer, Gretchaninov, I think. It was called "Oh, could I but express in song!" and Newman commented, "This composer evidently cannot."

24. *New York Times*, from the Associated Press, February 16, 1952.

25. This lack of selectivity vitiates an otherwise valuable collection of material by C. D. MacDougall called *Hoaxes* (New York, 1958²).

26. Clifton James tells the story in detail in *I Was Monty's Double* (New York, 1958).

27. W. Voigt, *Wie ich Hauptmann v. Köpenick wurde, mein Lebensbild* (Berlin, n.d., c. 1909).

28. Adrian Stephen, *The "Dreadnought" Hoax* (London, 1936).

29. *Aeneid* 4.437: *Talibus orabat talesque miserrima fletus.* . . .

30. The story of Partridge is told in the Dictionary of National Biography and supplemented by W. A. Eddy in "The Wits *vs.* John Partridge, Astrologer," *Studies in Philology* 29 (1932) 29-40. Professor James Clifford of Columbia has been kind enough to check my account of the hoax and to add some details. The name is sometimes (e.g. in Swift's *Accomplishment of the First of Mr. Bickerstaff's Predictions*) spelled Partrige. The Merlin quotation is from the end of Tennyson's *Vivien*.

31. Details of this and many other literary deceptions are given in a delightful book called *Artifices et Mystifications Littéraires* by Roger Picard (Montreal, 1945). Mérimée had already invented a Spanish playwright called Clara Gazul; and a few knowing readers suspected Hyacinthe Maglanovitch because his portrait showed him playing the *guzla*—not because that is not a real Balkan instrument, but because it is an anagram of Gazul. Maglanovitch is said to mean "son of mist," a suitable name for a poet of the mountains like Ossian; and Mérimée chose the name *illyrique* because he thought many romantic poems were *il-lyriques*, non-lyrical.

32. The stories of *Spectra*, Fern Gravel, and Ern Malley are told in an amusing book, *The Spectra Hoax*, by W. J. Smith (Middleton, Conn., 1961).

33. *Aeneid* 2.739, Aeneas speaking of his lost wife; 9.436, a dead boy compared to a drooping flower.

34. *Aeneid* 6.307, of the ghosts of girls dead before marriage (a quotation of *Georgics* 4.476); and, very significantly, of girls in doomed Troy, *Aeneid* 2.238.

35. Swift, *On Poetry* 255-256; Butler, *Hudibras*, Part 1, Canto 3,735-736.

36. Teofilo Folengo, called Merlinus Coccaius (1491-1544), the Benedictine monk who was the father, although not the first writer, of macaronic verse, says, "Ars ista poetica nuncupatur ars macaronica, a macaronibus derivata, qui macarones sunt quoddam pulmentum, farina caseo butyro compaginatum, grossum rude et rusticanum. ideo macaronica nil nisi grossedinem ruditatem et vocabulezzos debet in se continere." (Quoted from J. A. Morgan, *Macaronic Poetry*, New York, 1871, 148-149.)

37. Pope, *Rape of the Lock*, Canto 1 and Canto 3 fin.; John Philips, *The Splendid Shilling*; Pope, *Dunciad*, Book 4 init. *The Splendid Shilling* is a little jewel of satiric parody. Philips, who was Milton's nephew, wrote it, not to mock his uncle's magnificent poetry, but to amuse and teach one of his own undergraduate friends who was a spendthrift, by heroically exaggerating the woes of insolvency and

the comforts of the affluent man who possesses a Splendid Shilling.

38. Vergil, *Aeneid* 4.173-188; Butler, *Hudibras*, Part 2, Canto 1, 45 and 47-48.

39. Pope, *Dunciad* 2. 157-184.

40. Swift, *Legion Club* 151-152. There is a good discussion of this poem in Maurice Johnson's *Sin of Wit* (Syracuse, N.Y., 1950) 100-105.

41. Catullus 66, from Callimachus' *Lock of Berenice*: cf. *The Rape of the Lock* 5.127-130:

A sudden star it shot through liquid air,
And drew behind a radiant trail of hair.
Not Berenice's lock first rose so bright,
The heavens bespangling with dishevelled light.

42. Spence, *Anecdotes* (ed. S. W. Singer, London, 1820) Section V, 1737 . . . 39, p. 194.

43. Details of Juvenal's parody of Statius are given in G. Highet, *Juvenal the Satirist* (Oxford, 1954) 79 and 256-259, notes 1, 5, 11, and 12.

44. The *Moschaea* by Teofilo Folengo (1491-1544) is in the slightly inappropriate meter of elegiac couplets, and is written in the "macaronic" blend of Latin and Italian (mostly Latin): its chief modern inspiration seems to be Ariosto. Lope's *Gatomaquia* is in a loose lyrical meter: it begins with an imitation of Vergil's *Aeneid* 1.1a-d (the autobiographical lines cut out by Vergil's executors) and contains some good parodies of Ariosto. Addison called his poem ΠΥΓΜΑΙΟ-ΓΕΡΑΝΟΜΑΧΙΑ, and based it on the curious little piece of geographical lore about central African pygmies and southward-migrating cranes in *Iliad* 3.2-7. Macaulay thought it might have given a hint to Swift for his *Voyage to Lilliput* (see Macaulay's essay on Addison). In his learned and eccentric book cited in n. 15, G. W. Waltemath mentions an *Alopekiomachia* or *Battle of Foxes*, in Latin elegiacs, published in 1498 by Sebastian Brant, who wrote *The Ship of Fools*, but I have been unable to see it. We should also notice a long satire on monarchy and court-life, called *Gli Animali Parlanti* (1802). Its author, Giovanni Battista Casti, mistakenly claims in his preface that he is the first to satirize men engaged in politics under the guise of animals; he adds that *Reynard the Fox* and other books of its type have nothing in common with his work—whereas most readers would see them as belonging to exactly the same tradition at different stages of development. The poem is amusing, as when Casti derives the human courtiers' *baciamano* from the animals' respectful *leccazampa* to King Lion; but twenty-six cantos of it are too much. There is a witty English abbreviation and adaptation of it by W. S. Rose, in the style of Byron: *The Court and Parliament of Beasts* (London, 1819).

45. Lines 1-4 of *Le Lutrin* correspond to *Aeneid* 1.1-7, even in such a small detail as the asymmetry of the two parts of the theme:

> *arma / uirumque qui* etc.
> *les combats / et ce prélat terrible, qui* etc.

The invocation to the Muse in lines 9-12 corresponds to *Aeneid* 1.8-11: even Vergil's amazed question (unusual in epic poetry), *tantaene animis caelestibus irae?*, is neatly parodied by Boileau:

> Tant de fiel entre-t-il dans l'âme des dévots?

Pope did the same in lines 7-12 of the first book of his *Rape*, ending with

> In soft bosoms dwells such mighty rage?

(I often wonder how many famous parodic passages of English satire were based by their authors on the Greek and Roman originals, and how many suggested to them by Boileau. Thus, Johnson's famous phrase at the beginning of his adaptation of Juvenal 10, "from China to Peru," is inspired less directly by Juvenal than by Boileau, *Sat.* 8.3:

> De Paris au Pérou, du Japon jusqu'à Rome.

And surely the great effect at the end of Pope's *Dunciad*, the yawn of Dulness, is modeled on the yawn of Mollesse at the end of the second book of *Le Lutrin*?) In his first book, Boileau goes on to model the anger of Discord and her indignant speech upon Juno's outburst of rage in *Aeneid* 1.36-49, while her transformation into an aged servant of religion and her visit to the treasurer Auvry are parodies of the demon Allecto's visit to Turnus in *Aeneid* 7.406-466.

46. *Absalom and Achitophel* 1. 8-10.

47. Reported by Dean Lockier in Spence's *Anecdotes* (ed. S. W. Singer, London, 1820, Section II, 1730 . . . 32, p. 60).

48. W. Frost, in *"The Rape of the Lock* and Pope's Homer," *MLQ* 8 (1947) 342-354, shows that, although Pope's translation of Homer appeared later than the publication of *The Rape*, Pope parodied verses from his translation while working on it, and inserted the parodies into his satire.

49. François de Callières' *Histoire Poétique de la guerre nouvellement declarée* (sic) *entre les anciens et les modernes* was published in 1688 at Paris, without an author's name. It is in the form of a prose version of a classical epic, in twelve books, with an introduction. The introduction describes the formal opening of the Battle of the Books—the famous session of the new French Academy at which Charles Perrault read his poem *Le Siècle de Louis le Grand*, claiming that contemporary French writers equalled or surpassed the ancient Greek and Latin authors. (For this phase of the Battle,

see G. Highet, *The Classical Tradition*, Oxford, 1949, c. 14, particularly pp. 280-282.) It goes on to say that the supporters of the moderns applauded, the lovers of the ancients were disgusted, and a third group—who believed that in some fields the ancients excelled the moderns, and the moderns surpassed the ancients in others— left the meeting pensively. One of them (obviously de Callières, although he does not name himself) then dreamed the adventure described in the epic parody which follows: a war between Ancients and Moderns, stimulated by the goddess Renown, who carried a description of the meeting up to Parnassus and recited Perrault's poem. Then the Ancients seized one peak of Parnassus, the Moderns the other. (The mountain does in fact have two peaks.) The battle of Helicon ensues, with a number of Homeric duels: Corneille is defeated by Sophocles and Euripides, Malherbe by Pindar, Statius by Marini; the contest of Seneca with Lope de Vega is a draw. Racine and Boileau then join the Ancients, and are welcomed. At last peace is made on a compromise decreed by Apollo, who ends the poem by complimenting Racine and Boileau and the great LOUIS. This amusing little book is difficult to find, and is not often read; but anyone who goes through it carefully is bound to see that Swift's *Battle of the Books* was (as Wotton suggested) an imitation of it, with some gaps and some original additions. Like de Callières, Swift opened with the seizure of the two peaks of Parnassus, and proceeded to a war, with an elaborate order of battle and a series of duels; he made the goddess Fame fly from earth to heaven with news of the conflict, and caused Jupiter to interest himself in it, like Apollo in de Callières' parody. But he was too inexperienced to work out an original and consistent conception, and perhaps ashamed to copy de Callières too closely. Thus, he presented Bentley both as a librarian (superior to all the books) and as one of the warring book-champions. And—a much greater sign of immaturity—he could not finish his piece. He promised to give "a full impartial account" of a battle which happened "on Friday last." But as soon as he started describing the fight itself, he pretended to be translating from an *ancient* record interrupted by "gaps in the manuscript"; and he broke off after a dozen pages with *"Desunt caetera"* ("the rest is lacking") long before the termination of the conflict, which he therefore, unlike de Callières, left undecided. Swift's own episodes, the fable of the spider and the bee and the flight of Momus, are far better than his imitation of the French author. The resemblance between the two satires is examined in some detail by E. Pons, *Swift* (Strasbourg, 1925) 271-274. For de Callières' satire several earlier inspirations have been suggested; but one which appeals particularly to me is the fight in the bookshop described in the fifth canto of

64. *Hudibras*, Part 1, Canto 1, 359-362.

65. *Hudibras*, Part 2, Canto 1, 585-590:

> You will find it a hard chapter,
> To catch me with poetic rapture,
> In which your mastery of art
> Doth show itself, and not your heart;
> Nor will you raise in mine combustion
> By dint of high heroic fustian.

66. Aristophanes, *The Frogs* 1309-1363.

67. *The Frogs* 1477-1478, translated by W. B. Stanford.

68. *The Frogs*.

69. Fielding's parodies cover a wide range of English baroque drama, beginning with Dryden, whom he cites very often. It is strange to see him annotating his own line, spoken by Princess Huncamunca, in Act 2, Scene 4,

> O Tom Thumb! Tom Thumb! wherefore art thou Tom Thumb?

with a reference to Otway's *Marius*:

> Oh! Marius, Marius, wherefore art thou Marius?

Otway's play was indeed partially based on Shakespeare's *Romeo and Juliet*; but did Fielding not recognize the Shakespearean original of this question?

70. Carey, *Chrononhotonthologos* (1734). The prologue to this play correctly defines mock-heroic parody as opposed to burlesque:

> To-night our comic muse the buskin wears,
> And gives herself no small romantic airs;
> Struts in heroics, and in pompous verse
> Does the minutest incidents rehearse.

71. *"Savonarola" Brown* appears in Beerbohm's *Seven Men*, which came out in 1919. The quotations are from Acts 2 and 3.

72. *Henry IV, Part 2*, 2.4.176-180, parodying Marlowe, *Tamburlaine the Great, Part 2*, 3.1-2.

73. The duel of Menelaus and Paris (*Iliad* 3.324-382) is touched upon in *Troilus and Cressida* 1.1.113-117 and 1.2.228-231. The parade of the Trojan heroes in *Troilus and Cressida* 1.2.190-265 is adapted from Helen's description of the Greek heroes in the famous wall scene, *Iliad* 3. 161-244. The slaying of Hector by Achilles in a duel (*Iliad* 22) is degraded in *Troilus and Cressida* 5.8 into the butchery of an unarmed man by Achilles and a troop of his Myrmidons.

74. *Troilus and Cressida* 1.3.142-184; cf. *Iliad* 9.186-191.

75. *Troilus and Cressida* 2.1 and 5.7; cf. *Iliad* 2.211-277.

76. This was suggested by O. J. Campbell, in *Comicall Satyre and Shakespeare's "Troilus and Cressida"* (San Marino, Cal., 1938). He followed this book with an admirably sensitive study, *Shakespeare's*

Satire (New York, 1943), which has particularly valuable chapters on those difficult plays *Measure for Measure, Timon of Athens,* and *Coriolanus.* Mr. Campbell describes the two latter as "tragical satires." The reference to *Hamlet* is 2.2.201-210. (The prince was evidently reading Juvenal 10.) If Chapman was the rival poet of whom Shakespeare speaks with such envy in the *Sonnets,* it is a little easier to see why, after Chapman's translation had (at least in part) appeared, Shakespeare should take such a fierce delight in mishandling Homer's and Chapman's heroical world.

77. Air 6 in *The Beggar's Opera,* "Virgins are like the fair Flower in its Lustre," is a vulgarization of a stanza from Catullus's beautiful wedding song, 62.40-48.

78. Chorus of Peers, from Act 1 of *Iolanthe.*

79. Sergeant's song with chorus of Police, from Act 2 of *The Pirates of Penzance.*

80. Bunthorne's recitative, from Act 1 of *Patience.*

81. Buttercup's song, from Act 2 of *H.M.S. Pinafore.*

82. The parody of Gilbert and Sullivan is *Perseverance, or Half a Coronet, an Entirely Original Operetta by Turbot & Vulligan,* with words by A. P. (now Sir Alan) Herbert and music by Vivian Ellis. It was produced in 1934 as part of Cochran's revue *Streamline.* The scene is the terrace of the House of Commons, with fishing-boats moored in the Thames to provide a picturesque chorus of fishing-girls. The plot turns on the fact that the Earl of Bunion had twin sons, but nobody knows which was born first and which should therefore inherit the title. The final chorus is at once a criticism of Gilbert and Sullivan and a parody of one of their most famous songs, "Take a pair of sparkling eyes," from Act 2 of *The Gondoliers:*

> Take a dainty paradox,
> Dress it like a chocolate box—
> Take two babies, mix them well;
> Take one spinster, give her H—
> Take some logic, chop it thin;
> Take some tunes and rub them in:
> One patter song, and don't forget
> Your unaccompanied octette.
> Take a little love, but hush!
> Not enough to raise a blush:
> By degrees you'll get a
> Rather popular operetta.

83. *Il Mattino* came out in 1763, *Il Mezzogiorno* in 1765. *Il Vespro* and *La Notte,* which Parini did not complete, were published after his death, in 1801. Although the empty-headed young nobleman is described in general terms, and is a type which often recurs in history

and indeed in satire (Pope's Sir Plume in *The Rape*, Juvenal's Rubellius Blandus in 8), still, contemporaries recognized him as Prince Alberico di Belgioioso.

84. There is a good analysis of Goncharov's satirical novel *Oblomov*, "the superfluous man," in chapter 9 of Marc Slonim's *Outline of Russian Literature* (New York, 1958).

85. *Mattino* 792-793.

86. Flattering poets, *Mezzogiorno* 905-939; "concilio di Semidei terreni," *Mattino* 61-62.

87. The myth of primitive equality, *Mezzogiorno* 2.250-338, with some resemblance to Lucretius's picture of primitive mankind in 5.925-957. *Mezzogiorno* 298-301 is adapted from Juvenal 14.34-35.

88. Pope, *Prologue to the Satires* 308.

89. "Precettor d'amabil Rito," *Mattino* 7; "Or io t'insegnerò," *Mattino* 11; further parodies of the didactic manner in *Mattino* 30-32, 395-397, 941-943.

90. His lordship dressing, compared to Achilles and Rinaldo, *Mattino* 249-253; the myth of Cupid and Hymen, *Mattino* 313-391; his lordship, enraged by his hairdresser's carelessness, compared to a bull escaping from the sacrificial altar, *Mattino* 542-554, cf. Vergil, *Aeneid* 2.223-224; Mars invoked to gird on his lordship's dress sword, *Mattino* 808-814. Parini compares himself to Iopas singing at the banquet given by Dido to Aeneas and to Phemius the minstrel of King Alcinous in the *Odyssey*, *Mezzogiorno* 7-23.

91. *Rape of the Lock* 2.5: these are "le gentili Dame e gli amabili Garzoni" who offer sacrifices to themselves on the altars of Fashion, in Parini's dedication to his poem.

92. *Lilliput*, c. 6 fin. Swift parodied one of the world's greatest didactic poems in his *Description of a City Shower*, which is inspired by the weather prognostications in Vergil, *Georgics* 1.424-457, and then goes on to parody scenes from the *Aeneid*: lines 47-52 = *Aeneid* 2.50-53, lines 57-60 = *Aeneid* 9.30-32. The point of the satire is the ignoble squalor of the city as contrasted with Vergil's rural and heroic worlds. In this as in so many other satirical traits Swift was the predecessor of James Joyce. And he was a devoted and skillful parodist. His *Intended Speech against Peace*, an attack on Lord Nottingham, parodies a political oration; his *Windsor Prophecy*, an attack on the Duchess of Somerset which is said to have ruined his chances of obtaining preferment in the church, parodies a medieval document. And although his greatest work is not, in form, a parody, it contains parodic distortions: the petty pygmies of Lilliput, the gross giants of Brobdingnag, the squinting intellectuals of Laputa, and the filthy Yahoos—are these not parodies of human beings?

93. Jefferson to Langdon (1810), from *A Jefferson Profile as Revealed in his Letters*, ed. S. Padover (New York, 1956), 194.

94. Horace, *Sermones* 1.10.44.

95. Vergil, *Catalepton* 4, 6, 7, and 12 imitate Catullus. The tenth poem is a clever parody of Catullus 4, *Phaselus ille.*

96. Chaucer, *Sir Thopas* 1914-1919; *Prologue to Melibeus* 1 (2109), 7 (2115), and 12 (2119).

97. Swift, *Ode to Dr. William Sancroft late Lord Archbishop of Canterbury* 231-239.

98. The Sapphic-Horatian-Southeyan ode *The Friend of Humanity and the Knife-Grinder* was written by George Canning and John Hookham Frere. It was aimed at a particular poem of Southey called *The Widow* and at a particularly "assiduous member of the Society of Friends of the People," George Tierney, M.P. (So Mr. Dwight Macdonald on p. 37 of his *Parodies*, New York, 1960.) I wish it did not remind me quite so strongly of the lyrics for Schubert's *Winterreise.*

99. "Peter Pindar" was John Wolcot (1738-1819). He is vulgar but sometimes funny. Samples:

> A desultory way of writing,
> A hop and step and jump mode of inditing,
> My great and wise relation, Pindar, boasted:
> Or (for I love the Bard to flatter),
> By jerks, like Boar-pigs making water.

(This is from *Lyric Odes to the Royal Academicians, for 1783*, 6. 1-5.) Here is George III on discovering a louse on his plate at dinner:

> "How, how? What, what? what's that, what's that?" he cries,
> With rapid accent, and with staring eyes:
> "Look there, look there; what's got into my house?
> A Louse, God bless us! Louse, louse, louse, louse, louse."

(From *The Lousiad*, Canto 1.)

100. C. S. Calverley, *Complete Works* (London, 1926). On pp. 28-29 there is a sweet Sapphic *Ode to Tobacco.*

> Sweet, when the morn is gray;
> Sweet, when they've cleared away
> Lunch; at the close of day
> Possibly sweetest.

101. Quoted from Dwight Macdonald, *Parodies* (New York, 1960) 224.

102. Both Henry Reed's parody and Mr. Eliot's remarks appear on p. 218 of Dwight Macdonald's anthology of parodies.

103. Cicero, *Orator* 151. There is no other evidence for the assertion.

104. Pope, *Prologue to the Satires* 204.

105. There is a good edition of the *Epistulae Obscurorum Virorum* with notes and English translation by F. G. Stokes (London, 1909).

Conrad Dollenkopf's interpretations of Ovid (Mr. Stokes explains) are not pure fantasy, but are taken from medieval paraphrases and commentaries. As for his grotesque etymologies (MAVORS = mares vorans; MERCVRIVS = mercatorum curius), they are no worse than some we find in medieval scholiasts. Letter 1.43 is astonishingly frank in dealing with sexual scandal: after repeating, with horror, a story about a monk making love to a trollop in Mainz Cathedral, the correspondent goes on to say that the Order is really as bad as the Templars once were.

106. For its first version see C. Read, *Le Texte primitif de la Satyre Ménippée* (Paris, 1878).

107. Hor. *Serm.* 1.1.24-25. The satire was a composite effort. Its principal contributors were Pierre Le Roy (who apparently thought of it first), Jean Passerat, Florent Chrestien, Nicolas Rapin, and Pierre Pithou.

108. The complete "Gettysburg Address in Eisenhowese" appears on pp. 447-448 of Dwight Macdonald's *Parodies* (New York, 1960).

109. Note, for instance, Ernest Hemingway's *Torrents of Spring* (1925), a brisk douche on Sherwood Anderson; Stella Gibbons' *Cold Comfort Farm* (1932), a chilling pastiche of English novelists of the mystical Soil; and *Parody Party*, ed. Leonard Russell (London, 1936), containing Cyril Connolly's superb parody of Aldous Huxley, *Told in Gath*. Besides Mr. Macdonald's anthology quoted above, there is a good collection edited by Burling Lowrey, *Twentieth-Century Parody, American and British* (New York, 1960).

110. Clifton Fadiman, "The Wolfe at the Door," from his *Party of One* (New York, 1955).

111. Peter De Vries, "Requiem for a Noun, or Intruder in the Dusk," reprinted from *The New Yorker* in Dwight Macdonald's *Parodies* (New York, 1960).

IV. THE DISTORTING MIRROR

1. On the Eskimos and the Negroes see R. C. Elliott, *The Power of Satire* (Princeton, 1960) 70-74. From J. Dollard, "The Dozens," *The American Imago* 1 (1939) 3-25 (a reference which I owe to Mr. Elliott), it appears that the commonest form of Negro abuse is an insult to the opponent's mother:

> Your ma behind
> Is like a rumble seat.
> It hang from her back
> Down to her feet.

The peculiar name "Dozens" may come from an obscene song in which the singer counts up from one to twelve acts of sexual intercourse with his rival's mother.

2. If Hernández had not wished to bring his poem to a happy conclusion, with the gaucho riding off into the distance, I think there would have been a real knife-fight: for the Negro was the brother of a man killed in a brawl by Martín Fierro at the beginning of his career, and was bent on revenge. (The brawl is in section 7 of the first part of the poem, and the song-duel in section 30 of the second, *La Vuelta de Martín Fierro*.) Walter Owen's vigorous translation, *The Gaucho Martín Fierro* (Oxford, 1935), which first introduced me to the poem, has a most interesting preface, with three pages on the once widespread custom of song-contests "in all the lands where the guitar is the instrument of the people." It should be noted, however, that sometimes they were simply contests in wit, and did not always or necessarily descend to mutual abuse.

3. The wit of the contest was not much superior to that of the Negro "Dozens," referred to in note 1 above. Sarmentus began: "I say you look like a wild horse." So the Negro sings:

> You weren't born fair,
> I sure can swear.
> You were born by an alligator,
> And suckled by a mare.

On Horace's journey to Brindisi see pp. 201-204.

4. The text of the poem is in *The Anglo-Latin Satiric Poets and Epigrammatists of the Twelfth Century*, ed. T. Wright (London, 1872). The title is a rather unconvincing coinage from the Greek elements *archi-*, "leading" or "superior," as in "archangel" and "archbishop," and *threnos*, "lament."

5. Thus, the abodes of the various hypostatizations are described in terms like the abode of Hunger in Ovid's *Metamorphoses* 8.788f. The style and even the meter of the poem resemble Ovid more than any other Latin poet, as when the skin of the Psylli is called

> parma ueneniferi iaculis imperuia dentis,

or Bacchus is invoked as

> Bacche corymbiferis Phrygiae spectabilis oris,

two lightly dactylic lines with exactly the same metrical pattern, each with a purely Ovidian word in it: *uenenifer* from *Met.* 3.85, *corymbifer* from *Fast.* 1.393. The description of a drinking bout in Book 2 (p. 268 Wright) begins:

> Consedere duces, et Bacchi stante corona
> surgit ad [h]os paterae dominus septemplicis Aiax
> Anglicus, et calice similis contendit Vlixes,

which is a parody of the contest for the arms of Achilles in *Metamorphoses* 13. This passage lets us hear the very shouts of our boozy Germanic ancestors:

> Ergo uagante scypho distincto gutture "Wesheil!"
> ingeminant, "Wesheil!"

The first words of Architrenius, *Velificatur Athos*, are a reminiscence of Juvenal 10.174; and there are other close adaptations of Juvenal. His attack on gourmandise (5.94-96),

dum gula saeuit

retibus adsiduis penitus scrutante macello proxima,

becomes in *Architrenius* (p. 269)

Ha, gula, quae mundum penitus scrutatur!

6. Hor. *Ep.* 1.11.27.

7. More in his preface says that his book is *festivus et salutaris*, no doubt thinking of Horace's various descriptions of the satirist's function.

8. Rabelais, Fourth Book, c. 2. In Medamothy Epistemon bought a fine picture, representing Plato's Ideas and the atoms of Epicurus.

9. For an amusing and perceptive account of satire in the modern fantasies called "space fiction," see Kingsley Amis, *New Maps of Hell* (New York, 1960) cc. 4 and 5.

10. Lucian, *Menippus* 21; see R. Helm, *Lucian und Menipp* (Leipzig, 1906) c. 1, especially note 5 on p. 37.

11. Lucian, *Icaromenippus*; Helm (quoted in n. 10) c. 3.

12. Ariosto, *Orlando Furioso* 34. 73-85; Milton, *Paradise Lost* 3. 444-497. Note the "low" contemptuous words which show that Milton has here stepped from epic to satire: "embryos and idiots," "trumpery," "rags," "the backside of the world." Milton explicitly corrects Ariosto in this passage, saying that all earthly vanities go to this distant Limbo and dwell there,

Not in the neighbouring Moon, as some have dreamed:

Those argent fields more likely habitants,

Translated Saints, or middle Spirits hold,

Betwixt th' angelical and human kind. (3.459-462.)

13. In *YCS* 1 (1928) 1-40, A. R. Bellinger shows that Lucian's dialogues approached drama: he read them aloud to his audiences, clearly differentiating the various speakers and describing the changes of scene.

14. Rabelais, Second Book, c. 30.

15. The mysterious name *Apocolocyntosis* does not appear either in the text of Seneca's skit or as its title in the manuscripts, which call it either "Seneca's joke on the death of Claudius," or "The apotheosis of Claudius in satire, by Seneca." The word is found only in the historian Dio Cassius (Book 61, epitome), where it apparently refers to this satire. Its meaning is fairly clear. It is a satirical deformation of "apotheosis" and means "transformation into a fool." (1) Officially Claudius was transformed into a god, but in reality (as interpreted by this satire) he was rejected by the gods and be-

fooled. (2) The piece contains many allusions to the contrasts *god*) (*fool* and *monarch*) (*fool*; and Nero made a pun on Claudius's death involving the Greek word for "fool" (Suetonius *Nero* 33.1). (3) In contemporary Roman slang *cucurbita* meant "fool" (Petronius 39), and the Greek for *cucurbita* is κολοκύνθη. (*Gurdus* also meant "fool," says Quintilian 1.5.57; and so does *gourde* in modern French.) So if we wanted a typically slangy and vulgar title to correspond to *Apocolocyntosis*, we could choose *Dopification*. However, Mr. Robert Graves has suggested with characteristic ingenuity that the word means "elimination by colocynth," and that it refers to the fact that Claudius, after his first dose of poison failed to take effect, was finished off with an enema of colocynth administered by the expert poisoner Lucusta: colocynth, or wild pumpkin, being a purgative so powerful as to be lethal in large doses. (When the sons of the prophets tasted it at Gilgal, they cried out, and said, "There is death in the pot." See II Kings 4.38-41.) This explanation, published in V. P. and R. G. Wasson's *Mushrooms, Russia, and History* (New York, 1957), is certainly possible; but it is unlikely, because to attach such a name to the satire would be for Seneca to admit that Claudius was murdered, whereas his death (although its concomitants are touched upon in chapters 3 and 4) is not represented as other than natural. Claudius was murdered and duly apotheosized in October. In December came the Saturnalia, when normal relations were turned upside down and jollity reigned supreme. Since Claudius is called *Saturnalicius princeps* in the eighth chapter of the *Apocolocyntosis*, and since the whole piece is built on absurd contrasts and violent reversals, it seems likely that Seneca wrote it to be read at the Saturnalia of Nero's first year as Emperor.

16. Julian, *Symposium* 336a-b. The title by which the work is now generally known, *The Caesars*, is not found in the manuscripts. Although it is technically a Menippean satire, blended of prose and poetry, there are very few snatches of verse in it.

17. Quevedo, *El Sueño de las Calaveras*: Júpiter estaba vestido de sí mismo.

18. Dante, *Inferno* 34.

19. Quevedo, *Las Zahurdas del Plutón* med., cf. *Calaveras* ad fin.

20. Voltaire, *Micromégas*, c. 4. A contemporary satirical comedy on the same theme is Gore Vidal's delightful *Visit to a Small Planet*.

21. *The Singular Adventures of Baron Munchausen*, by Rudolph Raspe and others, ed. J. Carswell (New York, 1952), Introduction, xxvii-xxix.

22. Rabelais, Second Book, c. 32.

23. Rabelais, Second Book, c. 22; Second Book, c. 7.

24. There is a good edition of Caxton's English translation of *Reynard* by D. B. Sanos (Cambridge, Mass., 1960).

25. This is from c. 28 of a verse adaptation of *Reynard* by F. S. Ellis (London, 1894).

26. Chaucer, *Nun's Priest's Tale* 3312-3316. The poem has been translated into unrhymed pentameter English couplets by G. W. Regenos under Chaucer's title, *The Book of Daun Burnel the Ass* (Austin, Texas, 1959). The Latin text has been edited, with introduction and notes, by J. H. Mozley and R. R. Raymo (*University of California English Studies* 18, Berkeley, Calif., 1960).

27. On these two poems see F. J. E. Raby, *History of Secular Latin Poetry in the Middle Ages* (Oxford, 1934) 1.269-276 and 2.151-152.

28. The *Metamorphoses*, and a short Greek version of the same plot (dubiously attributed to Lucian and called *Lucius or The Donkey*), are both probably adapted from a lost Greek tale by one Lucius of Patras; but Apuleius has put a vast amount of his own experience and imagination into his book.

29. The speech in which Apuleius defended himself against the charge of practicing magic is his *Apologia* or *De Magia*, one of the principal documents for magic in antiquity. There are an old but still useful edition by H. E. Butler and A. S. Owen (Oxford, 1914) and a valuable study, *Die Apologie des Apuleius von Madaura und die antike Zauberei* by Adam Abt (Giessen, 1908). In the speech Apuleius is rather vague about the relation between magic and religion, whereas in the *Metamorphoses* he understands the difference very well. Even allowing for his desire to make light of the charges against him, it would appear that he wrote the *Metamorphoses* at a more mature stage of his life. For the later belief in his wizardry, see the letter from Marcellinus to St. Augustine, asking for help in his discussions with pagans who said that the miracles of Jesus were less important than those of Apollonius, Apuleius, and others; with St. Augustine's reply: *CSEL* 44, ed. A. Goldbacher (Vienna, 1904) 136.1 and 138.19.

30. *Simia quam similis, turpissima bestia, nobis!* So said Ennius in one of his satires: fragment 23 on p. 390 of Warmington's *Fragments of Old Latin* I (Cambridge, 1935).

31. *Greatauk, duc du Skull, ministre de la guerre*, appears in Book 6, c.1. Porpoisia is *la Marsouinie*, inhabited by *les Marsouins*, a word which, detached from zoology, means "ugly brutes." Is it possible that Anatole France could have been thinking of the Germans?

32. E.g. this sentence in Book 6, c. 11: "Le gouvernement de la république demeura soumis au contrôle des grandes compagnies financières, l'armée consacrée exclusivement à la défense du capital, la flotte destinée uniquement à fournir des commandes aux métallurgistes."

33. Book 4, c. 3; and Book 8, "Les Temps Futurs: l'histoire sans fin."

34. "Likely impossibilities rather than unlikely possibilities." (Aristotle, *Poetics* 1460a27).

35. From an article in the Paris magazine *Arts* (1961).

36. *His Monkey Wife* also contains some deft satire on English snobbery. Thus, the chimpanzee Emily learns to curtsey, and wonders if she is to be presented at court—particularly after reading in a society paper: "In England the Primate takes precedence of all but Royal Dukes." (Chapter 3.)

37. Hor. *Serm.* 1.1.24.

38. Butler, *Hudibras*, Part 1, Canto 1. 139-142.

39. Swift, *Mr. Collins's Discourse of Free-Thinking* (1713).

40. Swift, *Polite Conversation, The Third Dialogue.*

41. So Kiessling-Heinze in their edition, and E. Fraenkel in pp. 105-112 of his sensitively written *Horace* (Oxford, 1957).

42. Lejay in his admirable edition of the satires points to the contrast in lines 27 to 33 of the poem: on the one hand, Maecenas, Cocceius Nerva, and Fonteius Capito; on the other hand, *ego*, smearing my sore eyes with black ointment.

43. Horace on inquisitive acquaintances, *Serm.* 2.6.40-58. Note that in 37, when he made the journey to Brundisium, Horace had just recently become one of Maecenas's intimates.

44. The idea was copied in England by Oliver Goldsmith, whose amiable Citizen of the World (1760-1762) was a Chinese.

45. The structure of Aristophanic comedy was first clarified by the brilliant Tadeusz Zielinski, *Die Gliederung der altattischen Komödie* (1885).

46. Pantagruel contains Panurge within himself (as is shown, for instance, by the lawsuit in chapters 10 to 13 of the Second Book), and he contains Friar John, without the weaknesses of either.

47. These satirical scenes are from Voltaire's *Candide*, cc. 11-12; Waugh's *A Handful of Dust*, c. 6, "À côté de chez Todd"; *Gulliver's Travels, Brobdingnag*, c. 5; Juvenal 6.425-433; and Swift, *The Lady's Dressing-Room.*

48. This is from a good study of Strachey by a man who knew him for thirty years, Clive Bell's *Old Friends* (New York, 1957) 32.

49. O. Henry was deeply sympathetic to the men who gave him the material he used in *The Gentle Grafter*. They were his fellow-convicts in the penitentiary at Columbus, Ohio, and they told him the stories when he made his rounds at night as a pharmacist, treating minor ailments. (See pp. 139-142 of *The Caliph of Bagdad*, by R. H. Davis and A. B. Maurice, New York, 1931.)

50. Another satiric touch which readers who do not know Persian will certainly miss is that Morier gave some of his characters names which, to the uninstructed, sound well, but are denigratory: Mírzá

Ahmak (Doctor Fool), Námard Khán (Lord Coward), and Mullá Nadan (the Reverend Ignoramus). (This is from E. G. Browne's introduction to *Hajji Baba* as issued by the Limited Editions Club, New York, 1947.) Distorted or ridiculous names are always a sure sign of satire. So in Gogol's *Inspector*, the chief of police is called Skvoznik-Dmukhanovsky, the school superintendent Hlopov, and the judge Lyapkin-Tyapkin: their names mean, roughly, Rascal-Puftup, Bed-bug, and Bungle-Steal. (I owe this to the notes in the translation by J. L. Seymour and G. R. Noyes in J. Gassner's *Treasury of the Theatre*, vol. 1, revised edition, New York, 1958.)

51. On the purpose of the *Satyrica* see p. 115. Although Petronius was working in the medium of Menippean satire, he had Horace's satires in mind. (He admired Horace, for he coined the elegant epigram which describes his style, *Horatii curiosa felicitas*.) The banquet itself, with its explanatory host, its collapsing ceiling, and its final flight of the guests, is a huge expansion of *Serm.* 2.8; and the legacy-hunting incident, *Sat.* 141, is a gruesome variation on a theme from Horace's satire on legacy-hunters, *Serm.* 2.5.84-88.

52. From O. Weinreich's excellent introduction to his *Römische Satiren* (Zürich, 1949) CII-CIII, I learn that the banquet of Trimalchio was enacted by noblemen and ladies at the court of Hanover in 1702, apparently with no idea that they were mimicking the canaille; and again at St. Cloud during the regency of the Duke of Orleans; and that Frederick the Great wrote a poetic letter praising his chef for maintaining a cuisine more refined than the gross luxury of Nero's time. The French scholar Jérôme Carcopino, in his *Daily Life in Ancient Rome* (tr. by E. O. Lorimer, New Haven, Conn., 1940), built heavily on Petronius. It would be interesting to see a *Daily Life in the United States* based partly on the domestic manners of Louis B. Mayer or Al Capone. In the *Satyrica*, the amused disgust of Encolpius and his friends is frequently underlined: at first ironically—admiratione saturi (28.6), nihil amplius interrogaui ne uiderer numquam inter honestos cenasse (41.5)—and then more and more frankly: hominem tam putidum (54.1), cum Ascyltos . . . omnia sublatis manibus eluderet et usque ad lacrimas rideret (57.1), Giton . . . risum iam diu compressum . . . effudit (58.1), tot malorum finis (69.6), pudet referre quae secuntur (70.22), ibat res ad summam nauseam (78.5), to the final escape from the intolerable, tam plane quam ex incendio (78.8).

53. Régnier is inspired in 10.33-69 by Hor. *Serm.* 1.9; his portrait of the pedant (115-241) comes from Caporali's *Del Pedante*, even to the joke *pedetemptim* in 217; and the passage 290-317—including the outrageous comparison of the soup full of dead flies to the Gulf of Patras full of floating wrecks after Lepanto—from Caporali's *Sopra*

la Corte. The sequel (*Sat.* 11), in which he loses his way and is offered a miserable lodging and lively entertainment by a lady of free disposition, is inspired in part by the episode of Polyaenos and Circe in Petronius, *Sat.* 126-139 (which is actually quoted in 229-242) and in part by the more appropriately sordid incident in Petronius, *Sat.* 6-8.

54. Waugh, *Vile Bodies*, c. 8.

55. Proust, *Du Côté de chez Swann*, Deuxième Partie.

56. The wife gives her husband long curtain lectures: "mai ne' lor letti non si dorme" = Juvenal 6.268-269 (but Boccaccio goes on to report one of the lectures, in fine conversational Italian). Even the most chaste would rather have one eye than one man = Juv. 6. 53-54. Wives go off to brothels and return "stanche ma non sazie" = Juv. 6.115-132. They will not go anywhere with their husband, but they are brave in facing disgraceful adventures = Juv. 6.94-102. "Nothing is harder to endure than a rich wife" = Juv. 6.460 (now thought spurious, but believed in Boccaccio's time to be authentic). They know what is done in India and Spain, they know the source of the Nile, who is pregnant, everything = Juv. 6.402-412. They teach their daughters how to rob husbands and to receive clandestine letters from lovers = · Juv. 6.231-241. They deny their guilt even when taken in the act = Juv. 6.279-285, with an impudent variation: "non fu cosi: tu menti per la gola"—no doubt inspired by medieval stories of the trickery of women, like *Decameron* 7.9.

57. Lucretius 4. 1173-1184.

58. Juvenal 6. 461-464, 471-473.

59. E.g., Tertullian, *On the Costume of Women*. The *Hamlet* quotation is 3.1.151-152.

60. Boileau, *Sat.* 10. 195-200.

61. Swift, *The Lady's Dressing-Room* 43-50. The same topic re-appears in Swift's *A Beautiful Young Nymph Going to Bed*; in c. 5 of *Brobdingnag*; and, with a typical Swiftian elaboration, in *Strephon and Chloe*, a poem whose point is that even a girl who apparently does not sweat must excrete. (The use of the idealistic pastoral names Strephon and Chloe is parodic satire.)

62. Swift, *The Legion Club* 219-230. Another eighteenth-century satirist greatly admired Hogarth: Georg Christoph Lichtenberg (1742-1799), one of whose last works was an *Ausführliche Erklärung der Hogarthischen Kupferstiche* (1794). It rather shocked Goethe, who preferred the Antique. See C. Brinitzer, *A Reasonable Rebel* (tr. B. Smith, New York, 1960) 181.

V. CONCLUSION

1. The fullest discussion of the origins of the name *satura* in antiquity is in Diomede in vol. 1 of Keil's *Grammatici Latini* 485.30-

486.16. The connection between food and types of literature is wittily and informatively discussed by O. Weinreich, *Römische Satiren* (Zürich, 1949) x-xiv.

2. In Greece there were satyr-plays, in which mythical themes were treated lightly with touches of grotesquerie and romance; they were acted after the three tragedies which each competing author submitted. They also have nothing whatever to do with satire.

3. The passage describing these stage *saturae* is Livy 7.2, which is generally believed to be based on Varro. One other possible derivation for *satura* should be mentioned: the Etruscan word *satir*, which means "speech." But we know only this word, and have no other evidence to support the connection.

4. See, for instance, Naevius's "local jokes" about the favorite delicacies of people from the towns of Praeneste and Lanuvium, and his charming character-sketch of the coquette from Tarentum: E. H. Warmington, *Fragments of Old Latin* II (Cambridge, Mass., 1936) 80-81 and 98-101.

5. See note 22 on chapter 2 of this book, page 250.

6. Horace, *Sermones* 1.1.24.

7. Persius 1.119-123.

8. Juvenal 1.30-39 and 63-72.

9. Juvenal 1.81-87.

10. Juvenal 1.147-171.

11. An intelligent contemporary author, Pamela Hansford-Johnson, has said quite frankly, "Satire is cheek"—a remark quoted with approval by her husband C. P. Snow, in his recent *Science and Government*. Sir Charles adds, "It is the revenge of those who can't really comprehend the world or cope with it," which is a natural comment for a man who admires success, but is a little surprising in a novelist who himself uses satire so deftly.

12. See a brief but interesting article by M. Mack, "The Muse of Satire," in *Studies in the Literature of the Augustan Age*, ed. R. C. Boys (Ann Arbor, Michigan, 1952) 218-231. Mr. Mack challenges the belief of many critics that satire expresses the rage and hate of the satirist himself. Satire, he says, would be better treated as a branch of rhetoric. He stresses what he calls the "fictionality" of the speaker in Pope's formal satires. It is a mistake, he continues, to believe that we hear the voice of Alexander Pope; what we hear is that of a *persona*, who is sometimes a projection of the ideal satirist, sometimes an ingénu, sometimes a public defender. This seems to me to be a useful caveat for readers of narrative satires, even when they are autobiographical in form: Encolpius is not Petronius, and Gulliver is not Swift (although sometimes he resembles him pretty closely). Naturally it is true for satires in the form of parody. And it is true—

within limits—for monologue satires. Yet it would, in my view, be difficult to maintain that in most monologue satires (if they are ostensibly spoken by the satirist) there is more fiction than truth. Thus, the satirist often tells us facts which apply to no one but himself: Pope in his prologue to the satires gives his address ("TWIT'NAM"), describes his appearance, and names his particular personal friends and enemies. Again, although satire, like rhetoric, does exaggerate and suppress and distort, yet, like rhetoric, it is supposed by its hearers to contain much more truth than pure fiction and to be inspired by emotions genuinely felt. By its hearers? Yes, and by its writers. One of the greatest of them welcomed death as the final cure for the torments of the typical satiric emotion, "cruel indignation," which he said could then no longer rend his heart. (So Swift, in his epitaph.)

13. This information comes from J. M. Cohen's introduction to his new translation of Rabelais (Penguin Books, 1955).

14. Dryden, preface, "To the Reader," *Absalom and Achitophel* (First Part).

15. Rabelais, First Book, cc. 13-15 and 21-22; the ideal prince's education, cc. 23-24.

BRIEF BIBLIOGRAPHY

(1) *Corpusculum Poesis Epicae Graecae Ludibundae*: (1) *Parodia et Archestratus*, ed. P. Brandt (Leipzig, 1888); (2) *Sillographi*, ed. C. Wachsmuth (Leipzig, 1885²).
An excellent edition of the Greek mock-epic poems, packed so tightly with information that it is difficult to use, but invaluable for specialists.

(2) J. W. Duff, *Roman Satire* (*Sather Classical Lectures* 12, Berkeley, Cal., 1936).
Short and attractively written introductory discussion.

(3) R. C. Elliott, *The Power of Satire* (Princeton, 1960).
An intelligent but sometimes confusing book tracing the roots of satire back to primitive ceremonies and making it akin to a magical incantation. The central idea may be difficult to accept, but Mr. Elliott well conveys the violence and combativeness which lie behind most satiric writing.

(4) J. Geffcken, "Studien zur griechischen Satire," *NJbb* 27 (1911) 393-411 and 469-493.
A brilliant essay on satirical writing in Greece outside the drama; packed with uncommon information and suggestive ideas.

(5) I. Jack, *Augustan Satire: Intention and Idiom in English Poetry 1660-1750* (Oxford, 1952).
Careful and sensitive analysis of such great poems as *Hudibras*, *Absalom and Achitophel*, and *The Rape of the Lock*, and of the literary and spiritual worlds in which they were created.

(6) E. Johnson, *A Treasury of Satire* (New York, 1945).
A fine big anthology of excerpts from works which are either wholly or in part satiric, together with a heartily written introduction, appreciative rather than analytical.

(7) U. Knoche, *Die römische Satire* (Göttingen, 1957²).
A soberly written book by an expert classicist: covers nearly every essential fact.

(8) Dwight Macdonald, *Parodies: an Anthology from Chaucer to Beerbohm—and after* (New York, 1960).

An admirable collection of parodies in English: most of the finest (Calverley's *The Cock and the Bull*, Carroll's nonsense poems, printed together with their originals), many less widely known masterpieces (three of Proust's *Pastiches et Mélanges* and a magnificent "little review" essay by W. B. Scott), and a good Appendix by the editor.

(9) J. Peter, *Complaint and Satire in Early English Literature* (Oxford, 1956).
This looks like two different books tied together: one on medieval satire in England, the other mainly concerned with Marston and Tourneur. However, it is learned and subtle, and will be useful for specialists.

(10) J. Sutherland, *English Satire* (Cambridge, 1958).
Seven short chapters outlining the history of satiric writing in England: good on the eighteenth century, they say little on modern satire, and not quite enough on such important figures as Butler and Byron.

(11) C. E. Vulliamy, *The Anatomy of Satire* (London, 1950).
This book (from which I unwittingly borrowed my title) is a useful anthology of quotations from satirical works, and of satirical excerpts from other types of writing. The pieces are mostly English, although some come from French, Greek, and Latin. Definition, however, is rather vague, and the citations are mostly too short to give the full impact of satire.

(12) H. Walker, *English Satire and Satirists* (London, 1925).
The best historical treatment of English satirical literature: it is in thirteen chapters, beginning with *Architrenius* and the *Speculum Stultorum* and ending with Butler's *Erewhon*. Full, rich, thorough, with a useful introduction which stresses the wide diffusion of the satiric spirit and emphasises its distinction from the spirit of comedy.

(13) O. Weinreich, *Römische Satiren* (Zürich, 1949).
A representative group of selections from the Roman satirists, translated into fluent German prose and verse, with valuable notes, and what the French call a "well nourished" introduction of a hundred pages.

(14) H. Wolfe, *Notes on English Verse Satire* (London, 1929).
A good clear introduction to the subject, particularly useful

on such problems as the distinction of satire and lampoon. It contains valuable comments on some satirists who are nowadays neglected, such as Belloc and Chesterton.

(15) D. Worcester, *The Art of Satire* (Cambridge, Mass., 1940).
A bright but diffuse book dealing mainly with satire in English, but bringing in some works in other languages. It should not be used without careful checking, for there are many bold statements (particularly about Greek and Roman literature) which are quite wrong, and many unjustifiable generalizations. Still, the author's distinction of "high" and "low" burlesque is good, he has a fine discussion of Rabelais, and in general his enthusiasm for the subject conveys itself to the reader—which is an essential virtue in any work of aesthetic appreciation.

INDEX

Figures in bold type indicate an important reference. Figures within parentheses mean that the subject of the note is not actually named in the passage cited.

A

Abraham a Sancta Clara, **48**, 76-77, 241, **254-55**, 257
abuse, 38, **152-54**, 201, 232-33, (253), 269, 270; in satire, 26, 211, 233
Abyssinia, 95-96, 204
Academy: French, 102, 262; Plato's, 30
Achaeans, 81
Achilles, 123, 258, 265, 267, 270
actors and acting, 68, 93
Addison, Joseph, 107, 108, 138, 261
adventure, tales of, 11, 37, 39, **113-15**, 150, 175-77, 181-83, **198-204**, 217-18
Aeneas, 7, 108, 267
Aeschylus, 121, 157, 248, 257
Aesop, 180, 252
Africa, 181, 182, (189), 204, 261
Agitprop, **62**, 64
Ajax, 270
Aladdin, 176
Alcibiades, 148
Alcmena, 120-21
Alexander the Great, 31, 165, 166, 219
Alexandrines, *see* meter
Alfred the Great, 85
allegories, 160, 180
alliteration, 135
Álvarez de Toledo y Pellicer, Gabriel, 108
Amadís de Gaula, 114
Ambert, 239
amoebaean song, 153
Amour, 103, 206, *and see* sex
Amphitryon, 120
anagrams, 97, 142, 260

anapaests, *see* meter
anarchism, 184
Anchises, 7
Anderson, Sherwood, 269
anecdotes, 32, 34, 41, 46, 48
angels, **72-73**, 85, 87, 133, 168
Angry Penguins, (101), 102
animals: in fable, 177-78; in satire, 39, 107-08, **177-90**, 228, **261**; *and see* ants, apes, bears, birds, cats, cattle, cocks, donkeys, foxes, frogs, gadflies, hens, horses, insects, leeches, lice, lions, mice, owls, penguins, pigs, rats, ravens, rhinoceroses, sheep, wasps, wolves
anthems, national, 77, 91
anticlimax, 18, 92
Anti-Jacobin Review, 133
Antioch, 43-44
anti-romance, 115, 150-51
antithesis, 18, 130, 137, 172, (182-83), (227)
Antony, Mark, 201-03, 253
ants, 177-78, 187
apes, 10, 90, 183, **189-90**, 212, 237, 273, 274
Apollo, 103, 104, 112, 263
Apollonius of Tyana, 273
apophthegms, 34
Apuleius, *Apologia* or *De Magia*, 273; *Metamorphoses*, 16, 113, **181-83**, (207), 209, 249, **273**
Arabia and the Arabs, 97, 118, 173, 251
Arabian Nights, (175), (176), 251
Aramaic, 139
archaisms in satire, 37, 83
Archestratus of Gela, 251
Archilochus, 38, 251
Architrenius (The Man of Many Sorrows), **160-61**, **270-71**, **280**
Archytas, 160
Argentine literature, 152, 270
Ariosto, Ludovico: *Orlando Furioso*, 112, 113, 115, 163, 261, (267), 271; satires, 47

INDEX

Aristophanes: as a dramatist, 26-29, 153, 207, 248, 274; as a satirist, 3, 26-29, 41, 50, 120, 132, 137, 198, 207, 241, 258; influence, 26-29, 36, 122, 163, 248, 250-51; *Birds*, (28), 186; *Clouds*, 26, (28), 56, 197-98; *Frogs*, 14, (120), 127, 163, (210), 248, 250; *Knights*, 26, 153; *Lysistrata*, (28); *Peace*, 163, 209, 251; *Wasps*, (28), 187, 248

Aristotle: Lyceum, 30; *Nicomachean Ethics*, (55, 56); *Poetics*, 13, 187, (233), (251), 258

Arthur's knights, 115, (165)

Ascanius, 108

Aspasia, 137, 138

asses, *see* donkeys

astrology, 97-99

Athena, 83, (104), 259

Athenaeum, 199

Athenaeus, 259

Athens and the Athenians: political and social life, 15, 57, 137, 153, 187, 258, 259; art, literature, and philosophy, 40, 41, 42, 56; *and see* comedy, tragedy

atomic bomb, (173), 184-85

Attila, 23

Augustine, Saint, 273

Augustus, 166, 167, 201

Aurora, 111

Australia and the Australians, 101-02, 149

Austria and the Austrians, 48, 200

autobiographical narrative, 37, 50, 114, 218, 277

B

Bach, J. S., 91

Bacon, Francis, 142

Balaam, 113

ballads, 132, 135, 229

baroque age, 47-48, (112-13), 121, 129, (184), 199, 227-28, 230, 265

Bath, Wife of, *see* Chaucer

Batrachomyomachia, see *Battle of Frogs and Mice*

Battle of the Books, 262-63

Battle of Frogs and Mice, 16, 39, 80-83, 89, 105-06, 107, 187, 255, 258

beards, 44, 95, 257

bears, 178

Beaumont, Francis, 121

Beerbohm, Max, 77-78, 122-23, 145-46

bees, 39, 187, 263

beggars, 16, (31), 33, 43, 124, 165, 243

Belgioioso, Prince Alberico di, 266-67

Belial, 86, 236

Bell, Clive, 217, 274

Bellamy, Edward, 171

Belloc, Hilaire, 281

Benchley, Robert, 177-78

Bennett, Arnold, 146

Bentley, Richard, 263

Berman, Shelley, 51

Bernard, Saint, 46

Bernard of Morval, *On the Contempt of the World*, 44-45, 254

Berni, Francesco, 47, 53, 115, 222

Bible, 139, 140, 142, 217; parodied, 132, 168, 257, 258; Old Testament, 214, 217; II Kings, 272; Psalms, 88, 257; Proverbs, 66, 177, 254; New Testament, 139; Gospels, 159; Matthew, 168, 258; Luke, 72; Acts, 31

Bildungsroman, 182

biography, 216-19

Bion of Borysthenes, 26, 30, 31-35, 40, 48, 51, 63, 240, 249, 254-55

birds, 68, 108, (185), 186

bishops, 15, 54, 133, 138, 144, 180

blank verse, *see* meter

Bloomsbury, 95, 195

Boccaccio, Giovanni: *Il Corbaccio*, 224, 226, 276; *Fiammetta*, 226

Boiardo, Matteo Maria, *Orlando Innamorato*, 115

Boileau, Nicolas, 16, 48, 61, 240, 263; *Art Poétique*, 112; letters, 61; *Le Lutrin (The Lectern)*, 108, 109, 262, 263-64; satires, 16, 222, 227, 262

Bologna, 110-11
Boswell's *Life of Johnson*, 143
bourgeois, 187, (208)
Bowles, Paul, *Sheltering Sky*, 151
Brady, Diamond Jim, 222
Brahms, Johannes, 90
Brant, Sebastian: *Alopekiomachia*, 261; *Ship of Fools*, 48, 224, 228
Brecht, Bertold, *Dreigroschenoper (Three-Penny Opera)*, 124
Brindisi, 153, 201-04
Britain and the British (social and historical), 6, 11, 12, 24, 83-88, 93, 94-97, 122, (138), 161, 171-72, 195, 204, 217, 219
Bromyard, John, 46
Brontë, Charlotte, (144)
Browning, Robert, 54, 55, 123, 135, 241, 255
Buckingham, George Villiers, Duke of, *Rehearsal*, 121
Bumble, Mr., 158
Bunyan, John, *Pilgrim's Progress*, 142-43
burlesque: defined, 103-07; examples, 109-13, 116-17, 118-20, 120-21, 123-24, 264
Burnett, Frances Hodgson, 151
Burns, Robert, *Holy Willie's Prayer*, 71-72, 76
Busche, Hermann von den, 140
Butler, Samuel (1612-1680), *Hudibras*, (16), (104), (105), 107, 119-20, 191, 279, 280
Butler, Samuel (1835-1902), *Erewhon*, 161, 280
"Buttle, Myra," *The Sweeniad*, 125-28
Byng, Admiral John, (12), 247
Bynner, Witter, 100-01
Byron, 48, 49, 134-35, 196, 201, 230, 240, 261, 280; *Childe Harold*, (135); *Don Juan*, 113, 201, 204; *English Bards and Scotch Reviewers*, 16, 48, 240; *Hours of Idleness*, 48; *Vision of Judgment*, 62, 80, 83-89, 127, 259
Byzantine satire, 257

C

Caesar, *see* Julius Caesar
Calas, Jean, 23
California, 149, 205
Caligula, 166
Callières, François de, 109, 262-64
Callimachus, 38, 40, 251, 261
Callot, Jacques, 200
Calverley, C. S., 135, 268, 280
Calvinism, 71-72, 76
Campbell, O. J., 265-66; Roy, 49, 195, 241, 247
Candide, *see* Voltaire
cannibalism, 10, 20, 58-60, 145, 204, 211, 212-13
Canning, George, 268
canular, 102
Čapek, Karel, *R.U.R.*, 187; and Josef, *The Insect Comedy*, 187
Capone, Al, 275
Caporali, Cesare, 222, 275-76
Carey, Henry, *Chrononhotonthologos*, 121-22, 265
caricature, 22, 69, 146, 158, 183, 190, 195, 196, 224-30
Caroline, Queen, 122
Carroll, Lewis, 176, 280
cartoons, 22, 169-70
Casaubon, Isaac, 47
Casella, Alfredo, 90
Casti, Giovanni Battista, *Gli Animali Parlanti*, 261
Catherine the Great, 204
Catiline, 253
Cato, 160
cats, 108, 178, 196
cattle, 36, 96, 180, 185, 231
Catullus, 106, 132, 261, 266
Céline, Louis-Ferdinand, *Voyage au Bout de la Nuit*, 190
Cercidas, 36, 40
Cervantes Saavedra, Miguel de, 168, 240-41; *Don Quixote*, 106-07, 116-20, 158, 173, 199-200, 207, 208, 210, 241-42; *Galatea*, 117
Chabrier, Emmanuel, 90
Chaplin, Charlie, 22
Chapman, George, 123, 266

character-portrait, character-sketch, 39, 40-41, 46, 53, 111, 138, 220, **224-28**, 233, 277
Charles I, 85; II, 108
Chatterton, Thomas, 85
Chaucer, Geoffrey, 42, 85, 232; *Canterbury Tales: Knight's Tale,* (189); *Nun's Priest's Tale,* (179), 273; *Tale of Sir Thopas,* 132; *Wife of Bath's Prologue,* 46-47, 53, 254
chefs, *see* cooks
Chesterton, Gilbert Keith, 281
choliambic, *see* meter
Chorism, 100
chorus: in comedy and satire, 28-29, 41, 122, 126, 153; in opera, 124, 125; in tragedy, 69-70, 132
Chrestien, Florent, 269
Christianity: doctrines and preachers, 31, **44-47**, 168, 169, 227, 236, 249, 253, 254; growth and conflicts, 6, 43, **44**, 139, 167, 213-16; criticized, 6-7, 42, 43, **71-72**, 127, 128, 167-68, 191, 205-06, **213-16**
Christmas, 145-46
church, Christian, (6), 44, 45-46, 71, 98, 108, 124, 128, 130, 139, 160, 169, 178, 179, 184, 191, 195, 205-06, 213-16, 267
Cicero, 103, 137, 138, 253
Cicirrus, 153
Cid Campeador, El, 118
Cid Hamet Benengeli, 118
Claudian, 42, (253)
Claudius, emperor, **165-67**, 251, **271-72**
Cleon, 26, 55, 153
Cloudcuckooland, 186
Clough, Arthur Hugh, 88
clowns, 50, 67, 106, 112, 156, (201)
Cobbett, William, 142
cocks, (61), 120, 153, 178
Cole, Horace de Vere, **94-97**
Coleridge, S. T., 196
Collier, John, *His Monkey Wife,* **189-90**, 274
colloquialism, (3), 18, 19, 20, 29, 32, 37, 41, 50, 51, 63, **103-05**, 233, 253, 272
comedy: humor and humorous writing generally, 67, 144, 150, 178, 179; the dramatic genus, 104, 157, 179, 196-98, 207; a type of literature allied to, but distinct from, satire, **150**, **154-56**, **196-98**, 207, 244, **248-49**, 255, 280; Greek Old Comedy, 25-29, 30, 41, 83, 153, 248, 252, 255, 258, 274, *and see* Aristophanes; Greek New Comedy, 30, 53, 113, 121, 153, 232, 248, *and see* Menander; Lucian's "comedies," 43; Roman comedy, 53, 121, 232, 233
commedia dell' arte, 232
Communist party, 62, (172), 184, **185-86**
"complaint," 45, 254
Connolly, Cyril, parodying Huxley, 269
Conrad, Joseph, 74, 145, 205
Constantine, emperor, 167-68
cooks and cookery, 53, 103, 275; in satire, 21, 59, 60, 111, 221, 230; *and see* dinners, food
Cooper, James Fenimore, 144
coqs-à-l'âne, 61
Corbeil, Gilles de, 46
Corneille, Pierre, 263
couplets, *see* meter
Cowley, Abraham, 133; Malcolm, 101
Cowper, William, 85
crabs, (81), 82, (83)
Crates, 36
Cratinus, 248
Cruikshank, George, 228
cryptography, 142
Cupid, 130, 182, 267
Cynics, 32, **33-34**, 36, 51, 111, 164, 165, 169, 185, 233, 250
Cyrus the Great, 165, 219

D

Dadaism, 192
Damon, S. Foster, 101
Dante, 84, 86, 88-89, 103, 163, 164, 169, 212
Dark Ages, **5-6**, (12), 13, 29
Daumier, Honoré, 228

dead, world of the, *see* Hades, *and* hell
Debussy, Claude, 90, 176
decasyllables, *see* meter
"declamations," 253
Defoe, Daniel, *New Voyage Round the World*, 150; *Robinson Crusoe*, 150
Demeter, 153
democracy, 15, 125, 126, 137
Democritus, 244
Demosthenes, 56, 138
Denham, Sir John, 18
descriptive satire, 220-30
Despard, Col. Edward, 60-61
devils, 45, 87, 148, 154, 168, *and see* Satan
de Vries, Peter, **147**
dialect, 32, 50, (51), 111, 153
dialectic process, 33, (56)
dialogue: dramatic, 27, **232-33**; philosophical, 32, **33**, 56-57, 63, 249, *and see* Plato; political, 62-63; satiric, 26, 27, 43, 53, **62-65**, 164, (233), **252-53**, 256, 271
diamerdis, powder of, 164
diatribe, **40**, 48, 51, 249, **250**, and chapter III passim
Dickens, Charles, 212; *Oliver Twist*, 158; *Our Mutual Friend*, 222-23; *The Pickwick Papers*, **198-99**
didactic poetry, 36, 160, 252, 267; satirized and parodied, **128-31**, 267
diminutives, 103, 104
d'Indy, Vincent, 90
dinners in satire, 21, 39, 49, 64-65, 204, 221-23, 243, 258-59, *and see* cooks, food
Dio Cassius, 271
Dio Chrysostom, 34
Diogenes, **33-34**, 36, 165
Dionysus, 120, 163, 210, 250
display speech, 53, 249
Disraeli, Benjamin, 125
doctors, 97, 197, 208, 209, 237, 241
doggerel, 107, 132
dogs, 33, 39, 183, 185, 229, 230
Dóhnanyi, Erno von, *Variations for Piano and Orchestra*, 82-83
Dominicans, 138, 139

Domitian, emperor, 42, 107
Donatus, 255
donkeys, (7), 31, (61), 106, 108, 113, 120, 179-80, 181, (182), 207, 209, 234
Donne, John, 47
Donnervetter, Ludwig, *All Is Everything*, 74
"Dooley, Mr.," 50
"Dozens, the," 152, 269
drama, 15, 33, 41, 47, 55, 103, 149, 156, 158, 255; drama satirized, 69-70, 106, **120-28**, 135; dramatic satire *or* satiric drama, 14, **157**, 158-59, **186-88**, **197-98**, 232-33, 255; *and see* 47
drawings, 193, **228-30**
"Dreadnought," H.M.S., 95-97
Dreyfus case, 184
drum matches, 152
Dryden, John, 133, 241; on satire, 109, 241; *Absalom and Achitophel*, 108, 109, 279; *Alexander's Feast*, (133); *Amphitryon*, 121; dramas, 265; *Mac Flecknoe*, 17, **108-09**; *Song for St. Cecilia's Day*, (133)
Duchamp, Marcel, 67-68
Dulness, the hypostatization, 7, 104-05, 127, 262
Dunbar, William, 154
Dunn, Alan, 169-70
Dunne, Finley Peter, 50
Dürer, Albrecht, 228

E

Ecbasis Captivi, **180**
Eiffel Tower, sold, 210
Eisenhower, Dwight D., 52, **143**
Eldorado, 10, 11, 162
elegiac poetry, 15, (104), 106; *and see* meter
Eleusinian procession, 153
Elijah, 109
Eliot, T. S., 102, **125-28**, 136; *Ash Wednesday*, 128; *Murder in the Cathedral*, 125, 126; *The Waste Land*, 126, (127), 128
Elisha, 109
Elizabeth, Queen, 85
emperors, *see* monarchs
Encolpius, *see* Petronius

encomium, 53, (165), (204)
England and the English (social and historical), 19, 45-46, 49, 58-60, 122, 126-27, 138, 159, 161, 171, 189, 193, 196, 204, 205, 228-30, 270, 274
Ennius: *Annals*, 107; *Hedyphagetica*, 39, 251; satires, 41, 53, 232-33, 248, 252, 255, 273
epic, 3, 15, 42, 103, 114, 160, 178, 258, 262; parodied: (a) burlesque, 103-07, 109-13, 114, 135, 149, 178-79, 264, 265, 281; (b) mock-heroic, 36, 39, 80-83, 103-07, 107-12, 149, 251, 252, 253, 258-59, 263-64, 265, 279
Epictetus, 34, 165
Epicurus, 271; Epicureans, 30, 115, 226, 243
epideictic speech, 53, 249
epigrams, the genus, 26, 104, 179, 253; in satire, 167
Epistemon, 164, 165, 271
Epistulae Obscurorum Virorum (*Letters of Obscure Men*), 139-40, 141, 268-69
Erasmus, 139; *Praise of Folly*, 16, 48, 53-54, (247), 255
Eskimos, 152
ethnocentrism, 205
Etruscan, 277
Eulenspiegel, Till (Owlglass), 208, (212)
Euphuism, 141
Euripides, 26, 32, 120, 127, 132, 248, 263
Eutropius, 42
excretion, 105, 111, 212, 227, 276
existentialism, 11
extravert satire, 65

F

fables, 32, 41, 46, 177-78, 179, 180, 252, 263
Fadiman, Clifton, 146-47
Falstaff, 107, 123, 210
Fame, 105
farce, 154-56, 231
farrago, 231, 234

Fathers, Unmarried, 74
Faulkner, William, 147, 151
Fescennine verses, 153
fessus, 103-04
Ficke, Arthur Davidson, 100-01
fiction, parodied, 143-47; *and see* anecdotes, fables, narrative satire, novels, stories
Fielding, Henry: *Jonathan Wild the Great*, 218-19; *Joseph Andrews*, 143-44; *Tom Jones*, 109; *Tom Thumb the Great*, 121, 265
Flaubert, Gustave, *Bouvard et Pécuchet*, 191-93
Fletcher, John, 121
flyting, (26), 152-54, (201), (232-33)
Folengo, Teofilo, 260; *Battle of Flies*, 107-08, 261
folklore, 32
folk-poetry, 99, 251, 258
Fontenelle, Bernard Le Bovier de, 170
food, and literature, 231, 233, 277; satirized, 34, 39, 53, 251-52, 271, 277; *and see* cooks, dinners
fools, 29, 34, 38-39, 48, 53-54, 66, 122, 159, 164, 179-80, 200, 201, 210, 216, 224, 271-72, *and see* lunatics
Fools' Mirror (*Speculum Stultorum*), 179-80, 273
foxes, 56, 158, 178-79, 180, 181, 188, 261
Fraenkel, E., (203), 248, 274
France and the French (social and historical), 91, 102-03, 112-13, 125, 141, 159, 184, 209, 210, 227, 228, 238-40, 262, 272, 275
France, Anatole, *Penguin Island*, 113, 184-85, 273
Franco, General Francisco, 126
Franklin, Benjamin, (255)
Frederick the Great, 275
Frere, John Hookham, 268
friars, 46
Friend of Humanity and the Knife-Grinder, The, 134, 268
frogs, *see Battle of Frogs and Mice*

G

gadflies, 122
Galileo, 172
Gargantua, see Rabelais
Garth, Sir Samuel, *The Dispensary*, 107
Gavarni, 228
Gay, John, *Beggar's Opera*, 124, 266
Gazul, Clara, 260
Genêt, Jean, 151
Genghis Khan, 23
George III, 61, **84-88**, (89), 127, 268; George IV, 122
Germany and the Germans (social and historical), 9, (61), 93-94, 96, 99, 138, 140, 182, 195, 200, (208), 270, 273, 275
giants, 149-50, 159, 164, 209, 212, 258, (259), 267
Gibbon, Edward, *Decline and Fall of the Roman Empire*, 7, **213-16**
Gibbons, Stella, *Cold Comfort Farm*, 269
Gilbert, W. S., and Sullivan, A., **124-25**, 196, (197), 266
Gilbert, Stuart, 264
Gillebertus, 46
Gilles de Corbeil, 46
Gillray, James, 228
Giraudoux, Jean, 121
Glyn, Elinor, 151
Gnostics, 214
God, 23, (71-72), 85, 130, 135, 136, 157, 168, 169, 213, 214, 215
God Save the Queen, 77
gods, pagan *or* Olympian, 31, 36, 42, 53, 80, 83, 106, 107, 110-11, 120-21, 164, **166-67**, 181, 186, 211, 216, 231, 271-72
Goebbels, Paul Joseph, 216
Goering, Hermann, 23
Goethe, 3, 276; *Faust*, 90, 191, 200, 211
Gogol, Nikolai, 241; *Revizor (The Inspector-General)*, 209, 275
Goldsmith, Oliver, *A Citizen of the World*, 274
"Goliards," 46, 132, 228
Golias Against Marriage, 46

Goncharov, Ivan A., *Oblomov*, (129), 267
Gordon, General Charles George, 217
Gorgias, 136
Gounod, Charles, 90
Goya, Francisco, 131
Graes, Ortwin von, 139-40
the Grail, 115, 162
Grandville, Gérard, 228
Grant, Duncan, 95, 97
Gravel, Fern, *Oh Millersville!*, 101
Graves, Robert, 272
Greek language, 25, 42, 43, 95, 135, 139, 180, 255, 272
Greek people (social and historical), 25, 30-31, 37, 38, 43, **120-21**, 153, 166, 181, 216, 227, 253, 258, 259
Gretchaninov, Alexander, 259
Grimmelshausen, Hans Jakob von, *Der abenteuerliche Simplicissimus*, 39, **200**, 209
Grock, 67
Gropius, Walter, 195
Grundy, Mrs., 161
Guggenheim Museum, 170

H

Hades, land of the dead, 21, 120, (163), 164-65, 212, 250; *and see* hell
Haggard, Rider, *King Solomon's Mines*, 11
Haiti, 181
Hal, Prince, 210
Hall, Joseph, 47
Handel, G. F., 85
Hannibal, 96, 108
Hansford-Johnson, Pamela, on satire, 277
Hanswurst, 48
Harte, Bret, *Condensed Novels*, **144-45**, 146
Hasek, Jaroslav, *The Good Soldier Schweik*, 200, 209
Hastings, Warren, 85
Hauteville, Jean de, *Architrenius*, 160-61

heaven, (7), 71, 84-85, 87, 88, 127, 163, 164, 165, 166, 167, 250
Hebrews: Hebrew language, 138, 139; *and see* Jews
Hector, 123, 265
Hegemon of Thasos, 258, 259
Helen of Troy, 110, 265
Heliodorus, 114
hell: the place of punishment, 45, 71, 87, 154, 166, (169), 212, (215), (236), 237; the abode of the dead, 163, 166
Hemingway, Ernest: *For Whom the Bell Tolls*, 11; *Torrents of Spring*, 269
Henry, O., *The Gentle Grafter*, 218, 274
hens, 185
Heraclitus, 244
Herbert, A. P., *Perseverance*, (125), 266
Hercules, 120, 121
heresy and heretics, 44, 139, 170, 236, 253
Hermes, 121
Hernández, José, *Martín Fierro*, 152, 270
Hesiod, 258
hexameters, *see* meter
Hipponax, 38, 155, 238, 251, 258
historical writing, 104, 117, 118, 166, 176, 213-16, 253; *and see* biography
Hitler, 22, 61
hoaxes, (91), 92-103, 208, 209, 238-39, 260
Hobbes, Thomas, quoted, 6
Hogarth, William, 85, 228, 276; "Gin Lane," 228-30
Home, Daniel Dunglas, 54
Homer, 32, 39, 103, 123, 251, 259; style and language, 80-82, 95, 106, 252; *Iliad*, 37, 39, 81, 123-24, 142, 234, 258, 259, 261; *Odyssey*, (10), 38, 109, 114, 163, 248, 250, 253, 259, 267; parodies of, 32, 36, 39, 80-83, 106, 108, 109, 114, 123-24, 248, 250, 252, 253, 259, 263, 264, 265-66
homilies, 179, 180, 226; *and see* sermons

homosexuality, 49, 53
Horace, 3, 64-65, 180, 201-04, 234, 235, 236, 240, 274, 275; on satire, 24-26, 29, 30, 35, 39-40, 47, 141, (191), 234, 235, 236, 248, 250, 252, 271; *Epodes*, 30, 38, 251, 264; lyrics ("Odes"), 30, 133, 134, 268; *sermones* (including both satires and letters), 30, 35, 40, 250, 251; *Letters*, 24, (25-26), 30, 35, 61, (161), (180); *Satires*, 24, 30, 35, 37, 39, 41, 45, 65, 180, 235, 236, 250, 275; individual satires: 1.1, 64, 234, 250, 252; 1.2, 252; 1.3, 252; 1.4, (25), 248, 252; 1.5, 153, 201-04, 248, 253, 274; 1.6, 203, 252; 1.7, 253; 1.8, 253; 1.9, 203, (222), 253; 1.10, (24), 132, 248, 250, 252; 2.1, 252; 2.2, 252; 2.3, (30), 250, 252; 2.4, 53, 252; 2.5, 252, 253, 275; 2.6, (203), 252; 2.7, 65, 252; 2.8, 64-65, 221, 252, 253, 275
horses, 36, 52, 159, 183, 209, 270
Housman, A. E., 69-70, 80
Hugo, Victor, 48, (144)
Hulagu, 23
"humanists," 139
humor, 32; *and see* comedy, satire
Hutten, Ulrich von, 140
Huxley, Aldous, 195, 269; *Ape and Essence*, 173; *Brave New World*, 174; *Point Counter Point*, 196
Hymen, 130, 267
hymns, 10, 72, 77, 91, 132

I

iambics, *see* lampoon *and* meter
Illyria, the poet of, 99-100, 260
imagery, 20, 69, 104, 119, 130, 133, 134, 153, 154, 249
Imagism, 100
imitation distinguished from parody, 68-69
improvisation, 27, 32, (35), 40, 41, 51, 152, 232-33, 242
incongruity, 13, 21, 42, 44, 55, 67, 150, 213, 229
Inquisition, Holy, 10, 11, 99, 172
insects, 107-08, 175, 187, 188, 209
introvert satire, 65

invective distinguished from satire, 42, 44, 151, **155-56**, 250, 253, 254, 258
Ionesco, Eugene, *The Rhinoceros*, 188
Iopas, 267
Ireland and the Irish, 15, **57-60**, 105, 110, 134, 159, 230
irony, 15, 18, 41, 46, **55-61**, 129, 213-16, 241, 255; "dramatic irony," 57, **255-56**
Islam, 205
Issoire, 239
Italy and the Italians, 37, 51, 54, 110-11, 141, 231, 232-33

J

Jack, Ian, *Augustan Satire*, 256, 279
Jack Pudding, 48
Jäger, Johann, 140
James, Clifton, 92-93, 94, 96; Henry, 145
Jaques, 47
Jarrell, Randall, *Pictures from an Institution*, 196
Jefferson, Thomas, **131**
Jensen, Oliver, **143**
Jerome, Saint, 44, 61, 253-54
Jesus, 31, 46, 72, (160), 168, 169, 213, 215, (257), 273
Jews, 10, 34, 61, 72, 108, **138-39**, 205, 214
Jewsbury, Miss Anne, 79
Joan, Saint, 86, **112-13**
Johnson, Samuel, 14, 142, 143, 247; *Vanity of Human Wishes*, 262
Jonson, Ben, *Volpone*, 188, 213
Joyce, James, *Ulysses*, **109-10**, 240, 264, 267
Juan, Don, 210
Judas Iscariot, 169
Julian the Apostate, 37, 43-44; on Christianity, 43, 168; *The Beard-Hater (Misopogon)*, 43-44; *The Drinking-Party (Symposium)*, (37), **167-68**, 251, 272
Julius Caesar, 166, 167, 219
Jung, C. G., 121
"Junius," 61-62, 85, 87

Juno, 111, 112, 262
Jupiter, 111, 168, 263
Juvenal, 16, 37, **41-42, 43**, 141, 160, 240-41, 250, 253; on satire, 15, 231, 234, 235; individual satires: 1: 15, 16, 48, 231, **234**, 252; 2: 252; 3: **3-5**, 12, 13, 16, 19-20, 21, 252, 253; 4: 42, 107, 252, **253**, 261; 5: 221; 241, 243, 252, 271; 6: (212), 224, 226-27, 252, 253; 7: 252; 8: 252, 267; 9: 53, 252, 253; 10: 252, 262, 266, 271; 11: 243, 252; 12: 252; 13: 252; 14: (130), 252, 267; 15: 252, 253; 16: 252

K

Kennedy, John F., 52; Walter, 154
kings, *see* monarchs
Kipling, Rudyard, 145-46
Knish, Anne, 100-01
Knox, Ronald, *Essays in Satire*, **142-43**
Koestler, Arthur, 172
Köpenick and its Captain, 93-94, 96
Kreuger, Ivar, 92

L

Labouchere, Henry, 77, 257-58
Laforgue, Jules, 136
Lamb, Charles, 191
lampoon, 26, 30, 61, **151-54, 155-56**, 166, (238), 281
Langland, William, *Piers Plowman*, 47, 254
Laocoon, **89-90**
lassus, 103-04
Latin language, classical, 24, 45, 95, 103-04, 108, 139, 160, 181, 221, 231; post-classical, 44, 45, 139, 140, 141, 160, 179, 180, 199
lectures, 32, 33, 41
Lee, Charles, 79
leeches, 122, 237
Leers, 35-36, 37
Leibniz, Gottfried, 8, 22-23, 207
Leporello, 210
Le Roy, Pierre, 269

Le Sage, Alain René, *Gil Blas de Santillane*, 218
letters, poetic, 61, 65, 256, 275; *and see* Horace *and* Pope; prosaic, 61-62, 139-40, 201, 205-06, 253
Letters of Obscure Men (Epistulae Obscurorum Virorum), **139-40**, 141
Lewis, D. B. Wyndham, *The Stuffed Owl*, 79; Percy Wyndham, *The Apes of God*, 195; *One-Way Song*, 49-50
lice, 237, 268
Lichtenberg, Georg Christoph, 276
Limbo, 21, (163), 164, 271
Lincoln, Abraham, *Gettysburg Address*, 143
Linklater, Eric, *Juan in America*, 204
lions, 36, 178, 180, 261
Livy, 103, (232), 277
"local gags," 233, 277
London, 19, 131, 176, 223, 229-30
Longfellow, Henry Wadsworth, 88
Louis, Saint, 113; Louis XIV, 159, 184, (262), 263; Louis XVI, 131; Louis-Philippe, 228
Low, David, 22
Lowrey, Burling, *Twentieth-Century Parody*, 269
Lucian, 35, 37, **42-43**, 107, 164, 240, 250, 251, 253, 255, 271; *Ignorant Book-Collector*, 43; *Lucius or Donkey*, 273; *Nigrinus*, 43; *Paid Companions*, 43; *Pictures*, 253; *Professor of Oratory*, 32; *True History*, 149, **176-77**
Lucilius, **24-29**, 30, 38, 41, 107, 180, 203, 233, 234, 241, **248-49**, 252
Lucius, (181), 182, 207; *and see* Apuleius, *Metamorphoses*; Lucius of Patras, 273
Lucretius, 130, 267; as a satirist, 3, 226
lunatics, 39, (84-85), (89), 105, 116, 117, 119, 120, 159, **163**, 166, 200, 207, 208, 216, 217, 230, 237, 250, 255
Luther, Martin, 140
Lyceum, 30

lyric poetry: Greek, 25, 36, 120, 132, 133; Latin, 30, 132, 133; other, 48, 100-01, 126, 127, **131-36**, 260
lyrical satire, including parodies of lyric poetry, 36, 45, **100-02**, 127, **131-36**, 199, 211, 261
Lysias, 137

M

macaronic poetry, 104, 107-08, 231, 260, 261
Macaulay, Thomas Babington, 24, 261
McCarthy, Mary, *The Groves of Academe*, 196
Macedonians, 259
Mack, Maynard, 277-78
MacLeish, Archibald, 136
McTwaddle, Dr. Mary, 74
Madariaga, Salvador de, 117
madmen, *see* lunatics
Maecenas, 64, **201-03**, 221, 250, 274
magic, 181, 182, 209, 273, 279
Maglanovitch, Hyacinthe, 99-100, 260
Malherbe, François de, 263
Malley, Ern, 101-02
Malory, Sir Thomas, 116, 179
Man of Many Sorrows, The (Architrenius), **160-61**, **270-71**, **280**
Manet, Édouard, 68
Maoris, 161
Map, Walter, 46, 254
maqama, 251
Margites, **38-39**, 178, 200, **251**
Marini, Giovan Battista, 263
Marlborough, Duke of, 85
Marlowe, Christopher, 123, 265
Marot, Clément, 61
marriage, satires on, 39, 46, 130, 224-27, 254; *and see* women
Marston, John, 47, 280
Martians, 170
Marx, Karl, 184
the Mass, 257
Matro, *Attic Dinner*, 252, **258-59**
Maurois, André, *Voyage au Pays des Articoles*, **161-62**

Maurras, Charles, 126
Mayakovsky, Vladimir, *Klop* (*The Bedbug*), **174-75**
Mayer, Louis B., 275
Medamothy, 162, 271
Megerle, Johann Ulrich = Abraham a Sancta Clara
Melbourne, Viscount, 142
Menander, 198, 207
Mendès, Catulle, 258
Menelaus, 123, 124, 265
Menippean form of satire, 36, 37, (39), 141, 272, 275
Menippean Satire, The (*Satyre Ménippée*), **141**
Menippus, 36, 37, 111, 163, 164, 165, 166, 167, 169, 233, 240, **250-51**, 252
Mephistopheles, 211
Mercury, 111, (121), 269
Mérimée, Prosper, 99-100, 260
Merlin, 98-99
metaphor, *see* imagery
metaphysicotheologocosmolonigology, 9, *and see* optimism
meter, 29, 37, 103, 104, 248, 251, 270; individual types: Alexandrines, 113; anapaests, 28, 134; blank verse, 123, 129, 130; choliambic, 38; couplets, rhyming, 122, 230; decasyllables (French), 113, (264); elegiac couplets, 36, 179, 181, 261; (dactylic) hexameters, 36, 39, 44, 80, 84, 88, 112, 160, 251, 252, 270; heroic couplets, 107, 109; iambics, 26, 30, 36, **38**, 39, 86, 132, 251; octosyllables, 61, 104, (107), 112; *ottava rima*, 86, (88); Sapphic stanza, 134, 268; scazon, 38; Spenserian stanza, 135; trochees, 28, 252
mice, *see* Battle of Frogs and Mice
Michael the archangel, 87, 88
Michelangelo, 90, 122
Mickiewicz, Adam, 100
Middle Ages, 44-47, 72-73, 114, 115, 116, 132, 160, 172, **178**, 179, 250, 254, 269, 280
Miller, Henry, **50**, 255
millionaires, 4, 43, 52, 184, 195, 221
Milton, John, 49, 85, 86, 89, 140, 260; *Paradise Lost*, 163-64, 271

mimicry, 68-69, 77-78, 93, 123, 155, 233
Minerva, 130, 199, *and see* Athena
miracles, 31, 85, 87, 157, 164, 165, 184, 205, 207, 214, 215-16, 273
Mirbeau, Octave, *Le Jardin des Supplices*, 151
misanthropy, **235-36**
misogyny, 39, 46, *and see* women
missionaries, **31-34**, 184
Mix, Miss, 144
mock-heroic, defined, **103-07**; examples, 36, 39, **80-83**, **107-12**, 118, 120, 121-23, 124-25, 219, 252, 253, 258-59, 263-64, **265**, 279
Modena, 110-11
Mohammed, 205
Molière, *Amphitryon*, 121; *Tartuffe*, (157), 197
Moloch, 86, 221
"Momism," 50
Momus, 104, 263
Mona Lisa, 67
monarchs and monarchy, 5, 11, 31, 42, 77-78, **84**, 86-87, 94, 95-96, 108, 131, 142, 157, **165-68**, 176, 178, 179, 180, 210, 212, 216, 228, 240, 261, 272
money, satirized, 10, 11, 34, 36, 43, 46, (51), (53), 54, 64, 76-77, 212-13, 260-61; *and see* millionaires
monkeys, *see* apes
monks and monasticism, 54, 169, 180, 181, 257, 260, 269
monocles, 223-24
monologue: non-satirical, 31-34, 36, 40, 44, 55, 146, 250, 253, 255; satirical, 5, **13-14**, 16, 35, 37, 39, **40-41**, **41-66**, 148, 224, **252-53**, 254, 255, **277-78**
Montagu, Lady Mary Wortley, 227-28
Montesquieu, Charles de, *Persian Letters*, **205-06**
Montgomery, Gen. Bernard, 93, 96
Moore, Tom, 134
More, Thomas, 247, 255; *Utopia*, 162
Morgan, Emanuel, 100-01

Morier, J. J., *The Adventures of Hajji Baba*, 218, 274-75
Morris, Besaleel, 17-18; William, (135)
motion-pictures, 156, 173
Muller, Charles, 90
Munchausen, Baron, *see* Raspe
Murry, John Middleton, 196
Muses, 103, 104, 133, (135), 244, 262
music, 26, 67, 82-83, **90-92**, 101, 133, 152, 153, 161, 176, 187, 189, 208, 221, 259
Musonius, Rufus, 34
Mussolini, 23, 110
myths, 126, 130; Greek and Roman, 112, 120, 121, 140, 277

N

Naevius, Gnaeus, 25, 233, 277
names, satiric, 54, 80-81, 97, 99, 101, 105-06, 114, 125, 128, **140**, 184, 199, 221, 223, 234, 271, **274-75**, 276
Napoleon I, 91, 178; Napoleon III, 48
narrative satire, **9-12**, 13-14, (18), 37, 39, 80, 114, 116, **148-230**, 253, 277
Navy, Royal, (12), **94-97**, 125, 138, (197)
Nazis, (9), (23), (61), 188
Negroes, 152, 195, 269, 270
neologisms in satire, 37, 104
Nero, 115, 165-67, 272, 275
Nerval, Gérard de, 100
New York World-Telegram, 73-75, 257
New Zealand, 161, 173
Newhart, Bob, 255
Newman, Ernest, 259
newspapers, 51, 171, 172
Nietzsche, Friedrich Wilhelm, 168
Nigel of Canterbury, *Speculum Stultorum*, 179-80
night-clubs, 51-52
Nightingale, Florence, 216-17
Nivard of Ghent, *Ysengrim*, 180-81
nobility and gentry, 34, 54, 106, **129-31**, 138, 178, 189, 193, 208, 212, 241, 243, 266, 275

"novelette," 193
novels, 49, 50, 109-10, **143-47**, 149-51, **156-58**, **188-90**, **190-96**, **198-200**, **204-05**, 206, 222-24, **269**, 277

O

Oblomov, by I. Goncharov, 129, 267
obscenity, as an element of satire, 15, 18, 20, 26, 27, 29, 41, 50, 51, 110, 212, 232, 233, 242, 249, 256; in other genera, 32, 34, 102, 153, 201, 242, 269
observer, satirical, 47, 50, 115, (123-24), 198, 200, 203, 204, 205, 218
Octavian (later Augustus) 201-03
octosyllables, *see* meter
Odysseus, 10, 38, 114, 163, 250; *and see* Ulysses
Offenbach, Jacques, 125
Oldham, John, 48
Olympians, *see* gods
opera: comic, 26; romantic, 100; tragic, 82; parodic, **124-25**
optimism, (8), 10, 22-23, 171, 207, 236, 237, (243); *and see* metaphysicotheologocosmolonigology
oratory: in general, 33, 44, 102, 103, 141, 240, 273; Greek, 15, 25, 53, 57, 104, 114, 137, 141; Latin, 104, 141, 165, 167; parodied, 15, 53, **75-76**, **137-38**, 141-42, 143, 267; *for* pulpit oratory, *see* sermons
Origen, 191
Orpheus, 125; Orphism, 169
Orwell, George, 240; *Animal Farm*, **185-86**; *Nineteen Eighty-Four*, **171-73**
Osric, 158
ottava rima, *see* meter
Otway, Thomas, 265
Ovid, 179, 270; *Art of Love*, 128-29, 252; *Metamorphoses*, 140, 160, (182), 269, 270
Owl, Stuffed, 79
Owlglass, Till, (Eulenspiegel), 208, (212)
owls, 17, 79
Owst, G. R., *Literature and Pulpit in Medieval England*, 45-46, 254

Oxford, 193-95, 240; 17th Earl of, 142
oxymoron, 227

P

Pachmann, Vladimir de, 67
pagans, 6, 44, 72, 165, **167-68, 213-16**, 236, 273
painting, 20, 67-68, 120, 131, 161, (227), 242, 271
Pallas Athena, 104
Pan, 104
Pandarus, 22, 123
Pangloss, *see* Voltaire
Pantagruel, **210-11**, *and see* Rabelais
Panurge, **210-11**, *and see* Rabelais
papists, *see* Roman Catholics
parabasis, **28-29**
parables of Jesus, 72
paradox, in satire, 17, 18, 40, 51, 53, 167, 172, 242, 249, 266
parasites, 53, 252, 255, (259)
Parini, Giuseppe, *Il Giorno* (*The Day*), **129-31**, 241, 266-67
Paris, city and university, 16, 102, 108, 160, 171, 180, 223, (238), 239; prince, 112, 123, 124, 265
Parnassus, 112, 263
parody: defined, **69**; generally, 258, 269, 279-280; in satire, **6-7, 13-15**, 18, 29, 39, 40, 46, 49, 51, **67-147**, 166, 167, 169, 241, 248, **256-69**; in allied forms, 32, 48, 160, **256-57**
parodic satire, **6-7, 13-15**, 29, 46, 53, **67-147**, 148, 149, 169, 231, 240, 242, 252, 253, **256-69**, 276, 277
paronomasia, *see* puns *and* word-play
παρρησία, 34
Parthenon, (83), 259
parties, horrible, **219-20, 221-24**
Partridge, John, **98-99**, 260
Pascal, Blaise, 175
Passerat, Jean, 269
pastoral literature, 135, 153-54, 207, 276
Patroclus, 123

patrons and patronage, 64, (201-04), 221, 243
Paul, Saint, 31, 249
Peacock, Thomas Love, 16, 195-96, 198; *Melincourt*, **189**
Pegasus, 133
Pegler, Westbrook, **73-75**
Pellinore, Sir, 116
Peloponnesians, 259
penguins, 184
Perceval, Spencer, 85
Pericles, 137
Perrault, Charles, *Le Siècle de Louis le Grand*, 262
Persia and the Persians, 31, 205-06, 218, 259, 274-75
Persius, 41, 234, 248, **252-53**
persona of the satirist, 277-78
pessimism, 171, 185, (235), 236, 237, 243
Pétain, Marshal, 126
Peter, Saint, 88; Peter the Great, 159
Petrarch, 89
Petronius, 3, 241; *Satyrica*: name, **232, 264**; purpose, 115; character, 14, 37, **114-15**, 209, 212-13, 221-22, 253, 275, 277
Pfefferkorn, Johann, 139
Pharisees, 72
Phemius, 267
Philips, John, *The Splendid Shilling*, (104), 260-61
Phillips, Stephen, 123
Philo, 34
philosophy, general, 8-9, 30-31, 174, 179, 183, 244, 250, 251; Greek, 30-37, 40, 43, 44, 63, 215, 233, 236, 250; medieval, 73; *and see individual philosophers and schools*
phlyákes, 120
"photography," satiric, 3, 190, 200, 203, 222
picaresque stories, 114, 199, 200, **217-19**
Picasso, Pablo, 68
Piers Plowman, 47, 254
Pigres of Halicarnassus, 258
pigs, 39, 59, 116, 122, 185, 226, 264, 268

Pindar, 133, (135), 263, 268
"Peter Pindar" (John Wolcot), 135, 268
Piosistratus, Sextus Amarcius Gallus, 45
Pistol, 107, 123
Pithou, Pierre, 141, 269
Piwonka, M. Puelma, 248, 250, 251, 256
Plato, 15, 30, 33, 56, 63, 65, 136, 160, 169, 271; *Apology* or *Defence of Socrates*, 40; *Gorgias*, 56-57, 136; *Menexenus*, 15, 57, **136-38**; *Phaedrus*, 137; *Protagoras*, 136; *Republic*, 164; *Symposium*, (179)
Plautus, 121, 233
plays, *see* drama
Plutarch, 219
polemic, 43, 44, 56
politics as a theme for satire, 24, 26, 27, 42, 51-52, 73-75, 75-76, 77, 80, 107, 108, 191, 199, 201-04, 219, 261, 267, 268
Pompey, Sextus, (201), 202
Popes and the Papacy, 102, 111, 139, 140, 141, 165, 206
Pope, Alexander, 3, 15, 48, 61, 109, 130-31, 240, 277, 278; *Dunciad*, **6-7**, 12-13, 17-18, (104), 105, 109, 127, 128, 262; *Epilogue to the Satires*, 63-64; Homer, 109, 262; letters in verse, 61, 256; *Moral Essays*, 256; *Prologue to the Satires*, (138), 278; *Rape of the Lock*, (104), (106), 109, 130, 231, 262, 267, 279
porpoises, 184, 273
portraits, 69, 111, 131, 220
Poseidon, 114
Pound, Ezra, 79, 102, 136
practical jokes, *see* hoaxes
prayers, **71-72**, **76-77**, 163
preaching, *see* sermons
Priapus, 114
priests, 12, 46, 54, 102, 108, 117, 126, 140, 166, (179), 206, 208, 212, 228, 249
princes, *see* monarchs

Prisoner's Exit (Ecbasis Captivi), 180
Prodicus, 136
Progress, Inevitable, *see* metaphysicotheologocosmolonigology
Prometheus, 130
prose, non-fictional, parodied, 136-43
prostitutes, 31, 32, 96, 116, 121, 124, (193), 249, 269
Protagoras, 136
Protestants, 108, 141, 240
Protocols of the Elders of Zion, 92
Proust, Marcel, 182, 223-24, 280
proverbs, 48, 76, 177
Psyche, 182
pterodactyls, 92
puella, 104
Pulci, Luigi, *Morgante*, 264
pulpit oratory, *see* sermons
Punch and Judy, 48
puns, 32, 46, 48, 120, 167, 259, 272; *and see* word-play
puppets, 48, 241
purgatory, 163, 226
Puritans, 119
Pushkin, Alexander, 100

Q

Quevedo y Villegas, Francisco Gómez de, *Visions*, 86, **168-69**, 212, 241, 259
Quintilian, 140
Quixote, *see* Cervantes
quotations, 32, 257; in satire, 16, 42, 43, 45, 62, **104**, 130, 160, 226

R

Rabelais, François, 3, 47, 50, 97, **115**, 119, 133, 176-77, 208, 212, **239-40**, 241, 281; Almanac, 97; *Gargantua*, 148, (212), **239-40**, 243; *Pantagruel*, 97, 148, 162, 164-5, 168, 169, 176, **210-11**; *Prognostification*, 97-98
Racine, Jean, 235, 263
Ralph, James, 17-18
Ranke, Leopold, 99-100

Rapin, Nicolas, 269
Raspe, Rudolph, *Baron Munchausen*, 158, **175-76**
rats, 122
Ravel, Maurice, 90
ravens, 185, 188
Read, Herbert, 102
Reboux, Paul, 90
Reed, Henry, 136
Reformation, 140
Régnier, Mathurin, 47, 222, 275-76
religion, 8, 273; Greek, 31, 36, 42; satirized, 36, 42, **70-72**, 76-77, 80, **138-41**, 148, 173, 190, 271-72
Renaissance, 47, 114, 115, 132-33, 138, 184, 222, 224, 228
Reuchlin, Johann, 139-40
revue, 232
Reynard the Fox, 158, **178-79**, 183, (212), 261
rhapsodists, 258
rhetoric, 32, 104, 114, 116-17, 141, 277-78
rhinoceroses, 188
rhymes, burlesque, 104
Richard I, 85
Richardson, Samuel, *Pamela*, 143
Rinaldo, 267
Robeson, Paul, 195
Rochester Philharmonic Orchestra, 91
rococo, 130
Romains, Jules, 102, 239; *Knock*, 209; *The Pals (Les Copains)*, 102-03, **238-39**
Roman Catholics, (6), 7, (42), 58, 98, 126, 128, 141, 169, 205-06, 240
romance, romantic fiction, 11, 14, 103, 109, **113-20**, 150-51, (156), 157, 190, 193, 198, 200, 201, 242
Romance of the Rose, 47
Rome and the Romans (social and historical), 4-5, 6-7, 15, 20, 34, 42, 43, 96, 107, 108, 141, **167**, 201-03, 211, 214, 216, **221-22**, 232, 234
Romulus, 108, 166
Roosevelt, Eleanor, 74-75
Roppel, Earl, 101
Rose, W. S., *Court of Beasts*, 261

Round Table, Knights of the, 115, 165
Rowlandson, Thomas, 228
Royal Society, 159
Rufinus, 42
Ruskin, John, *Aratra Pentelici*, 19-20
Russell, Lillian, 222
Russia and the Russians, 91, 159, **174-75**, 185, 204

S

Sade, Marquis de, 151
Sahl, Mort, 51-52, 255
salt = wit, 26, 30, 34, 249
Sancho Panza, *see* Cervantes
Sapphic stanza, *see* meter
sarcasm, 41, **57**
Satan, 85, 86, 87, 89, 99, (169)
satir, 277
SATIRE: name, 180, **231-33**, 276-77
  definitions, 5, **14-22**, 45, 47, **150**, 163, 182, 231, 233, 237-38
  neighbors, 26, **151-56**, 197
  the satiric emotion, **12-13**, **21-23**, 68-69, 112, **150**, 172, 188, 193, 208, 210, 216, **235-38**, **278**
  subjects, 3, 5, 8, **16-18**, 22-23, 40-41, 51, 65, 159-60, **209-10**, 234, 242
  patterns or forms, **13-14**: monologue, 5, 13, 40-41, 148, 224, and chapter II; *parody*, 7, 14, 148, and chapter III; narrative and drama, 13-14, 116, **148**, **156-58**, and chapter IV
  characteristics: critical spirit, 17, 20, 25, 26, 29, 35-36, 48, 50-52, 55, 64, 65, 89, 97, 176, 252; desire to shock, 5, 18, 20-21, 41, 51, 65, 168, **211-12**; distortion, 5, **123**, **156-58**, 159, 190-91, 196-97, 198, 228; humor, 5, 12, 15, 18, 21, 30, 35, 40, 47, 110, 192, 212-13, 228, **233-34**, 242; improvisatorial tone, 27, **40-41**, 48, 51, 233, 242; informality, looseness of form, 3, 5, 10-11, 27,

29, 35, 40, 51, 180, 201, **206-08**, 233; *interest in personalities*, 3, 16, 26, 29, 40, 195-96; *photographic clarity*, 3, 45, 200, 203, 222; *realism*, 3, 5, 16, **18-20**, 42-43, 123; *topicality*, 4, 5, **16-18**, 26, 40, 42, 51; *variety*, **18**, 24, 40, 44, 61, **62**, 201, 231, 233, 237-38, 254; *special vocabulary*, 3, 17, **18**, 19, 20, 28, 29, 41, 51, **103-05**, 113, 119, 242, 271; *wit*, 35, 40, 48, 61, 123, 254; *and see* abuse, anecdotes, animals, caricature, colloquialism, dialogue, fables, incongruity, irony, names, obscenity, paradox, puns, word-play

SATIRE, ROMAN: **24-30**, **35**, **39-40**, 41-42, 45, 51, 53, 107, 113-15, 165-67, 181-83, **232-33**, 234, **248-56**, 261, 264, **271-77**, 279-80; *and see individual satirists*

SATIRICAL WRITING, GREEK: 25, **26-39**, 42-44, 107, 120-21, 132, 136-38, 163, 164, 167-68, 176-77, 178, 186-87, 233, **248-55**, 258-59, 271, 272, 274, 279; *and see individual satirical writers*

SATIRISTS: *motives*, 17, **26-27**, 146, **155-56**, 158, 167, 212, 218, **234-38**, **238-43**, 264, **277-78**; *difficulties and dangers*, 15, 16-18, 42, 51, 55, 138, 222, **234-35**

satura, 18, 40, 153, (180), 207, 231, 232, 233, 237, 256, **276-77**

Saturn: god, 111; planet, 170, 223; Saturnalia, 65, 167, 272

Satyre Ménippée, **141**, **269**

satyr-play, 258, 277

satyrs, 41, 231-32, 264, (277)

Sausage-Seller, 153

Scarron, Paul, *Virgile Travesti*, 112, 119

scazon, *see* meter

Sceptics, 36, 51

scholasticism, 72-73

Schönberg, Arnold, *Three Satires*, **91**

Schubert, 268

Schweik, The Good Soldier, by Jaroslav Hasek (1883-1923), 200, 209

Scotland and the Scots, 71-72, 152, 154, 196, 223, 240

Scriblerus Club, 73, 121

sculpture, 6, 12-13, 19, 20, 161, 228; parodied, 89-90, 102

Sebastian, Saint, 90

self-parody, 78-79, 85, 133, 258

Semitic languages, 221, 251

Semonides, 39, 226

Seneca, 34, 165-67, 263; *Apocolocyntosis* or *Pumpkinification of Claudius*, 16, 37, **165-67**, 251, 253, 255, **271-72**

Serbia, 100

sermones, 40, 45, 46, 256; *and see* Horace

sermons, 41, 44, **45-46**, 48, **102**, 213, (228), 249, 254

servants, 10, 24, 129, 143-44, 198, 210; *and see* slaves

Settle, Elkanah, 7, 13

sex, 37, 60, 112-13, 114-15, 173, 174, 181, 184, 204, 206, 248, 269

Shadwell, Thomas, 17, 108-09

Shakespeare, 3, 28, 47, 49, 85, 103, 122, 123, 142, 147, 157, 174, 197; *All's Well*, 197; *As You Like It*, 47; *Coriolanus*, (189), 266; *Hamlet*, 17, 57, 124, 158, 227; *Henry IV*, (107), 123, (210); *Measure for Measure*, 266; *Othello*, 22; *Richard III*, 52-53; *Romeo and Juliet*, (123), 265; *Sonnets*, 266; *Timon of Athens*, 57, 266; *Troilus and Cressida*, 14, 22, 123-24, **265-66**; *Twelfth Night*, 197

Shaw, Bernard, 174; *Arms and the Man*, (157); *The Doctor's Dilemma*, 197

sheep, 79, 185

Shelley, 49, 196; *Oedipus Tyrannus*, 122; *Prometheus Unbound*, 122

shepherds, 153, 207

Simplicissimus, see Grimmelshausen

Sindbad the Sailor, 175, 176

Sitwell, Edith, 90; family, 195

Skelton, John, 47
slang, *see* colloquialism
slaves, 12, 22, 31, 36, 65, 166, (182), 203, 211, 221, 240
Slavs, 11, 100
Smith, Horace and James, *Rejected Addresses*, (14), 134-35, 141-42, 247; Sydney, 24; William Henry, 125
Snow, C. P., on satire, 277
Socrates, 26, 33, 40, 41, 55-57, 63, 137-38, 148, 179, 197-98, 236, 249
soldiers of fortune, 38, 53, 157, 175, 200; boastful soldier, 175
song, 101, 211, 259; combats in, 152-54, 269-70
sonnets, 79-80
sophists, 30, 33, 136, 181, 249
Sophocles, 235, 257, 263
Southey, Robert, 84-89, 134, 196, 268
space fiction, 163, 271
Spain and the Spaniards, 86, 118, 141, 168, 189, 217
Spectra hoax, 100-01
Speculum Stultorum, 179-80, 280
Spenser, 85, 119; Spenserian stanza, *see* meter
spider and bee, 263
σπουδογέλοιος, 36, 233-34, 250
Squire, J. C., 247
Stalin, 23, 185
Standard Speech to the United Nations Organization, 75-76
Statius, 107, 253, 261, 263
Steinberg, Saul, 147
Stephen, Adrian, 95-96; J. K., 79-80; Virginia, 95-97
Stilicho, 42
Stoics, 30, 41, 165, 168, 250
Stone Age, 151, (177), 183
stories, short, 122, 145, 146, 208
Strachey, Giles Lytton, 49; *Eminent Victorians*, 216-17; *Queen Victoria*, 49
Stranitzky, Joseph, 48
Stratocles, 259
Strauss, Richard, 82, 208
Stravinsky, Igor, 90
Stuffed Owl, The, 79

Sullivan, *see* Gilbert
supernatural intervention, 80, 83, 104-05, 126, 130, 157
"Sweeney," 126, 127
Swift, Jonathan, 3, 22, 50, 109, 131, 133, 138, 159-60, 185, 227, 235, 240, 267, 278; *Accomplishment of the First of Mr. Bickerstaff's Predictions*, 98; *Battle of the Books*, 109, 263; *Beautiful Young Nymph Going to Bed*, 276; *Cantata*, 133; *Mr. Collins's Discourse against Free-Thinking*, (191); *Complete Collection of Genteel and Ingenious Conversation*, 191-92; *Description of a City Shower*, 267; *Elegy on Partridge*, 99; *Gulliver's Travels*, 15, 149-50, 158, 159-60, 174, 176, 185, 207, 208, 277; *Lilliput*, 131, 149, 159, 170, 207, 209, (212), 261, 267; *Brobdingnag*, 138, 149-50, 159, 207, 209, (212), 267, 276; *Laputa*, 149, 159, 207, 267; *Houyhnhnms*, 149, 183, 207, 209, 267; *Intended Speech against Peace*, 267; *Lady's Dressing-Room*, (212), 227; *Legion Club*, (105), 230; *Modest Proposal*, 57-61; *On Poetry*, (104); Pindaric poems, 133; *Predictions . . . by Bickerstaff*, 98, 99; *Proposal for Correcting the English Language*, (22), 247; *Strephon and Chloe*, 276; *Vindication of Bickerstaff*, 99; *Windsor Prophecy*, 267
Swinburne, Algernon Charles, 135-36
swindles, 92, 209-10, 233
sylphs, 104
Symposium, by Julian, 167-68; by Plato, (179)

T

Tacitus, 216
Talmud, 138
Tassoni, Alessandro, 241; *La Secchia Rapita (Rape of the Bucket)*, 106, 109, 110-12, 264
Tchaikovsky, Peter, 90, 91-92

Teles, 249
television, 172, 232
"telling the truth in a jest," 47, 141, 191, 234, 235
Tennyson, Alfred, 123; *In Memoriam*, 142; *Locksley Hall*, 190; *Vivien*, (99)
Terence, *Phormio*, 255
Tertullian, 44, 191, 276
Thelema, Abbey of, 243
Theocritus, 153-54
Thersites, 39, **123-24**, 251
Thessaly, 181
Thirlwall, Connop, 255
Thomas Aquinas, Saint, 73
Three-Penny Opera, see Brecht
Thucydides, 137
Tiberius, emperor, 216
Timon, of Athens, *see* Shakespeare; of Phlius, 36-37
Tiresias, 163, 252
Tithonus, 111
Titian, 90
totalitarianism, 171-73, 188, 199
Tourneur, Cyril, 280
tragedy, 3, 13, (15), 23, 42, 157, 169, 179, 197, **235, 236**, 244; Greek, 13, 27, **69-70**, 80, (104), 120, 258, 277; Roman, (104)
Trajan, emperor, 240
translation, 69, 109, 123, 173
travel, tales of, **149-50, 159-62, 175-77**
Tree, Herbert Beerbohm, 123
Trimalchio, the name, 221; *and see* Petronius
triumphal procession, 211
trochees, *see* meter
Troy and the Trojans, 81, 112, 123, 265
Troy, Hugh, 92
Tyler, Wat, 86

U

Ulysses, 252, 270; *and see* Joyce *and* Odysseus
underworld, *see* Hades *and* hell
United Nations Organization, 75-76

United States of America (social and historical), 50-52, 100-01, 126, 152, (173), (174), 175, 204, 205, 222, 256, 275; American satirists, 50-52, **100-01, 196**, 272
Utopia, 162

V

Valjean, Jean, 144
Varro, M. Terentius, 37, (232), 252, 253, 277
vases, Greek, 120-21
vaudeville, 232
Vauquelin de la Fresnaye, Jean, 47
Vega Carpio, Lope Felix de, 108, 261, 263
Velazquez, Diego, 68
Venus, 160, 254
Vercingetorix, 102
Vergil, 84, 86, 95, **103-04**, 201, 202; *Aeneid*, 104, (108), 112, 132; individual books: 1: 108, 261, 262, (267); 2: 260, 267; 4: 95, (105); 6: 7, 260; 7: 108, 262; 9: 260, 267; *Bucolics*, 132, 153-4, 202; *Catalepton*, (132), 268; *Georgics*, 129, 260, 264, 267
Verus Caesar, 253
Victoria, Queen, 49, **77-78**, 142, 217, 257-58
Vidal, Gore, *Visit to a Small Planet*, 272
Villiers de l'Isle-Adam, Philippe-Auguste-Mathias, 116
Vinci, Leonardo da, (67), 228
Vinciguerra, Antonio, 47
Voigt, Wilhelm, **93-94**, (96)
Voltaire, 3, 73, 217; *Candide*, **8-12**, 14, **20-21**, 22-23, 39, 113, 158, 162, 163, 193, 200, 207, 209, 212; *L'Ingénu*, 200; *Micromégas*, **170**; *La Pucelle (Maid of Orleans)*, **112-13**; *Treatise on Toleration*, 23
voodoo, 181
Vorticism, 100
vulgarisms, 37, **103-04**, 116
Vulgate, 139

W

Walpole, Sir Robert, 219
Walter Map, 46, 254
Walter of Châtillon, 46
Walton, William, 90
war satirized, 39, **83**, 102, 103, 105-06, 107-08, **110-12**, 200, 239-40, 243, 255, 259
Washington, George, 85, 255
wasps, 28, 187
Watts, Isaac, 72
Waugh, Evelyn, 240; *Black Mischief*, **204**, 212; *Decline and Fall*, 158, **193-95**; *A Handful of Dust*, (212); *The Loved One*, **204-05**; *Scott-King's Modern Europe*, **199**; *Vile Bodies*, 223
Webb, Sidney, 174
Weill, Kurt, 124
Weinreich, O., *Römische Satiren*, 253, 275, 277, 280
Wells, H. G., *The First Men in the Moon*, 163; *The Sleeper Awakes*, 171, 174; *The Time Machine*, 171
Welsted, Leonard, 17-18
Whigs, 24, 98
Whitman, Walt, 115
Wife of Bath, *see* Chaucer
Wild, Jonathan, 218-19
Wilhelm II, 94
Wilkes, John, 85, 87
Williams, Vaughan, 187
Wilson, Edmund, 136

wit, 48, 270; *and see* satire
Wittgenstein, Ludwig, 31
Wolcot, John ("Peter Pindar"), 135, 268
Wolfe, Thomas, **146-47**
wolves, 17, 178, 180, 181, 237
women satirized, 39, 45, 46, **189-90**, 224, **226-28**, 235
Woolf, Virginia, 96
word-play, 40, 46
Wordsworth, William, 49, **78-80**
World Home Economics and Children's Aptitude and Recreation Foundation, 74
Wotton, William, 263
Wyatt, Sir Thomas, 47
Wylie, Philip, *Generation of Vipers*, 50-51

X

Xanthias, 210
Xenophanes, 35-36, 37
Xerxes, 258, 259

Y

Yalta, 51-52
Yiddish, 51
Young, Edward, 48
Ysengrim, 180-81

Z

Zeus, 42, 83, 120-21

OTHER TITLES IN LITERATURE
AVAILABLE IN PRINCETON AND
PRINCETON/BOLLINGEN PAPERBACKS

AESTHETIC AND MYTH IN THE POETRY OF KEATS, by Walter Evert (#63), $2.95

ANATOMY OF CRITICISM, by Northrop Frye (#234), $2.95

THE ANATOMY OF SATIRE, by Gilbert Highet (#280), $2.95

"ATTIC" AND BAROQUE PROSE STYLE: *Essays by Morris W. Croll*, edited by J. Max Patrick et al. (#177), $2.95

THE BEST PLAYS OF RACINE, translated by Lacy Lockert (#58), $2.95

C. P. CAVAFY: SELECTED POEMS, translated by Edmund Keeley and Philip Sherrard (#281), $2.95

CONFRONTATIONS: *Studies in the Intellectual and Literary Relations Between Germany, England, and the United States during the Nineteenth Century*, by René Wellek (#69), $2.95

THE CONTINUITY OF AMERICAN POETRY, by Roy Harvey Pearce (#19), $2.95

DANTE'S DRAMA OF THE MIND: *A Modern Reading of the Purgatorio*, by Francis Fergusson (#114), $2.95

THE DEED OF LIFE: *The Novels and Tales of D. H. Lawrence*, by Julian Moynahan (#33), $2.95

DOCUMENTS OF MODERN LITERARY REALISM, edited by George J. Becker (#66), $3.45

DOSTOEVSKY: *His Life and Work*, by Konstantin Mochulsky, translated by Michael A. Minihan (#243), $3.95

THE EARTHLY PARADISE AND THE RENAISSANCE EPIC, by A. Bartlett Giamatti (#168), $2.95

THE EDWARDIAN TURN OF MIND, by Samuel Hynes (#235), $2.95

ELIZABETHAN REVENGE TRAGEDY, by Fredson Bowers (#30), $2.95

ESSAYS ON ENGLISH AND AMERICAN LITERATURE, by Leo Spitzer (#113), $2.95

FEARFUL SYMMETRY: *A Study of William Blake*, by Northrop Frye (#165), $3.45

FRONTIER: *American Literature and the American West*, by Edwin Fussell (#189), $3.45

GEORGE SEFERIS: *Collected Poems*, translated by Edmund Keeley and Philip Sherrard (#236), $2.95

HEMINGWAY: *The Writer As Artist*, by Carlos Baker (#86), $2.95

THE HEROIC IMAGE IN FIVE SHAKESPEAREAN TRAGEDIES, by Matthew N. Proser (#127), $2.95

THE IDEA OF A THEATER, by Francis Fergusson (#126), $2.45

THE JAPANESE TRADITION IN BRITISH AND AMERICAN LITERATURE, by Earl Miner (#59), $2.95

JOSEPH CONRAD: *A Psychoanalytic Biography*, by Bernard C. Meyer, M.D. (#188), $2.95

THE LIMITS OF ART: Vol. 1, *From Homer to Chaucer*, edited by Huntington Cairns (P/B #179), $3.95

THE LIMITS OF ART: Vol. 2, *From Villon to Gibbon*, edited by Huntington Cairns (P/B #203), $3.95

THE LIMITS OF ART: Vol. 3, *From Goethe to Joyce*, edited by Huntington Cairns (P/B #217), $3.95

LINGUISTICS AND LITERARY HISTORY: *Essays in Stylistics*, by Leo Spitzer (#88), $2.95

THE LYRICAL NOVEL: *Studies in Hermann Hesse, André Gide, and Virginia Woolf* (#62), $2.95

MIMESIS: *The Representation of Reality in Western Literature*, by Erich Auerbach, translated by Willard R. Trask (#124), $2.95

THE NATURE OF ROMAN COMEDY, by George E. Duckworth (#244), $3.95

NEWTON DEMANDS THE MUSE, by Marjorie Hope Nicolson (#31), $2.95

NOTES ON PROSODY *and* ABRAM GANNIBAL, by Vladimir Nabokov (P/B #184), $2.95

THE NOVELS OF FLAUBERT, by Victor Brombert (#164), $2.95

THE NOVELS OF HERMANN HESSE, by Theodore Ziolkowski (#68), $2.95

ON THE ILIAD, by Rachel Bespaloff, translated by Mary McCarthy (P/B #218), $1.45

THE POETIC ART OF W. H. AUDEN, by John G. Blair (#65), $1.95

THE POETICAL WORKS OF EDWARD TAYLOR, edited by Thomas H. Johnson (#32), $2.95

THE POWER OF SATIRE: *Magic, Ritual, Art*, by Robert C. Elliott (#61), $3.45

A PREFACE TO CHAUCER, by D. W. Robertson, Jr. (#178), $4.95

PREFACES TO SHAKESPEARE, by Harley Granville-Barker (#23, 24, 25, 26), $2.95 each

PRINCETON ENCYCLOPEDIA OF POETRY AND POETICS, edited by Alex Preminger, with Frank J. Warnke and O. B. Hardison, Jr. (#282), $6.95

THE PROSE OF OSIP MANDELSTAM, translated by Clarence Brown (#67), $2.95

RADICAL INNOCENCE: *The Contemporary American Novel,* by Ihab Hassan (#237), $2.95

RELIGIOUS HUMANISM AND THE VICTORIAN NOVEL: *George Eliot, Walter Pater, and Samuel Butler,* by U. C. Knoepflmacher (#187), $2.95

SHAKESPEARE AND CHRISTIAN DOCTRINE, by Roland Mushat Frye (#4), $2.95

SHAKESPEARE AND SPENSER, by W.B.C. Watkins (#60), $2.95

SHAKESPEARE'S FESTIVE COMEDY, by C. L. Barber (#271), $3.45

SHAW AND THE NINETEENTH CENTURY THEATER, by Martin Meisel (#125), $3.45

SHELLEY'S MAJOR POETRY, by Carlos Baker (#27), $2.95

THE SPIRIT IN MAN, ART, AND LITERATURE, by C. G. Jung, translated by R.F.C. Hull (Vol. 15, complete and unabridged, in the Collected Works of C. G. Jung) (#252), $1.95

T. S. ELIOT'S DRAMATIC THEORY AND PRACTICE, by Carol H. Smith (#87), $2.95

THE THIRD VOICE: *Modern British and American Verse Drama,* by Denis Donoghue (#64), $1.95